Revised Edition by Thomas P. Rebel

SEA
TURTLES

and the Turtle Industry of the West Indies,
Florida, and the Gulf of Mexico

UNIVERSITY OF MIAMI PRESS
Coral Gables, Florida

First edition by Robert M. Ingle and F. G. Walton Smith
Published 1949 by University of Miami Press

Revised edition copyright © 1974
by University of Miami Press

Designed by Bernard Lipsky

Manufactured in the United States of America

Library of Congress Cataloging in Publication Data

Rebel, Thomas P   1947-
    Sea turtles and the turtle industry of the West
Indies, Florida, and the Gulf of Mexico.

    First ed. (1949) by R. M. Ingle and F. G. W. Smith.
    Bibliography: p.
    1. Sea turtles--Mexico, Gulf of. 2. Sea turtles--
Caribbean Sea. 3. Turtle fishing. I. Ingle,
Robert M. Sea turtles and the turtle industry of the
West Indies, Florida, and the Gulf of Mexico.
II. Title.
SH399.T9R4 1974   598.1'3'09162   73-159293
ISBN 0-87024-217-2

Illustration Credits: Dr. L. D. Brongersma and the Rijksmuseum
    van Natuurlijke Historie, Leiden, The Netherlands, from
    European Atlantic Turtles: pp. 18, 21, 22, 24, 25, 27, 29, 30
Florida State News Bureau: pp. 71, 93, 99, 114, 115
Marineland of Florida: pp. 51, 76, 90
Robert E. Shroeder: pp. 38, 107
Stuart News: p. 81
U.S. Fish and Wildlife Service: p. 33
Wometco Miami Seaquarium: pp. 42, 54, 77, 87

146317

CONTENTS

ILLUSTRATIONS

TABLES

PREFACE

A necessary preliminary to the proper development and control of our turtle resources is the evaluation of past, present, and potential productivity and the assembling of all available information regarding the biological and oceanographical factors that influence them. During the twenty-five years since the original publication of *Sea Turtles*, information on marine turtles has more than doubled and significant advances have been made in our understanding of their biologies. The summarized information included in this book, along with the annotated bibliography as a readily available reference source, should aid those persons concerned with identifying, studying, and conserving sea turtle resources in the Caribbean and the Gulf of Mexico.

I would like to gratefully acknowledge the cooperation of various government officials, fishery officers, and scientists too numerous to mention. Appreciation is also extended to Dr. F. G. Walton Smith and Dr. C. P. Idyll for their assistance with certain areas of this work and to Dr. Edward D. Houde and Francisco Palacio for translating articles and letters in French and Spanish. Robert M. Ingle and William E. Rainey deserve recognition for their help in reviewing the manuscript and their helpful comments.

Special thanks go to Dr. L. D. Brongersma and the Rijksmuseum van Natuurlijke Historie, Leiden, The Netherlands, for their kind permission to use the line drawings from their publication *European Atlantic Turtles*. My thanks also to the staff at the International Oceanographic Foundation for helping me locate the photographs.

Finally, I wish to thank Dr. F. G. Walton Smith, Dean Emeritus and Distinguished Professor of Oceanography at the Rosenstiel School of Marine and Atmospheric Science, University of Miami, for asking me to update his original book, coauthored by Robert M. Ingle, President, Conservation Consultants, Inc., and retired Chief, Bureau of Marine Science and Technology, Department of Natural Resources, Tallahassee. The book has almost tripled in size, and I am grateful for recognition as the author of this edition.

Thomas P. Rebel

SEA TURTLES

TAXONOMY

Seven species of sea turtles are found in the tropical and subtropical seas of the world. Of these, six species are indigenous to the Caribbean and Gulf of Mexico regions. Only three of the species normally found in the Caribbean have ever been plentiful enough for commercial exploitation on a wide scale; these are the green turtle, *Chelonia mydas,* the hawksbill turtle, *Eretmochelys imbricata,* and the loggerhead turtle, *Caretta caretta.* The olive or Pacific ridley, *Lepidochelys olivacea,* is only found in numbers in the Guianas. Immature individuals of Kemp's ridley, *Lepidochelys kempii,* also called the Atlantic ridley or bastard turtle, are captured on the west coast of Florida for their meat, and the eggs of this species have been harvested on the Mexican coast. *Dermochelys coriacea,* the luth, leatherback, or trunkback turtle, is not sufficiently plentiful to be of economic importance.

As might be expected, early workers in widely isolated parts of the globe have given different names to the same species, but work in the 1930s and 1940s dispelled much of the confusion. Stejneger and Barbour (1943) summarized the taxonomy of sea turtles, and their work is recommended for those interested in historical aspects. More recently, Oliver and Shaw (1953), Wermuth and Mertens (1961), and Loveridge and Williams (1957) consider the olive ridley and Kemp's ridley as subspecies, but other workers, including Carr (1956a) and Pritchard (1969d), have published sufficient reasons for retaining the binomial nomenclature.

Classification at the subspecies level is still subject to revision, and more study is necessary, especially with regard to statistical variation among populations. The trinomial nomenclature of the turtles normally found in the Caribbean is as follows: *Chelonia mydas mydas, Caretta caretta caretta, Eretmochelys imbricata imbricata,* and *Dermochelys coriacea coriacea.* A classification with a bibliography of original sources, dates, synonymies, and authors is given in the following list. For a more comprehensive listing of synonymies and authors refer to Garman (1884) and an even earlier discussion of taxonomy by Cope (1875). Sources previously mentioned in this section are also helpful.

Family Cheloniidae

GENUS *CHELONIA* (Type: *mydas*)   GREEN TURTLES
      Latreille, *Hist. Nat. Rpt.,* Vol. 1, 1801, p. 22.
Chelonia mydas (Linne) *Testudo mydas* (Linne) *Syst. Nat.,*
      Ed. 10, Vol. 1, 1758, p. 197, also *Chelonia mydas*
      (Schweigger) Konigsberg, *Arch. Natur Math.,* Vol.
      1, 1812, Pt. 3, p. 412, also *Chelonia agassizii* (Bocourt) *Ann. Sci. Nat.,* Ser. 5, *Zool.,* Vol. 10, Pts.
      1-3, 1868, p. 122.
      Type locality: Ascension Island, etc.
      Range: Tropical and subtropical oceans, occasionally
      straying to temperate waters.
Chelonia depressa (Garman) *Bull. Mus. Comp. Zool.,* Vol. 6,
      Pt. 6, 1880, p. 124.
      Type locality: Northern Australia.
      Range: Australian waters.
GENUS *ERETMOCHELYS* (Type: *imbricata*)
                            HAWKSBILL TURTLES
      Fitzinger, *Syst. Rept.,* 1843, p. 30.
Eretmochelys imbricata (Linne), *Testudo imbricata* (Linne)
      Syst. Nat., Ed. 12, Vol. 1, 1766, p. 350, also *Eretmochelys imbricata* (Agassiz), *Contr. Nat. Hist.
      U.S.,* Vol. 1, 1857, p. 381, also *Eretmochelys squamata* (Agassiz) *Contr. Nat. Hist. U.S.,* Vol. 1, 1857,
      p. 382.

Type locality: American seas, restricted to Bermuda Islands by Smith and Taylor, *U. Kansas Sci. Bull.*, Vol. 33, Pt. II, 1950, p. 315.

Range: Tropical and subtropical oceans, in littoral waters.

GENUS *CARETTA* (Type: *caretta*)
LOGGERHEAD TURTLES
Rafinesque, *Specchio Sci.*, Palmero, Vol. 2, No. 9, Sett. 1, 1814, p. 166.

Caretta caretta (Linne) *Testudo caretta* (Linne) *Syst. Nat.*, Ed. 10, Vol. 1, 1758, p. 197, also *Caretta caretta* (Stejneger) *Ann. Rep. U.S. Nat. Mus.*, 1902 (1904), p. 715.

Type locality: "About American Islands," restricted to Bermuda Islands by Smith and Taylor, *U. Kansas Sci. Bull.*, Vol. 33, Pt. II, 1950, p. 315.

Range: Tropical and subtropical oceans, straggling to temperate waters.

GENUS *LEPIDOCHELYS* (Type: *olivacea*)
RIDLEY TURTLES
Fitzinger, *Syst. Rept.*, 1843, p. 30.

Lepidochelys olivacea (Eschscholtz), also *Chelonia olivacea* (Eschscholtz) *Zool. Atlas*, Pt. 1, 1829, p. 2, pl. 3, also *Lepidochelys olivacea* (Girard) *Herpet. U.S. Expl. Exped.*, 1858, p. 435, also *Caretta olivacea* (Stejneger and Barbour) *Check List N. Amer. Amphib. Rept.*, Ed. 4, 1939, p. 170.

Type locality: Manila Bay, Philippine Islands.

Range: Tropical Pacific and Indian oceans; west coast of Mexico, straggling to the California coast; west coast of Africa and South American waters of Guianas.

Lepidochelys kempii (Garman), also *Thallasochelys (Colpochelys) kempii* (Garman) *Bull. Mus. Comp. Zool.*, Vol. 6, 1880, p. 123, also *Lepidochelys kempii* (Baur) *Amer. Natural.*, Vol. 24, 1890, p. 387, also *Caretta kempii* (Stejneger and Barbour) *Check List N. Amer. Amphib. Rept.*, Ed. 4, 1939, p. 170.

Type locality: Gulf of Mexico, restricted to Key West,

Florida, by Smith and Taylor, *U. Kansas Sci. Bull.*, Vol. 33, Pt. II, 1950, p. 358.

Range: Western Gulf of Mexico eastward to Florida, north to New England, and straggling to the Azores, British Isles, coasts of France and Netherlands, and occasionally to Mediterranean.

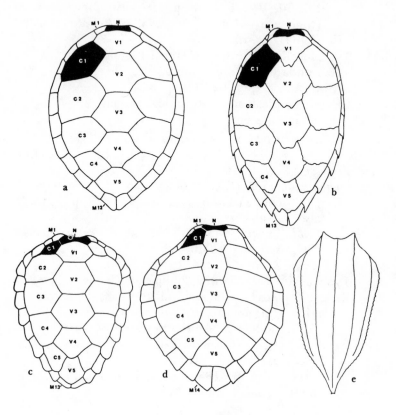

Fig. 1. The bony part of the carapace of a, *Chelonia mydas;* b, *Eretmochelys imbricata;* c, *Caretta caretta;* d, *Lepidochelys kempii;* e, *Dermochelys coriacea.* C, costal scutes; M, marginal scute; N, nuchal scute; V, vertebral scute.

Family Dermochelidae

GENUS *DERMOCHELYS* (Type: *coriacea*)
LEATHERBACK TURTLES
Blainville, *Bull. Soc. Philom. Paris,* 1816, p. 111 bis (119).

Dermochelys coriacea (Linne), also *Testudo coriacea* (Linne) *Syst. Nat.,* Ed. 12, Vol. 1, 1766, p. 350, also *Sphargis coriacea* var. *schlegelii* (Garman) *Bull. U.S. Nat. Mus.,* No. 25, 1884, p. 303, also *Dermochelys coriacea* (Boulenger) *Cat. Chel. Brit. Mus.,* 1889, p. 10, also *Dermochelys schlegelii* (Stejneger) *Bull. U.S. Nat. Mus.,* No. 58, 1907, p. 485.

Type locality: Mediterranean Sea, restricted to Palermo, Sicily, by Smith and Taylor, *U. Kansas Sci. Bull.,* Vol. 33, Pt. II, 1950, p. 315.

Range: Tropical and subtropical oceans, straggling to temperate waters.

Identification of sea turtles in the field is easily accomplished. A simple key is given for this purpose.

Key to the Sea Turtles of Florida, the West Indies, and the Gulf of Mexico

1. Back is covered with leathery skin . . . .
   ### LEATHERBACK TURTLE
   Dermochelys coriacea
1. Back is covered with shield or plates.
   2. Four pairs of shields or plates along the back. Color brown or black mottled with yellow.
      3. Shields of carapace do not overlap. Usually only one claw on front flipper. Jaw not beaklike. Single pair of prefrontal scutes on upper surface of snout . . . . GREEN TURTLE
      Chelonia mydas

3. Shields overlap. Two claws on
   front flippers. Upper jaw forms
   overhanging beak. Upper surface
   of snout covered by two pairs of
   prefrontals . . . . HAWKSBILL TURTLE
   Eretmochelys imbricata

2. Five or more pairs of shields or
   plates along the back. Color
   uniformly brown or black.
   4. Plastron with three (rarely
      more) inframarginal scutes
      on either side, each scute
      without pores. Color brown
      or reddish brown . . . . . LOGGERHEAD TURTLE
      Caretta caretta

   4. Plastron with four (sometimes
      three) inframarginal scutes on
      either side, each scute with a
      pore at its posterior border.
      Color gray to olive green.
      5. Five (rarely more) pairs of
         shields or plates along the
         back. Color gray. Carapace
         often as wide as it is long.
         Florida and Gulf of Mexico . . . .
         KEMP'S RIDLEY TURTLE
         Lepidochelys kempii

      5. Sometimes five but usually
         six to nine pairs of shields or
         plates. Color olive. Carapace
         usually not as wide as it is
         long. Guianas and surrounding
         areas . . . . OLIVE RIDLEY TURTLE
         Lepidochelys olivacea

Facing page: Fig. 2. Inframarginal scutes
(IM) of *Caretta caretta* and *Lepidochelys
kempii* separate the large scutes of the
plastron from the marginal scutes; p, inframarginal pores.

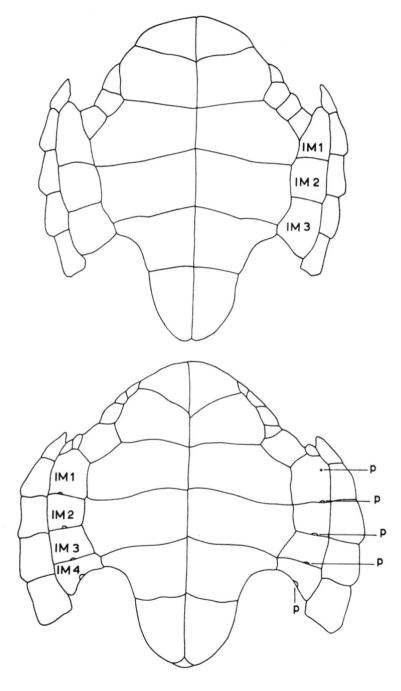

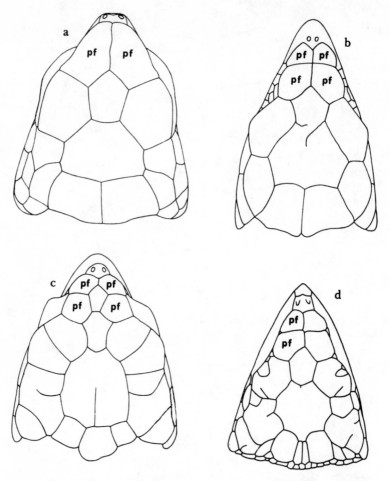

Fig. 3. Prefrontals (pf) on the upper surface of the head of a, *Chelonia mydas;* b, *Eretmochelys imbricata;* c, *Caretta caretta;* d, *Lepidochelys kempii.*

DESCRIPTION

Sea turtles are reptiles of the order Testudinata, so-called because of the bony plates on the outer surface of the body. These bony plates are usually fused to form a shell and may or may not be covered with horny shields. Dorsally the shell is known as the carapace and ventrally as the plastron.

Along the median line, dorsally, a row of plates called the neurals are fused with the vertebrae. The foremost plate of the carapace, found medially, is the nuchal. Lateral to the neurals on each side are the costals, which fuse with the ribs. The costals are surrounded by the marginals, which form the outermost edge of the carapace. (See Fig. 1.)

GREEN TURTLES

Green turtles have a single pair of scales, the prefrontals, on top of the head between the eyes. Four costal shields only are present on each side, and the shields of the carapace are not overlapping as they are in the hawksbill. There is, however, a slight overlap in the very young. The margin of the carapace is smooth, not serrate. The limbs are paddle shaped and have only one claw, although from time to time aberrant individuals appear with two claws. The carapace is light to dark brown, sometimes with a tinge of olive, with radiating wavy or mottled markings of darker color or with large blotches of dark brown. The plastron is yellowish. In the very

Fig. 4. *Chelonia mydas* Green turtle

young the carapace is black to gray, with margins on the shell and flippers; the plastron is dusky white.

The tail of the female barely reaches beyond the margin of the carapace. The tail of the male reaches some distance beyond. The eggs, usually soft-shelled and white in color and not quite spherical are 40 to 46 mm in diameter.

Geological records show that the green turtle was indigenous to the Florida region tens of thousands of years ago (Hay, 1908a, 1917). The green turtle is valued as food and is almost everywhere considered to be greatly preferable to other turtles in this respect.

Fig. 5. *Eretmochelys imbricata* Hawksbill turtle

HAWKSBILL TURTLES

Like the green turtle, the hawksbill has only four pairs of costal shields, but the shields characteristically overlap. The overlapping edges are rough and serrate. The margins of the carapace are markedly serrate, each marginal shield projecting from the posterior end as a pointed extremity. This marginal serration is less noticeable on the anterior end of the animal. Two pairs of scales, the prefrontals, are located between the eyes on top of the head. The paddle-shaped limbs are each equipped with two claws, rarely one. The jaws form a narrow hooked beak, hence the name hawksbill. Although all the turtles have something resembling a hooked beak, the hawksbill is distinguished by the narrowness of the anterior part of the skull.

Sexual dimorphism of the tail is the same as in the green turtle. The colored carapace of the adult is striking when clean; usually it is amber with streaks and markings of reddish brown, blackish brown, and yellow. The plastron is whitish yellow, often with a few black splotches. The young are usually black or brownish black with light brown on the keels, on the margins of the shell and flipper, and on the upper outer areas of the neck. Eggs are about 38 mm in diameter and white with a mucilaginous coating at the time of laying.

Eretmochelys imbricata is a smaller species than the green turtle, having a carapace of much less than three feet in length. The maximum weight is about 165 pounds. The principal value of the hawksbill is its translucent shields, which take a high polish and are sold as tortoiseshell. A large specimen yields up to eight pounds of commercial shell.

LOGGERHEAD TURTLES

The loggerhead or lantern back turtle is most easily distinguished by the five or more pairs of costal shields and the absence of inframarginal pores. In the first characteristic it differs from the green turtle and the hawksbill, which have only four costal pairs. The absence of pores in the plastron is the most easily distinguishable difference between the loggerhead and the ridley turtles. In addition, mature individuals are much larger than mature ridleys, with a relatively narrower carapace and larger head. Two pairs of large scales, the prefrontals, are found on top of the head between the eyes. Five or more costal shields are present on each side, the first one of each row making contact with the nuchal. Limbs are

Fig. 6. *Caretta caretta* Loggerhead turtle

paddle shaped, each with two claws. Sexual dimorphism of the tail is a feature of this species, similar to those previously mentioned. The adult carapace is reddish brown to brown, and the plastron is yellowish. In the young and half-grown loggerheads the shields of the carapace are keeled; the three dorsal keels can be seen easily in the field.

Deraniyagala (1930*a*, 1930*b*, 1933, 1934*a*, 1936*a*, 1943, 1945, 1952) cites good evidence that the loggerhead has broken up into several subspecies or races. There is enough divergence, he suggests, for the whole group to deserve family status. According to him, the loggerhead has not moved as widely over the globe as some of the other sea turtles and hence has not kept such a uniform genetic constitution.

Three and a half feet is a good length for the carapace of the loggerhead, and the weight rarely exceeds 350 pounds, but huge examples are known that approach small leather-backs in size (Carr, 1952). The turtle is not of much commercial importance although it dominates the catch in the Yucatán and Quintana Roo. It is edible, although commonly considered inferior to the green turtle. Actually the flesh of the loggerhead is as good as that of the green turtle (Ingle, 1972). The chief difference is that the latter has less sinewy parts in the muscle and is therefore more tender. The toughness of the loggerhead can be corrected, however, by patient removal of the many sinews. The presence of these sinews has probably made the loggerhead less desirable in the market. Smaller loggerheads are preferable to larger ones for eating; the larger ones, particularly the males, have a strong taste that some persons find objectionable. The loggerhead is an old inhabitant of the Caribbean; its remains have been found under geological formations tens of thousands of years old (Hay, 1908a, 1917).

RIDLEY TURTLES

The ridley turtle has five or more pairs of costals: Kemp's ridley usually has five, and the olive ridley has six to nine. The presence of inframarginal pores distinguishes the ridley from the loggerhead, and their discontinuous distribution makes identification between the species relatively easy. Ridleys have two pairs of prefrontals or scales between the eyes on top of the head. The carapace of the olive ridley, *Lepidochelys olivacea,* is olive or greenish white, whereas that of Kemp's ridley, *Lepidochelys kempii,* is dark gray, grayish brown, sometimes blackish, or olive green. Persons who are interested in the differences between the two species should read Pritchard (1969d).

Ridleys are the smallest of all species of sea turtles. They are of economic importance in only a few areas—the Mexican coast, the Florida coast, and the Guianas.

LEATHERBACK TURTLES

The leatherback turtle, or luth, differs greatly from the other sea-dwelling species. Its carapace is soft and is not fused with the vertebrae and ribs. Numerous small polygonal plates make up the carapace, which is covered with a leathery skin

Fig. 7. *Lepidochelys kempii* Ridley turtle

without any epidermal shields. In the male the tail extends beyond the hind limbs when placed edge to edge. Coloration of the adult is black or dark brown above, with scattered whitish flecks and white with irregular black marks below. The carapace of the leatherback turtle has five to seven keels running lengthwise along its back. In the very young these keels are tipped with yellow, contrasting with the black or dark brown color of the rest of the carapace. The limbs are black and edged with yellow. Full-sized eggs are approximately 5 cm in diameter and are soft and white. The leatherback normally lays several undersized eggs in each clutch.

Fig. 8. *Dermochelys coriacea* Leatherback turtle

It is the largest of all the species; individuals weighing as much as a ton are mentioned by Agassiz (1857a), but Pritchard (1971) finds the heaviest reliable record is around 1,600 pounds. The leatherback is usually not considered of any commercial value; however, certain native tribes of the South Pacific are known to use the oil of the luth in the manufacture of some of their domestic articles. This oil is used medicinally in the Virgin Islands and for boat sealant in parts of the animal's range, e.g., the Persian Gulf. Where breeding populations are dense enough, eggs are often taken for local consumption.

DISTRIBUTION

Sea turtles are not found in significant numbers outside tropical or subtropical oceans. They are occasionally swept into
northern latitudes by currents, and the colder temperatures
there often cause immobilization and death. This characteristic has caused them to be labeled by some as biological drift
bottles. For an extensive listing and discussion of sea turtle
occurrences in European Atlantic waters, the reader is referred to Brongersma (1972). They characteristically live in
salt water, although they are sometimes found in the brackish
water of estuaries. Sea turtles are independent of land, except
when they are laying eggs, and for this reason are widely
distributed within their temperature range.

GREEN TURTLES

Chelonia mydas has a wide distribution within 35° north
latitude and 35° south latitude. In the Western hemisphere
these turtles once occurred in relative abundance from the
North Carolina sounds throughout the Gulf of Mexico. On
American shores the northernmost point where they have
been recorded is Massachusetts. Occasionally they are seen
off the coasts of New Jersey and Long Island. They are the
most common sea turtles in Bermuda (Mowbray and Caldwell, 1958). They reach southward to the Argentine coast at
Mar del Plata and Necochea (Carr, 1952). In the Pacific they
are abundant as far north as southern California and as far

south as southern Chile at Chiloé Island (Carr, 1952). They are still found throughout the West Indies in varying numbers.

In the Windward and Leeward Islands they are fairly common. Adults are rarely seen in the Caymans, but the young are occasionally found. The coasts of Nicaragua and Costa Rica are abundant sources of green turtles in Central America; Nicaragua provides feeding pastures for turtles that nest in Costa Rica.

HAWKSBILL TURTLES

This species is rarely found north of Florida, although its appearance has been recorded at Woods Hole, Massachusetts, and probably at least one bona fide record exists of a hawksbill taken in European Atlantic waters (Brongersma, 1972). Other records previously ascribed to *E. imbricata* have been found by Brongersma (1972) to be incorrect or doubtful. He attributes their relative scarcity in these waters to their preference for warmer water than that sought by loggerhead and leatherback turtles, and to their overexploitation.

Hawksbills are present throughout the Caribbean. John Schmidt (1916) reports them from the Danish West Indies. E. F. Thompson (1947) states that young are frequently encountered in the Cayman Islands within enclosed waters, although the adults now rarely come in to lay. He further mentions that most of the hawksbills fished in Colombian waters at that time came from the vicinity of San Andrés, around the Seranna and Seranilla banks, and the outermost of the Mosquito Cays, and also from the Rasoline Banks, the Pedro Cays and the Morant Cays of Jamaica. Hawksbill distribution, of all the sea turtles, is perhaps the most confined to tropical waters.

LOGGERHEAD TURTLES

In the Atlantic, *Caretta caretta* is found throughout the Caribbean and as far north as Virginia, occasionally even in Nova Scotia and England. On American shores it is the most northward breeding of the sea turtles, up to South Carolina and sometimes Virginia. It has even been reported in the Mediterranean Sea and off the coast of Ireland. The logger-

Fig. 9. A 200-pound loggerhead collected off Virginia is examined by a Soviet oceanographer. The turtle was tagged and released.

head extends southward to the coast of Argentina and is common in both the Caribbean and the Gulf of Mexico.

RIDLEY TURTLES

This species exhibits the most unusual distribution of all the sea turtles. Kemp's ridley occurs from the Gulf coast of Mexico east to Florida on both the Atlantic and Gulf coasts. It is absent in the Caribbean, and individuals rarely straggle north of Florida. Brongersma (1967*a*) notes only eighteen records for *Lepidochelys kempii* in European waters.

The olive ridley, *Lepidochelys olivacea*, is also conspicuously absent from all but the southeast corner of the Caribbean. It inhabits Indo-Pacific waters, and its breeding grounds in the Atlantic are on the west coast of Africa and in the Guianas. Specimens have been taken from the Azores, off Surinam, Guiana, and French Guiana. It occasionally reaches temperate seas.

LEATHERBACK TURTLES

These turtles occasionally stray outside tropical waters and have been recorded in temperate latitudes more often than other sea turtles. Bleakney (1965) lists many records for Nova Scotia, and Brongersma (1967*a*) reports that this species has been reported forty-two times in British waters from 1756 to 1966. Additional European Atlantic records are given by Brongersma (1972). Considering the relative infrequency with which this turtle is seen even in tropical oceans, this number is high. Although widely distributed in tropical and subtropical seas, they are nowhere very plentiful in Atlantic waters. On American shores the southernmost range of *Dermochelys coriacea* is Mar del Plata, Argentina (Carr, 1952).

GROWTH AND AGE

Turtles grow to large sizes and frequently live for a considerable number of years. Additional data regarding growth rate
and age of maturity have been published in the last twenty
years but not in comparable quantities to other aspects of sea
turtle life history. No satisfactory method of determining age
by inspection has been derived for sea turtles.

GREEN TURTLES

Green turtles are about the same size as loggerheads, that is,
smaller than leatherbacks but larger than hawksbills and ridleys. The average varies according to the intensity with which
local fisheries scour an area. Ingle (1972) reports on the last
shipment of turtles from the Caribbean to Key West. The
average of this group was 162 pounds with a 35 inch carapace
length. The largest turtle weighed 300 pounds and had a 43
inch carapace length. Ingle's (1972) data on the Key West
importation activity indicate averages of 225 pounds and 35
inch carapace lengths during 1970. West Indian records cite
turtles of 850 pounds with a carapace of over 5 feet.

In the Danish West Indies John Schmidt (1916) found a
monthly increase in weight of 0.3 to 0.95 English pounds
(138 to 442 grams) in marked turtles that were weighed and
measured, released, later recaptured, and weighed and measured again. His observations are of value because they refer
to turtles living unconfined in their natural state. Unfor-

tunately, the measurements were limited to turtles within the intermediate size range, and the findings apply only to turtles of that size. Table 1 summarizes Schmidt's work.

Table 1. WEIGHT GAIN IN THE GREEN TURTLE

Initial weight, lb.	Average monthly increase, lb.	Percent of increase
5	0.63	12.6
11	0.73	6.8
15	0.64	4.3
15	0.31	2.1
18.5	0.31	1.6
20.5	0.95	4.6
26.25	0.50	1.9
44	0.58	1.3

From the data we can see that the weight increase per month is fairly constant; it does not depend upon the size of the animal (after the turtle weighs at least 5 pounds). The percentage of increase therefore becomes less as the animal grows larger. Schmidt does not believe that the seasons influence growth rate because in tropical waters the seasons are not well defined. For evidence regarding a seasonal difference in growth see the section on loggerhead turtles.

Caldwell (1962c) kept 25 green turtles on different diets and under different conditions for varying lengths of time up to 3 years. His growth estimates are a 100 mm increase in length the first year (from 50 mm at hatching to 150 mm), 115 mm the second year, and 115 mm the third year. Larger turtles caught and fed on cut fish and shrimp grew only about 50 mm a year. Kaufmann (1967) reports that 4 green turtles with an average weight of 25.8 grams and an average carapace length of 55.9 mm at 10 days of age were between 119.9 and 145.6 mm in carapace length and between 316.0 and 462.5 grams in weight at about 5 months of age. A green turtle released at 1 year of age had gained 12 pounds in 30 months when recovered by Witham and Carr (1968).

Schmidt declines to state unequivocally that the age of a

green turtle may be determined by its size. He presents conclusions from limited observations, stressing that such data are only of restricted value. Schmidt's findings are shown below:

Table 2. GROWTH OF GREEN TURTLES

Weight, lb.	Age, approximate years
5	1 to 1.5
10	2 to 2.5
20	3 to 3.5

Length

Age	Length, cm
first autumn	about 5
first winter or spring	?
second winter or spring	27
third winter or spring	35

The time it takes for a green turtle to reach maturity (about 35 inches carapace length) may vary from temperate to tropical regions. On the basis of data and assuming an arithmetic increase in length, Hendrickson (1958) estimates that maturity takes 4 to 6 years in tropical Sarawak. Caldwell (1962c) estimates that green turtles in temperate waters (where his data are from) reach maturity at 13 years of age or earlier. Caldwell's estimates are well based; Hendrickson, however, failed to consider that these turtles appear to grow less after the first 3 years and that a more reliable estimate of tropical growth might be maturity in 8 years.

Recent publication of 15 years of results from the tagging program at Costa Rica by Carr and Goodman (1970) shows negligible growth of mature female turtles (about one-half inch carapace length in 8 years). They assert that these turtles grow fairly rapidly until maturity and that the individual variation in size of nesting turtles probably is due mostly to their size at first laying. (The oldest recorded green turtle in captivity was at least 15 years old.)

Great variation occurs in the growth of turtles and in their climatic environments. These factors should be remembered when assessing growth potential among all sea turtles.

Fig. 10. *Left to right:* a 3-month-old Caribbean green turtle; a 10-month-old Pacific green turtle.

The freshly hatched green turtle is about 2 inches long. When it has reached one year of age, it is 8 to 10 inches long and about 2 to 5 pounds in weight. Moorhouse (1933) found that in very young turtles of 1 3/4 inches to 2 1/2 inches the carapace length increased about 1/8 inch to 3/8 inch in 16 days. According to him, 1-year-old turtles are about 8 inches long and 10-year-old turtles are 44 inches long. Flower (1937) mentions three green turtles that were 5 inches long and weighed 5 pounds. After nine years in captivity they all weighed 22 pounds. Harrison (1955, 1956a) lists a 14 1/2 pound *Chelonia* at three years and two months of age that weighed 18 1/4 pounds six months later.

Those interested in length-to-weight relations of green turtles should refer to Caldwell (1962b). His empirical relation is $\log W = -2.14 + 2.60 \log L$, where W is the weight in pounds and L is the length in inches.

HAWKSBILL TURTLES

These rarely exceed 3 feet in carapace length or 150 pounds

in weight. The record is a 280 pound specimen from the Cayman Islands. While the turtles are young, their growth rate appears to be about 4 inches per year.

The oldest known hawksbill was in the Berlin Zoological Garden; it was at least 16 years old. Earlier researchers believed the hawksbill matured to a weight of 25 to 30 pounds in little more than three years, but further investigations have indicated that they are mature at about 80 pounds (Carr, Hirth, and Ogren, 1966). Two 3-pound hawksbill turtles, received from Key West and raised in the aquarium in New York City, lived in captivity for seven and one-half years. One weighed 60 pounds and had a 26 inch carapace, and the other weighed 50 pounds and had a carapace 24 inches in length. The average rate of increase was about 7 pounds in weight and about 3.5 inches in carapace length per year.

John Schmidt (1916) reports the findings of Consul Schack, which are mentioned in Mortensen's *Marine Resources of the Danish West Indies*. Three young hawksbill turtles were kept in a small pool with the following results:

Table 3. GROWTH OF HAWKSBILL TURTLES

Turtle	Date measured	Length, cm	Breadth, cm
No. 1	April 21	10	6.5
No. 1	December 18	23	15.0
No. 2	April 29	9	6.5
No. 2	December 18	20	6.5*
No. 3	June 26	14	11.5
No. 3	December 18	24	16.5

*Probably an error in the original data.

By very logical assumptions, Schmidt states that these turtles must have been born in October, and as the size of newly hatched hawksbills is known (4 cm), we may conclude that they must add about 1 cm per month or about 5 inches per year. The growth in length of young hawksbills in the Danish West Indies may be summarized as follows:

first autumn	4 to 5 cm	2 inches
first winter	7 to 8 cm	3 inches
first spring	10 cm	4 inches
second autumn	20 cm	8 inches

Caldwell (1962c) reports that a single specimen from Costa Rica was maintained for about three years at the Marine Studios in Florida. Growth conditions were not optimal, but the turtle increased in length approximately 100 mm (4 inches) the first year, 60 mm the second, and 100 mm the third. Weight increases were, respectively, 160, 900, and 2,330 grams for the first three years. Three individuals kept at Cedar Key, Florida, showed a mean increase in length of 26 mm and a mean increase in weight of 50 grams in 195 days. They were fed cut fish. Five others, also on a fish diet but kept elsewhere, showed mean increases of 73 mm and 234 grams in 224 days. These growth rates are slower than those reported by Schmidt in the tropics.

In the case of the Pacific hawksbills, Hornell (1950) reports the attainment of 13 inches of carapace length in two years. Deraniyagala states that two young turtles increased in weight by about 10 pounds and 13 inches in 16 months to reach a length of 36.3 cm and a weight of 4,987 grams.

Twenty-five *Eretmochelys* were raised by Kaufmann (1967) to five months of age. He lists average carapace length and average weight at one day after hatching as 42.3 mm and 15.4 grams and the average at five months as 111.9 mm and 201.6 grams.

LOGGERHEAD TURTLES

The Atlantic subspecies is usually well under 300 pounds with a carapace little more than 30 inches long. Several records mention 450-pound individuals, and twice individuals have been reported at over 800 pounds.

Growth rate records are fragmentary, but they indicate an average annual increase of as much as 15 pounds in weight and 7 inches of carapace length during the first few years. Pope (1939) suggests that loggerheads become mature when they have reached a weight of about 200 pounds; however, it now appears that they mature at a smaller weight and a carapace length of about 31 inches (Caldwell, Carr, and Ogren, 1959). The oldest loggerhead turtles definitely recorded were at the Lisbon aquarium, where they died after 35 years.

One experiment conducted under artificial conditions provides information on seasonal variation in the growth of sea turtles. It is described in the Monaco Reports. Observations were made of three loggerhead turtles caught near the Azores and placed in a pool filled with salt water at Monaco, where they were fed fish. The temperature of the water was 21° to 23°C in the summer, 17°C in the winter. The turtles ate much more during the summer than during the winter, with a resulting greater growth in summer than in winter. The results are shown in table 4.

Table 4. GROWTH OF THREE LOGGERHEAD TURTLES

Date measured	Weight, kg.	Weight, lb. (approximate)
Specimen A		
23 August 1895	2.30	5
26 March 1897	4	10
7 April 1897	4	10
25 April 1897	4	10
18 September 1897	5.1	11
5 November 1897	5.2	11
15 December 1897	5.3	12
Specimen B		
3 September 1896	23.1	51
26 March 1897	25.6	56
7 April 1897	25.5	56
25 April 1897	25.5	56
28 May 1897	26.1	57
18 September 1897	30.38	67
5 November 1897	34.1	71
15 December 1897	35.2	77
Specimen C		
23 July 1897	0.68	1.5
18 September 1897	1.2	2.5
5 November 1897	1.3	3
15 December 1897	1.36	3

The results shown here do not agree with the findings of John Schmidt for other species in the Danish West Indies.

Fig. 11. Immature Atlantic loggerhead turtles. Note the pronounced keels on the larger specimen.

There is an obvious difference in weight gained between turtles of different sizes. For instance, specimen B, in the period between 25 April and 15 December 1897 gained 21 pounds in weight, an impressive increase for such a short period. With such a small number of samples, however, conclusions should be scrutinized with great care. It is frequently stated in the literature that in almost every brood there are one or more turtles with a growth rate considerably greater than that of the siblings.

Caldwell (1962c) reports that five individuals from 46.7 to 52.0 mm in length were held in a small tank at Jekyll Island, Georgia. They were fed shrimp and at the end of two months had mean increase in length of 21.9 mm. Flower (1937) mentions one loggerhead that when hatched weighed 20 grams and measured 48 by 35 mm. It was reared in captivity in Key West, Florida, for four and one-half years. At the end of that time it weighed 37 kilos (81 1/2 pounds) and measured 2 feet 1 inch by 1 foot 11 inches. It was exceptional, however, because it far outweighed and outmeasured the other four.

Kaufmann (1967) reared 26 *Caretta* on cut fish until the turtles were seven months old. Then many of the turtles died because the water became contaminated. His results are seen in table 5.

Table 5. GROWTH OF 26 LOGGERHEAD TURTLES

Age	Carapace length, *mm	Carapace width, *mm	Weight, g
after hatching	44.6 (42.5-46.2)	33.8 (31.0-39.9)	18.1 (17.1-19.1)
about 5 months	135.1 (113.6-152.0)	106.3 (86.8-121.2)	393.7 (249.0-523.0)
about 7 months	159.4 (141.1-181.0)	122.9 (112.5-140.0)	653.0 (493.5-869.5)

*The numbers within parentheses indicate mean range.

We can see that the variability among individuals continues to increase with age, but the average increase in length is about 2 cm per month.

Eighty-eight hatchling loggerheads were reared for six weeks at the NOAA Southeast Fisheries Center Laboratory on Virginia Key, Florida. They were fed mainly cut fish and were cared for and measured by Barbara Palko and myself; ten of these were retained for two more months.

Table 6. GROWTH OF 88 LOGGERHEAD TURTLES

No. of hatchlings	Age, weeks	Carapace length, *mm	Carapace width, *mm	Weight, *g
88	hatching	46.26 (40.5-47.8)	33.11 (30.0-35.2)	22.26 (20.7-23.7)
88	2	53.90 (47.8-56.5)	43.35 (40.5-46.4)	29.49 (24.4-35.3)
88	4	64.85 (56.0-68.9)	53.67 (47.8-58.7)	47.25 (34.6-55.1)
88	6	74.81 (62.5-79.6)	61.78 (54.5-66.2)	71.79 (50.5-88.7)
10	6	73.65 (62.5-79.6)	61.22 (54.5-66.2)	73.70 (50.5-88.7)
10	10	85.79 (70.7-95.5)	70.95 (63.8-77.7)	105.34 (72.8-134.8)
8†	14	95.38 (75.2-109.6)	78.28 (66.3-88.5)	151.64 (80.9-208.8)

*The numbers within parentheses indicate range.
†Two turtles were stolen from the laboratory.

G. H. Parker (1926) shows that some turtles grow considerably faster than others. He states that *Caretta* at hatching weighs about 20 grams. At four and one-half months it weighs 800 grams (larger than Kaufmann's), and at three years it reaches 19 kilos, or about 42 pounds.

Hughes, Bass, and Mentis (1967) give the weights and measurements of four *Caretta* grown in captivity for two and one-half years at 1,585, 1,750, 2,320, and 2,125 grams, and 20.0, 23.0, 25.0, and 21.5 cm carapace length. Under carefully controlled conditions, Uchida (1967) found that loggerhead turtles reached a maximum weight of 110 kilograms (220 pounds) and 1,040 mm (41 inches) carapace length. His specimens reached egg-laying size in six to seven years.

The authors of the original edition of this book observed firsthand loggerhead turtles raised in captivity in an aquarium at Key West, Florida. Although the animals there, by the manager's admission, received very little attention, mortality was only about 50% during the first year. The caretaker's opinion was that if reasonable, inexpensive measures had been taken, no young would have been lost the first year. Even under poor conditions of seawater, cleanliness, and light, yearling loggerhead turtles were found to be 8 inches long and about 2 pounds in weight.

In captivity loggerheads are generally voracious eaters and will soon take food from a person's hand. They are generally fed cut fish and shrimp.

RIDLEY TURTLES

The smallest of all sea turtles, neither sex of the ridleys reaches lengths much greater than 28 inches carapace length. Pritchard (1969*d*) lists the size range of 241 mature females in the Guianas as 24.5 inches to 29.125 inches. All were olive ridleys, *Lepidochelys olivacea*.

Field data on Kemp's ridley, *Lepidochelys kempii,* is given by Chavez, Contreras, and Hernandez (1967): 124 hatchlings were between 38 and 46 mm carapace length, with a mode of 42, and between 14 and 18 grams, with an average of 16.3; 203 mature females were between 59.5 and 75 cm carapace length; one specimen measured 63 cm (24.8 inches) and weighed 39 kilograms (about 86 pounds), another measured 69 cm (27 inches) and weighed 49.3 kilograms (about 108 pounds).

Data on growth rates of ridley turtles are very scarce. Caldwell (1962*c*) mentions an individual that weighed 8,178 grams and measured 260 mm when captured. After 316 days on a diet of cut fish, the turtle increased 45 mm in length and 1,589 grams in weight. A second Kemp's ridley, 279 mm in length and 2,838 grams in weight at capture, gained only 15 mm in length and 1,362 grams in weight after 330 days on the same diet. Nearly one year later it had increased an additional 46 mm in length and 1,816 grams in weight.

The growth rate of intermediate individuals appears to be about 2 inches per year; but, additional research is needed on these two species. Ridleys mature at about 25 inches carapace length (Carr and Caldwell, 1958).

LEATHERBACK TURTLES

Several leatherbacks taken off the west coast of North America have weighed in excess of 1,000 pounds, and a Vancouver specimen reached 1,450 pounds. The average weight is probably about 700 pounds. Pritchard (1971) found the carapace lengths of 192 mature females from French Guiana to be between 54 and 71 inches, with a median length of between 61 and 64 inches. Twenty adult females from Trinidad measured by Bacon (1969) had carapace lengths of 125 to 185 cm (50 to 73 inches).

The smallest nesting leatherback that Pritchard (1969d) mentions is 58.5 inches carapace length and 651 pounds. Caldwell (1958) gives the lengths (probably total lengths) of two large specimens captured in Florida as 74 and 79 inches.

Dermochelys generally shun food in captivity and often die within a few weeks or months of capture. The difficulty in rearing these animals has contributed to the lack of information on their growth rates. Deraniyagala (1936b) describes the growth of a captive specimen from about 3 inches long at the time of hatching to about 17 inches long at the end of 20 months.

HABITAT

Sea turtles are truly saltwater animals and are sometimes seen at considerable distances from land. They are dependent upon land only for egg-laying purposes and apart from this are not often seen out of water. Although normally found in strictly marine habitats, they can live under estuarine conditions.

Universal to all the species is the dearth of information regarding their first year of life. The hatchlings swim almost frantically out to sea and remain out of sight for the first year. The few records of turtles this age are generally based upon observations made considerable distances from shore and sometimes associated with drifting sargassum rafts. Hughes (1969a) states that posthatchlings at Tongaland, Africa, are carried by the Agulhas Current and are found near every major center between Durban and Cape Town. The size of the individuals found ranges from barely larger than hatchlings to almost twice this size, and a tagging program has been instituted to clarify their movement and origin.

GREEN TURTLES

These turtles are found in comparatively shallow water inside the reefs but not usually on the coral reefs themselves. Shoals and lagoons with marine grasses and algae are favorite places, and where this food is plentiful the turtles are seen in bays and inlets. Garman (1884) states that the turtles are found in most abundance on shoals near low sandy beaches or near uninhabited islands. *Chelonia* is a long distance migrant and may be hundreds of miles from land when migrating to or from the nesting beach. Carr (1967*a*) states that "the mature green turtle appears most usually to sleep on the bottom with its shell shoved under a ledge of rock or coral."

HAWKSBILL TURTLES

This species is usually found in shallower water than loggerheads and leatherbacks, usually in depths of less than fifty feet. The hawksbills seem to prefer cleaner beaches and more oceanic exposure than do the greens, although the two types often share the same nesting beach. Even though the hawksbill wanders a great deal, it seems more attached to one region than the other sea turtles. Typical habitats are coral reefs, shoals, lagoons, and lagoon channels and bays, where a growth of marine vegetation provides both vegetable and small animal food.

LOGGERHEAD TURTLES

Loggerheads are found in warm waters among islands, on the continental shelf, and near estuaries. They are also found in deeper waters in the neighborhood of food-bearing ocean currents. They have been caught on the red snapper banks in the Gulf of Mexico. Carr (1952) mentions that they sometimes enter streams and ascend them until "the water freshens, or until they die out in the salt marsh."

RIDLEY TURTLES

This turtle prefers coastal areas but is sometimes seen in large numbers in the open sea. Kemp's ridley is fairly restricted to the Gulf of Mexico, especially around the coasts of Mexico and Florida. Deraniyagala (1939*a*) states that the olive ridley is probably more of a bottom dweller than the other sea turtles. He gives the most frequent habitat as the shallow water between the reef and shore. In larger bays or lagoons the ridleys appear to seek out certain sequestered areas.

LEATHERBACK TURTLES

These are the most aquatic of all turtles. They are less well-known than the other species partly because they are less common, but also because they appear to prefer deep water. In more northern waters they will sometimes enter shallow bays, but in most of their range they are usually found in water over 150 feet deep, except when laying eggs.

FOOD AND ENEMIES

Sea turtles are beset by many kinds of parasitic worms, none of which appear to cause great pathology with the exception of one leech, *Ozobranchus branchiatus,* which has been held suspect by Nigrelli and Smith (1943) as the causative agent for papillomas. These growths sometimes occur around the periphery of the eyes and consequently could be an important factor in turtle mortality. Because this condition is fairly well-known in the *Chelonia mydas,* it may be important in any extensive turtle propagation scheme.

Sea turtles are frequently found more or less encrusted with barnacles. Hawksbills and loggerheads are generally more encrusted than are greens; barnacles are rare on leatherbacks. A rare burrowing barnacle, *Stephanolepas muricata,* has been mentioned by Hendrickson (1958) as a damaging ectoparasite on green turtles. Although the cases he mentions had only a few barnacles, he feels that severe infestations might be lethal to turtles. Dunlap (1955) mentions the existence of amoebae resembling *Entamoeba histolytica* in the intestinal contents of a leatherback from the Gulf of Mexico.

GREEN TURTLES

Green turtles are predominantly herbivorous, feeding upon such marine grasses as *Zostera, Cymodocea, Thallasia,* and *Halophila.* The roots are preferred according to Garman (1884). Green turtles also feed upon algae but are not entirely restricted to a vegetable diet; in captivity they prefer meat (Deraniyagala, 1939a). Hornell (1927) mentions their consumption of young oysters and Beebe (1937) found the stomach contents of a specimen captured near Clarion Island to consist of over 400 shell-less flying snails and 28 munidos or scarlett lobsterettes. Small mollusks and crustacea are also part of the diet, but apparently the young are more omnivorous than the adults. The turtles appear to bolt their food without mastication, but Parris (1958), observing sea turtles in captivity, states that they crush their food either intentionally or in maneuvering it to the back of the mouth. The young live on yolk and do not feed for several days. For the first year of their life they are mainly carnivorous, feeding on small, weak marine invertebrates (Carr, 1965). Brongersma (1972) adds that the green turtle's preference for vegetable food does not preclude its survival in the open ocean if sufficient animal food is available.

Little is known of the feeding habits of *Chelonia depressa*, but its inferior taste might be a result of an omnivorous or carnivorous diet (William et al., 1967).

Although turtles are timorous at all times, Garman and others agree that the adults are less so during the mating season. Townsend (1906) and Mellen (1925) as well as several others reported that green turtles frequently come ashore on lonely islands and reefs to bask in the sun. They sleep on the surface of the water.

Deraniyagala (1939a) records that green turtles are most abundant in the larger gulfs and lagoons of Ceylon during January and February when the salinity is markedly lowered by rain. The lagoon dwellers are usually distinguishable by a growth of algae on their shells which is not present on turtles from more open waters.

Reports from various sources indicate that sharks may mutilate adult turtles and even dispose of entire animals of considerable size. Norman Caldwell (1951) contains an eyewitness report of one of these attacks, and Brongersma (1972) reviews the literature on shark and killer whale predation of sea turtles.

The newly hatched turtles fall prey to both birds and fish. Moorhouse (1933) mentions that land crabs eat the hatch-

Fig. 12. The green turtle is characterized by four costal scutes, which never overlap, and by a single pair of elongated prefrontals on the upper surface of the snout.

lings. Hendrickson (1958), studying green turtles in Malaya and Sarawak, lists the ghost crab, *Ocypoda ceratophthalma*, as the most extensive predator. Crabs usually dragged the captured hatchlings to their burrows, where the head and neck were the first areas mangled. He also mentions lizards (*Varanus salvator*); snakes, including the python, *Python reticulatus*; and large fish, especially sharks, as enemies of the young. Additional workers have listed the following predators of green turtle hatchlings: raccoons, ocelots, dogs, and even jaguars (Carr, 1956a); monitor lizards and foxes (Bustard and Limpus, 1969); carnivorous ants (*Dorylus* spp.) and the rock monitor (McAllister, Bass, and van Schoor, 1965); dingos (*Canis familiarus dingo*); and rats (Limpus, 1971). Predators of the young and their eggs probably include most of the canivores and omnivores that live near a turtle nesting beach. Several workers have reported that if the nest is not uncovered in the first two or three days it remains relatively safe from predation until hatching.

Upon entering the water the young become rather easy

prey for large fishes and birds. For the first few days they are unable to dive well because the remains of the still undigested yolk lower their specific gravity.

HAWKSBILL TURTLES

Omnivorous feeders and very aggressive, hawksbills begin to eat grasses from the second day after hatching. Later they eat algae, *Cymodocea, Conferva, Sargassum, Pinna, Ostrea,* barnacles, fish, and Portuguese men-of-war. They feed mostly on such invertebrate items as sponges, sea urchins, and ectoprocts. Carr (1952) reports that two specimens from the Gulf of Fonseca had their alimentary canals "crammed with neatly cut, two-inch sections of the cylindrical fruits of the red mangrove." He mentions another specimen from the same locality that had eaten about 2 pounds of a mixture of mangrove leaves and dead bark and wood.

The stomach contents of two mature males taken on Tortuguero Bank during August 1964 were described by Carr, Hirth, and Ogren (1966). One contained only large amounts of a sponge, probably *Geodia gibberosa,* and the other contained (1) a sponge, apparently also *Geodia gibberosa;* (2) ectoprocts of the genera *Amthis* and *Steganoporella* and an unidentified calcareous species; (3) a hydroid, like *Sertularia;* and (4) two sea urchin spines. These authors suggest that the narrow beak of the hawksbill may be an adaptation for prying and probing for food in crevices and cavities among rocks and coral. Occasionally those species that feed on jellyfish may consume plastic bags by mistake, often resulting in death of the individual.

Barnacles are often troublesome, not because of their encrustations, but because one of them, *Stephanolepas muricata,* bores into the carapace, plastron, and flippers (Hornell, 1927; Nillson-Cantell, 1932).

The same predators in most cases attack young hawksbills as attack green turtles.

LOGGERHEAD TURTLES

Sometimes loggerheads eat marine grasses but not to the extent of either *Chelonia* or *Eretmochelys.* The adults are vicious and subsist largely on conchs, shellfish, and barnacles.

They will also feed on fish, sponges, and jellyfish. In the stomach of a *Caretta caretta gigas* weighing 100 pounds were 6 pounds of *Dromia, Calappa* (crabs), *Xancus* (chank shell), oysters, and *Clypeaster* (sea urchin). Three specimens from Madeira examined by Brongersma (1968g) contained the following: (1) remains of salpae, intestine, bones of a small fish, and a shell of the pteropod *Carolinia tridentata*; (2) remains of salpae and small elliptical bodies thought to be nematocysts of a medusa and a partly digested small fish; (3) a piece of plastic and numerous goose barnacles together with small pieces of bark.

Brongersma (1972, p. 162) comprehensively reviews the literature relating to the diet of loggerheads and summarizes as follows:

> On the high seas Loggerheads feed on Scyphomedusae, *Physalia physalia, Velella velella*, Salpae, Pteropods, *Ianthina, Nautilograpsus minutus, Lepas anatifera*, Squids (inter alia *Leachia*), Syngnathid fishes (*Enteluras aequoreas*), and perhaps also on other fishes . . . in shallow, coastal waters bottom dwelling organisms . . . and sponges. Apparently algae are sometimes taken in great quantity . . . sea-weeds will be taken together with other food. The turtles will swallow floating objects, sometimes inadvertently, sometimes because goose-barnacles are attached to these objects.

Loggerheads in captivity at Marine Studios, Florida, feed on stingrays, octopods, and squid (Vollbrecht, 1947). There they lie on the bottom in the winter months, coming to the surface about every three hours to breathe.

Baldwin and Lofton report that land crabs and raccoons successfully locate loggerhead nests at Cape Romain, South Carolina (Caldwell, 1959a). They estimated that 5.6% of the eggs were destroyed by raccoons. Routa (1967) estimated 7.8% destruction by these animals at Hutchinson Island, Florida. Ants are often found in nests that are excavated several days after laying.

Hughes, Bass, and Mentis (1967) mention that "considerable infestation (from 7 to 49 per turtle) of leeches (*Ozobranchus maggai* A'Pathy) were found adhering to the cloacal regions of some loggerhead females." They include the water mongoose (*Atilax paludinosus*) and the yellowbill kite (*Milvus aegyptius*) in the list of predators of the young.

As mentioned previously, this species is not as well-known as the other sea turtles. Carr (1952) lists the olive ridley, *Lepidochelys olivacea,* as mainly vegetarian, but it also feeds on

Fig. 13. Inframarginal pores and the very broad shell are special characteristics of Kemp's ridley.

sea urchins and mollusks. Caldwell and Erdman (1969) reported the stomach contents of a specimen caught off Surinam as 2 small catfish (9 cm length); 3 small, unidentified crab carapaces; 10 small, unidentified, and broken snail shells; and 2 liters of yellow green slimy liquid, probably jellyfish remains.

Kemp's ridley feeds primarily on invertebrates, particularly crabs. Smith and List (1950) reported parts of crabs of the genera *Callinectes* and *Hepatus* and numerous gastropod fragments in the stomach contents of a specimen from the Mississippi coast. Montoya (1966) lists gastropods, crabs, sea urchins, sea stars, medusae, and fish as occurring in the diet. Liner (1954) lists crab shells (*Callinectes* spp.) and occasional barnacles as stomach contents, and J. D. Hardy (1962) found blue crab fragments in one specimen. Two individuals caught in a shrimp trawl were found to be completely gorged with shrimp, presumably due to the easy availability of these animals (Carr, 1961*b*). Dobie, Ogren, and Fitzpatrick, Jr. (1961) examined the stomach contents of two ridleys from Louisiana and found the first turtle to contain crab fragments of *Callinectes sopidus* and *C. ornatus,* gastropods of the genus *Nassarius,* twigs, a fragment of wood, and a leaf; the second turtle contained gastropods of the genus *Nassarius,* clams of the genera *Nuculana,* and *Corbula,* and several mud balls of about 2 mm in diameter.

Ridley nests become easy prey for dog packs because the ridleys habitually nest in large numbers. Pritchard (1971) cites a communication from Montoya that large numbers of ridley hatchlings have been found in the stomachs of leatherbacks from Pacific Mexico.

LEATHERBACK TURTLES

These turtles feed on fish, eggs, bread, green algae, *Caulerpa,* hydrozoa, live young octopuses, and even tomatoes.

The leatherback has two- to three-inch long backward spines that line the mouth cavity and cover the surface of the J-shaped esophagus for its entire length. Bleakney (1965) believes these spines are a specialized modification for a diet of slippery prey like jellyfish. Ray and Coates (1958) state that the speed, size, and strength of the animals, as well as their very powerful jaws, make this animal a formidable predator. Pritchard (1971) notes that the deeply notched, sharp-edged jaws of the leatherback appear adapted for holding and cutting up soft-bodied prey, as opposed to the massive construction and crushing plates of *Caretta* and *Lepidochelys.*

An extensive review of the literature on the feeding habits of the leatherback turtle has been done by Brongersma (1969). In examining the contrasting opinions of various workers, he comes to the conclusion that the diet consists mainly of *Scyphomedusae* and Tunicates. Incidental food items are the animals that live in association with the medusae (juvenile fishes, amphipods) and with the Tunicates (amphipods) as well as the prey of the medusae (fish). A later discussion by Brongersma (1972) mentions that the diet is probably more varied than this. Pritchard (1971) relates that Montoya reports fish remains and large numbers of hatchling ridleys in leatherback stomachs from Pacific Mexico.

Leatherbacks are free from cirripedes because of the oily nature of their skin. Fishes, such as *Naucrates ductor* (Linn), often take up a position under the posterior of the carapace. *Leptecheneis naucrates* (Linn), the remora, attaches to these turtles and probably feeds upon the feces. A trematode, *Astrorchis renicapite* (Leidy), intestinal amoebae, flat parasitic worms, and nematodes are the parasites listed in the literature. Pritchard (1971) and Brongersma (1972) note the occasional presence of plastic bags in the gut and intestines of leatherback turtles. Apparently the turtles mistake the bags for jellyfish; the bags may cause mortality. Caldwell and Caldwell (1969) report the presence of leatherback turtle remains in the stomachs of three killer whales, *Orcinus orca*.

BREEDING HABITS

The sea turtles of economic importance are cosmopolitan and thus have been studied by different workers in various parts of the world. In comparing information from several sources, we should remember that the seasons are reversed in the antipodes. Observations from New Zealand, for instance, would not correspond month by month with observations from the Caribbean.

GREEN TURTLES

Detailed accounts of the breeding of green turtles are given by Moorhouse (1933), Hendrickson (1958), Carr and Giovannoli (1957), Carr and Ogren (1960), Hirth and Carr (1970), and Bustard and Greenham (1969). Owing to the general similarity between the habits of different species, only the breeding of green turtles will be described in detail. Further sources of information are mentioned in each section.

Breeding occurs within the same general range as that where coral reefs occur, between 30° south latitude and 30° north latitude. Copulation takes place before and during the laying season just off the beaches (Hornell, 1927). Carr (1965) believes that mating takes place only at the nesting ground and that this act fertilizes the female for the next mating season, two to four years later. The time of year when the nesting season begins and the duration of the nesting season vary from one area to another. In some areas it is a few months of the year whereas elsewhere the nesting season may be year round with one or two peaks of a few months.

Year-round seasons occur in Malaya, Sarawak, the Gulf of Siam, and the Seychelles. Hendrickson (1958) believes that the absence of a nonbreeding season in Sarawak is due to the absence of any gross annual temperature cycle. This lack of seasonal temperature fluctuations of any large magnitude is also found in the other areas with year-round breeding seasons.

True (1884) gives the Florida nesting season as April to July. Garman (1884) reports from local opinions that the breeding time for the green turtle is from April to June in Bermuda. He quotes other authors who agree on this season for Florida. During this period, copulation takes place and continues for a "considerable length of time." During copulation a strong nail on the first digit of the forward paddle of the male is bent downward to form a hook with which the male grasps the shell of the female. It is not uncommon to see females come ashore with broken carapaces, sometimes bleeding, after the aggressive attention of one or more males.

Thompson reports from prior records of the seventeenth century that the green turtle breeds in Jamaica during the late summer. Caldwell (1961) found limited summer nesting there. Ingle (personal communication, 1973) suspects that early records of green turtles may be misidentifications since these reports were generally made by laymen. In addition, earlier writers often associated edibility with the green turtle only. In this way other species of sea turtles were often rejected as possible alternatives by both first- and second-hand reporters.

There are only two important green turtle rookeries remaining in the Caribbean. The best known is Tortuguero, Costa Rica, where nesting occurs from July to September (Carr, 1967a). This rookery presumably supplies green turtles to the western Caribbean while a smaller colony at Aves Island in the Leeward Islands a hundred miles off Monserrat supplies the eastern Caribbean. The nesting season for Aves Island is mid-July to mid-October (Roze, 1955). James Parsons (1962, p. 4) points out that with the exception of Tortuguero "the largest breeding concentrations that have been recorded are found on uninhabited or sparsely populated islands. The type of beach characteristically favored seems to be steeply sloping, with a beach platform high and above the flood tide, and composed of a lightweight sand of medium coarse texture that does not pack easily into a hard surface." Bustard (1968) suggests that green turtles nest only where substantial vegetation in the form of large bushes or trees grows.

Important green turtle nesting in the Gulf of Mexico occurs in the area of the Yucatán Peninsula. According to James Parsons (1962), nesting is centered on the low coral islands off the northeast corner of the peninsula, particularly Isla Blanca, Isla Cancún, and the eastern coast of Cozumel. A second nesting area is located on Banco Chinchorro (Cayo Lobos) off southern Quintana Roo. Carranza (1967) lists Cayo Arcas, Puntarenas, and Triangulos Reef as areas of breeding activity from June to August.

John Schmidt (1916) quotes several sources on green turtle breeding in the Danish West Indies. These sources agreed that the exact time of breeding for green turtles was not known, although the turtle was assumed to reproduce from May to October inclusive. The avowed reason for this lack of knowledge is that the green turtle lays its eggs in the sand, not on the dry beach, but underwater. There is no scientific corroboration of this testimony. Instead, various workers have reported that eggs laid too close to the water invariably do not hatch. Boeke (1907) believed that the breeding season was from March to July although he was unable to secure eggs at that time. He did, however, obtain some eggs from a female in one instance and from the sand on another occasion, both times in the month of October.

Catesby's account (1731-1743) is the earliest one reviewed. He states that in the Carolinas and Florida the green turtle lays three or four times a year, with about a 14-day interval between laying. According to him, there is no breeding of *Chelonia* in the Bahamas. Audubon (1826) mentions that hundreds of turtles, including greens, are known to lay their eggs on Florida shores. Carr and Ingle (1959) recorded two nestings, one in July 1957 two miles north of Vero Beach and the other in June 1958 on Hutchinson Island,

Florida. From a survey of sea turtle nests on Hutchinson Island in 1967, Routa (1967) estimates that approximately 15 green turtles nested there that summer.

A study on Hutchinson Island during the summer of 1971 revealed 25 nestings of green turtles (Gallagher & Hollinger, 1972). Of these turtles, four were tagged. Two of the tagged individuals returned for second nestings. Compared with a total of 25 visits for green turtles (returns for second nestings included), there were 1,419 loggerhead nestings and one leatherback laying.

Deraniyagala (1939) reported that the few nestings made in Ceylon were during July to November. The peak of nesting is during February and March in Sarawak (Hendrickson, 1958). Off the eastern coast of Australia at Heron Island breeding has been observed from late October to February.

Hornell (1927) describes a migration from feeding areas to nesting grounds at Aldabras through the Mozambique Channel. No evidence of extensive migration was developed by the marking experiments of John Schmidt (1916) in the West Indies. More recent studies (covered in the section on migration), however, show that green turtles may be the most migratory of the sea turtles.

According to Garman, from two to four, sometimes five, lots of eggs are laid in a season. These layings each consist of 75 to 200 eggs each. The layings are 14 to 15 days apart. Moorhouse's data from the southwest Pacific is in complete accord with this 14-day interval. At Sarawak the internesting period averages 10.5 days (Hendrickson, 1958), and in Costa Rica the average is 12.5 days (Carr and Ogren, 1960).

Evidence has shown that green turtles nest in cycles of two, three, or even four years. In Costa Rica a three-year cycle is most predominant, and the two-year cycle is secondary. Carr and Carr (1970) suggest that the modulation from a two- to a three-year cycle or vice versa might be due to ecological influences. Favorable conditions would cause ripening of the eggs at an early date, and unfavorable conditions would cause modulation to a longer cycle.

Although most of Garman's data were obtained from fishermen and other residents untrained in scientific observation, it should be mentioned that these people believed that female turtles, when they return to multiple layings, pick the immediate vicinity of their previous visits to deposit their eggs. Hendrickson (1958) found that out of 5,748 turtles returning to lay eggs on two islands only 500 meters apart, only 215 (3.7%) changed islands. Site tenacity by female green turtles appears to be a fundamental though not infallible part of the nesting process.

Incubation varies, as might be expected, with the temperature and latitude. In the Seychelles it takes 47 days (Hornell, 1927). At Heron Island (Moorhouse, 1933) the incubation period is 72 days. Hendrickson (1958) found that at the peak of the nesting season in Sarawak (February and March) incubation times from 48 to 70 days were recorded, the average being 57.5 days (Carr and Ogren, 1960). In Ceylon the period is 50 to 60 days.

Carr and Ogren (1960) suggest that the nesting behavior of sea turtles can be studied on a comparative basis by breaking the emergence venture into 11 stages:

1. Stranding, testing of stranding site, and emerging from wave wash.
2. Selecting of course and crawling from surf to nest site.
3. Selecting of nest site.
4. Clearing of nest premises.
5. Excavating of body pit.
6. Excavating of nest hole.
7. Oviposition.
8. Filling, covering, and packing of nest hole.
9. Filling of body pit and concealing of site of nesting.
10. Selecting of course and locomotion back to the sea.
11. Re-entering of wave wash and traversal of the surf.

They believe that careful observation of each of these operations may provide considerable opportunity for ethologic comparison.

Minor differences in nesting behavior occur between green turtle colonies throughout the world; in general, however, the nesting process is remarkably similar not only among the green turtles but also among other species of sea turtles. A brief description of this process is provided by the following discussion. Those who wish to know more should refer to the sources previously mentioned in this section.

When coming ashore, the female turtle often stops to press her nose into the sand several times, as if "smelling" the area. She slowly crawls up the beach with occasional stops for "peering around" before selecting a nest site. When she reaches a suitable site, she uses her fore flippers to scoop out a shallow bowl, and simultaneously she uses her hind flippers to pile up the sand for covering the eggs later. The nest itself is then dug with the hind flippers alone. As the hole gets deeper, the female lifts her head and supports her weight with her fore flippers, a position which lowers the hind flippers and allows them to dig more deeply. She uses her flippers as scoops and lifts the sand out with care before flinging it backward from the hole.

The pit, when complete, is bottle shaped, and about 18 inches deep. The female shields the tail and orifice by folding the flippers backward before she begins to lay her eggs. The eggs are released two or three at a time from the extruded cloaca, along with copious mucus. Between 3 and 226 eggs are laid (usually slightly more than 100). The eggs are white, almost spherical, and soft, but turgid, and between 40 and 60 mm in diameter.

When the laying is finished, the female fills in the nest with her hind flippers and scatters the sand with her fore flippers. She continues to scatter sand as she returns to the water, thus obscuring the location of the nest. The total time taken is usually around two hours, and laying almost always occurs at night. One-hour layings have been noted, as well as those taking as long as seven hours, but these are exceptional.

Moorhouse (1933) made many useful observations on the behavior and breeding habits of the green turtle in particular during a stay on Heron Island from 31 October 1929 to 16 February 1930. Because turtles arrived mainly after nightfall and at any stage of the tide, patrols were made each night. During patrols, only those turtles that came on the shore and laid their eggs were counted. An exception to this procedure was in the case of marked turtles, which were counted each time they returned whether they laid or not.

During the season immediately preceding his visit, Moorhouse reports that nearly all the turtles were wiped out by the massive turtle hunts of the canning industry in that region. Because so many turtles came in to lay their eggs during the following season, when he was observing them, Moorhouse decided that possibly sea turtles did not lay each year but could skip several seasons before reproducing a second time. This assumption has since been supported by the work of Carr, Harrisson, Hendrickson, and others.

For recognizing the turtles under observation, each one was labeled with copper sheeting about 1-inch square attached to the carapace by a wire passed through a hole bored in one or the other of the pygal plates. The right bottom corner of each label was removed to orientate the label better for reading, and each label had a number punched in it. The labels proved a very satisfactory method of marking although five animals were not seen again after labeling. Other workers have found that tags attached to the carapace are unsatisfactory because of the abrasiveness of the males' shells during copulation. (Today a "cow ear" tag fastened on the margin of one of the fore flippers is a common tagging procedure.)

During the marking of the last few animals, the ones marked earlier had started returning for their second laying. Many of the animals had a total of seven layings, although in some cases they returned as often as twelve times. In many of the return visits the animal walked around the beach and, after perhaps digging a nest, went back to the water to return the following night at some other point on the beach to lay. Some of the animals in their wanderings on shore covered 600 yards in addition to digging nests.

Moorhouse states that the breeding season in the southern area of the Great Barrier Reef commences in late October and extends at least into mid-February. During that period females were observed in some cases to lay at least seven times. There is a strong indication that they may lay more times, since the turtles were still returning when the study was terminated.

The male green turtles were never observed on the beach, either during the day or night, although they frequently came close to shore.

Copulation occurred throughout the season. Mating pairs

were observed during October and November and again in January. During copulation the couple floated on the surface and frequently appeared to go to sleep, at which time it was possible to row right up to them.

According to Moorhouse, only the females of the green turtle come up on the beaches. Other workers have reported that occasionally a male is washed ashore while in the process of copulation. The females continue their trek until they are above the high waterline. Should they stop before this point, their efforts would be barren inasmuch as too much dampness in the sand adjacent to the eggs causes deterioration and death of the embryos.

Investigations have supported the legend that turtles are not easily disturbed while laying. Many workers report that hard abuse, loud noises, heavy blows to the carapace, etc., although deterrents before laying starts, are ignored by the female once laying commences. Carr and Hirth (1962) state that the Costa Rican green turtle may be startled by the slightest show of artificial light or by the slightest movement. They point out that on Ascension Island, however, the turtles are almost oblivious to outside interference from the time of stranding on the beach.

The average number of eggs laid by green turtles in different parts of the world varies as follows: Tortuguero, Costa Rica—110.0 (Carr and Hirth, 1962); Ascension Island—115.5 (Carr and Hirth, 1962); Sarawak—104.7 (Hendrickson, 1958); Bigi Santi, Surinam—142.8 (Pritchard, 1969d); Elanti and Dapp Island, Surinam—141.9 (Pritchard, 1969d); South Yemen—106 (Hirth and Carr, 1970). The apparent contrast among the above averages is overshadowed by the large amount of variability within each colony. As many as 226 eggs (Pritchard, 1969d) and as few as 3 (Hendrickson, 1958) have been recorded.

Sometimes the turtle will begin to dig a nest and then depart, the mission unfulfilled, only to dig another nest and complete the act in another part of the beach. Some writers have attributed this action to the desire by the turtle to confuse would-be predators. Moorhouse, after painstaking observations, lists four very practical reasons for this apparent deception. They are: (1) an impediment to digging, such as a log or a rock, (2) falling in of sand due to the weight of the animal, (3) interruptions by another turtle blundering in, or by man, and (4) an undesirable pit because the animal urinated in it.

Bustard and Greenham (1968) conducted further investigations at Heron Island. They listed two reasons why turtles failed to complete nesting: (1) obstruction of the turtle's digging by large or thickly matted tree roots, (2) collapse of the chamber sides due to insufficient support of the sand. The men found that very low moisture or an insufficient number of tree rootlets and root hairs were the primary contributions to the second reason. Statistical analysis for the presence of tree rootlets and moisture content for successful nest pits showed a high correlation.

There is some evidence that turtles arriving later in the breeding season are apt to destroy an incubated nest while digging a fresh pit. Moorhouse observed many nests thus destroyed and he also saw seagulls eating the excavated eggs. He attributed great loss of young to this occurrence and stated that although eggs thus disturbed may be recovered and planted in the sand they will not hatch. Bustard and Tognett (1969) used a stochastic model to show that nest destruction by female green turtles is density dependent and therefore is probably one of the important natural controls on maintaining a stable population. Few areas still remain today, however, where turtle populations have survived at a high enough level for this factor to be of any consequence.

Moorhouse noted a great variation in size of the carapace of laying females. The largest was 48 inches long by 42 inches wide whereas the smallest was 35 inches by 35 inches. However, a strong mode is obvious from his data. Of 50 turtles measured, 33 were between 40 and 43 inches in carapace length, 5 were less than 40 inches in length, and the remaining 12 were greater than 43 inches. Of 1,146 mature nesting females measured at Tortuguero (Carr and Hirth, 1962) the smallest measured 27.25 inches in carapace length and the largest was 46.25 inches, with the average being 39.40 inches. The average size of nesting females in the China Sea population studied by Hendrickson (1958) was 38.50 inches. Nesting green turtles at Ascension Island (Carr and Hirth, 1962) ranged from 33.00 to 55.50 inches and averaged 42.55 inches in carapace length. Yemeni turtles were between 31 and 45 inches, the average being 37.8 inches (Hirth and Carr, 1970).

The eggs of the green turtle are spherical and vary somewhat in size. These differences are listed in table 7.

Table 7. SIZE OF GREEN TURTLE EGGS

Area	Number examined	Size range, mm	Mean size, mm	Source
Tortuguero	400	41.1-50.1	45.7	Carr and Hirth, 1962
Ascension Island	100	49.0-58.7	54.6	Carr and Hirth, 1962
Shell Beach, Guyana	4	46-47 x 47-49	46.25 x 48	Pritchard, 1969d
Abul Wad Beach, Aden State, Yemen*	100	40-45	42.5	Hirth and Carr, 1970
Sharma Beach, Quaiti State, Yemen*	50	37.5-47.5	42.3	Hirth and Carr, 1970

*Peoples Democratic Republic of Yemen.

When laid, the egg is not completely filled and is therefore slightly dented. After several days in the nest this depression disappears. The hypothesis that filling out is a result of absorption of water from the surrounding damp sand is bolstered by the increase in egg weight during incubation. Cunningham and Harwitz (1936) report that the weight increase was greater than the volume increase and conclude that this difference accounts for an increased turgidity. Moorhouse washed sand, thoroughly dried it, and covered it carefully after putting it over several green turtle eggs. The eggs thus treated did not increase in weight but in fact shriveled.

Shriveling was also noted in eggs that had been left unprotected from the sun and air. The yolk of these eggs was intact, but the white was depleted. The yolk of a newly laid egg is largely water and contains very little albumin. When heated in the fresh state, the yolk will not coagulate, but coagulation is possible after desiccation.

The parchmentlike egg shell is applied in layers, the outer layer of which contains lime. This outer layer is not essential to development, although it probably serves a protective function. Eggs from which some of the slimy layers had been lost developed normally.

Although the growth of eggs in a given clutch is fairly uniform, the rate of growth and development in eggs from individual nests differs considerably. Such factors as sunlight and weather conditions probably limit these different growth rates.

Eggs that were incubated in the nest where they were laid and that were not disturbed showed a higher percentage of hatchings than did those taken from the killed female. However, Moorhouse's data show a great loss of eggs from accidents and misfortunes which apparently occur in nature. He marked fifty nests immediately after the eggs had been laid. From the fifty, the following results were obtained:

11	Definite hatchings (22%)
10	Destroyed by other turtles
6	Destroyed by encroaching seas
23	Nothing known of outcome

Moorhouse found that on Heron Island the incubation period ranged from 9 weeks and 2 days to 10 weeks and 2 days. Different incubation times exist in different parts of the world, attributable mainly to temperature differences. After 1 day of incubation the eggs show a white spot at the upper pole. There the albumin becomes apposed to the shell, and in the center of the area the developing embryo is seen as a clear patch when viewed in reflected light.

Moorhouse briefly summarizes the main points of the embryology as

2 days old	Body of five somites
10 days old	Heart closed and beating regularly; flipper buds definite and eye well advanced
13 days old	Allantois a small saclike outgrowth
30 days old	Ribs and plates plainly marked off; eye enormously enlarged
38 days old	Carapace becoming colored; head, lower jaw, and flipper move at will

The definitive work on the embryology of turtles is probably that of L. Agassiz (1875a). Readers particularly interested in this subject are especially referred to his treatise and to Penyapol (1958).

Simkiss (1962), working with *Dermochelys* eggs, found

that the high degree of calcification of the juvenile turtle at hatching requires five times the calcium present in the egg yolk. A high magnesium content of 40:1 (16:1 in the average vertebrate) led Simkiss to postulate that these cations might be obtained from seawater. Bustard and Greenham (1968) measured chloride levels of water in fertile nests of green turtles and showed that the volume of water intake by eggs would be insufficient to obtain the required amounts of calcium and magnesium from seawater. They postulated that it may be obtained externally by means of metabolism of the egg mass. Later experiments by Bustard, Simkiss, and Jenkins (1969) were conducted with green and loggerhead turtle eggs incubated in silica or coral sand moistened with distilled water. Their results show that the source of calcium and magnesium must be from the egg shell.

In the opinion of Moorhouse, the annual production of young turtles could be greatly increased if certain simple operations were followed after the females were caught. He decried the practice of turning the animals on their backs and hauling them away before they get a chance to lay. His arguments and research are forceful on this point, and it is likely that if the 100 or more eggs available inside each captured female were allowed to develop the additional hatchlings would be a stimulant to the waning supply of green turtles.

He made two plantings to try to show the importance of saving the unlaid eggs. Five nests were made from eggs of slain females. The percentage of successful hatches from these nests was roughly calculated at 16%. This figure includes one nest that was disturbed when a loggerhead subsequently attempted to dig a nest. Moorhouse feels that this data should be included since the catastrophe is so common. It is probable, then, that the average percentage of hatchings from unlaid eggs would be somewhat higher than 16.

Since nematode worms abound when the eggs are not thoroughly cleaned, the practice of taking eggs from the oviducts and planting them must be accompanied by great care in the removal of offal.

It has been suggested that the young turtles hatching earliest turn upon the other eggs and young and that they eat them or so injure them that death ensues. There is no evidence that this idea is true; young turtles do not eat anything when newly hatched. Furthermore, they are copiously supplied with food in the form of yolk, which is sometimes still visible outside the body a short time after hatching.

Moorhouse tried to transplant several batches of eggs from the original nest after development had commenced but with no success. It is apparently very difficult to handle the developing eggs without an amount of injury sufficient to cause death. Hendrickson (1958) noted that eggs transplanted with little care before one day after laying had 47.1% hatching success. More careful transplantation was done by him on 14 nests for embryological study and 23 other nests which had, respectively, 46.7% and 40% hatching success. He concluded that (p. 507) "Concussion and rotation of developing eggs were almost uniformly damaging at later stages when the embryonic disc and overlaying albumin had become adherent to the shell, but eggs moved on the morning after laying seemed to suffer little from relatively rough handling."

At Tortuguero, 50.7% of 12,000 eggs removed and handled hatched in 1959 and 50.8% of 30,484 eggs hatched the following year (Carr and Hirth, 1962). Carr and Hirth (1962) also reported 54.4% of 1,208 eggs hatched on Ascension Island. Pritchard (1969d) records 97% fertility for the only clutch of eggs examined for fertility at Bigi Santi, Surinam. He notes that previous hatch percentages were from transferred eggs and that (p. 95) "Their [Carr and Hirth] statement that 'removal of eggs from the nest and installation in artificial nests impose no additional mortality' is probably incorrect." When nests are located with a stick, the yolk from the broken eggs reduces the hatch of the others considerably.

Bustard and Greenham (1968) reported a hatching success of 67% from 30,000 green turtle eggs that were transplanted to a hatchery closely approximating natural conditions. The men also artificially incubated eggs in groups of 5 and 10 in culture dishes containing dry, heat-sterilized coral sand and distilled water or other solutions of known chlorinity. Their results are shown on the next page:

Seawater, %	Cl (mgCl/kg)*	Hatch, %
0	0	53
25	365	33
50	730	27
75	1,095	0
100	1,461	0

*Chlorinity is measured in milograms of chlorine per kilogram solution or parts per million by weight.

Seawater, %	Temperature, °C	Hatch, %
0	15	0
25	20	0
50	27	60
75	32	60
100	38	0

They concluded that the eggs must be able to withstand normal variations of 2°C plus the effect of metabolic heating (about 6°C). Eggs are able to hatch in chloride concentrations much higher than those found in natural nests except where such nests are below the spring high tide mark. Incubation time varied from 80 days at 27°C to 47 to 49 days at 32°C. Weight gains caused by uptake of water were 40% and 35% in two eggs incubated at 32°C; 37% on one egg at 30°C; and 14%, 16%, and 27% at 27°C.

Various observers tend to agree that all the young from any one nest do not emerge on the same day or night. However, the young apparently all leave the nest by the end of 48 hours. Bustard (1967) suggests that this nocturnal emergence is primarily an adaptation to enhance survival by limiting the effects of high temperature and predators. Observers have noted that when an occasional hatchling comes to the surface during the day he will often remain motionless with just his head exposed until dark. In work with green turtle hatchlings at Bigi Santi, Surinam, Mrosovsky (1968) found that thermal inhibition of activity is a major factor in limiting the emergence of hatchlings to nighttime.

If the sand is wet, the young turtles are sometimes unable to escape and huddle together beneath the surface until conditions become such that they can leave.

Fig. 14. Loggerhead hatchlings leaving the nest.

Moorhouse states that only rarely do the young green turtles dig their way out of the sand during daylight, but that such hapless creatures as do wander forth into the light are quickly devoured by gulls and heron. On Heron Island, furthermore, a large nocturnal crab, *Ocypoda*, feeds on the young turtles as they emerge at night. On the same island house cats are known to be harmful predators. Once past these terrestrial hazards, the young turtle faces danger from sharks and large fishes.

Although abnormalities of the carapace are fairly common in the young turtles, the length of the carapace is usually uniform. The respective means of carapace lengths of 100 hatchlings at Tortuguero and at Ascension Island are 49.7 and 51.7 mm with ranges of 46.0 to 56.0 and 49.1 to 55.0 (Carr and Hirth, 1962). Hatchlings measured at Bigi Santi, Surinam, ranged from 51 to 55 mm with a mean carapace length of 53.5 mm.

The newly hatched young of the green turtle are black to dark gray above and white below. Bustard (1970) states that such coloration is a negative survival factor on light-colored sand, that is, the young turtles are more easily spotted by predators and have less protection against solar radiation than would occur if their shells were of lighter coloration on top. He argues, however, that this coloration may have adaptive significance for their development at sea. Five hatchlings with their shells painted white and five others with natural coloration were placed in conditions closely approximating those in the ocean. The temperature of the white colored turtles was only 0.3°C above water temperature, but the others had temperatures averaging 1.4°C above the ambient temperature. Bustard reasons that this higher body temperature causes higher metabolism and thereby faster growth through the nondiving stage of the very young. Other species that do not have this type of coloration may reduce predation by other means, according to Bustard. As an example he cites the rough carapace of the loggerhead, which becomes spinose several months after hatching.

HAWKSBILL TURTLES

These turtles breed in warmer water between 25° north latitude and 25° south latitude. Copulation takes place near shore, and eggs are laid on sand of fine, gravelly beaches. Garman gives the mating season in Bermuda as April to June. The only nesting record of the hawksbill in the continental United States was near Juno, Florida, in August of 1959 (Carr et al., 1966). According to John Schmidt (1916), the hawksbill lays eggs high on the beach in dry sand under bushes from June to October in the Danish West Indies. Carr et al. (1966, p. 2) make the following observation: "It seems clear that nesting takes place periodically or sporadically on all undisturbed Caribbean shores, both insular and mainland, wherever there is suitable sand beach." They give the nesting range of the Atlantic hawksbill as southern Florida and Bermuda to Brazil. The nesting range includes, or once included, "the tropical Gulf coast of Mexico and its islands, and the whole of the West Indies to the northern coast of Cuba and throughout the Bahamas" (Carr et al., 1966, p. 2). The following recorded nesting sites are listed by Caldwell, Rathjen, and Hsu (1969): Florida, Jamaica, the Pedro and Morant cays, the Cayman Islands, the Danish West Indies (Virgin Islands of the United States), Grenada, Tobago, Trinidad, Guyana, Surinam, French Guiana, Panama, Costa Rica, Mexico, the islands and keys off the Central American coast, and Aves Island.

At Tortuguero, Costa Rica, the nesting season is from May through November, with the first two months being the principal time (Carr et al., 1966). In Venezuela the season is from May to August (Roze, 1955). Pritchard (1969d, p. 132) found these turtles "nesting in fair numbers on Shell Beach [Guyana] in August." He also reported limited nesting in Surinam in June and July and heavier nesting in French Guiana, according to local reports. In the Seychelles breeding is most evident during September to November (Hornell, 1927). In Ceylon (Deraniyagala, 1933) breeding areas are changed according to the time of the monsoon and are found from April to May on the northwest coast and from November to February on the southeast coast. Breeding is recorded in Grenada in July and August.

Very little information is available on the nesting cycle of *Eretmochelys*, but what does exist suggests that these turtles may also lay in two- or three-year cycles and may nest several times a season at about two-week intervals. The nesting behavior of the hawksbill is similar to that of the green and has been described by Deraniyagala (1939a) and Carr et al. (1966). Those persons interested in minor behavioral differences should refer to the latter report.

Nests are about 17 inches deep and 10 inches in diameter. The average clutch size is around 160, and the average size of nesting females is about 33 inches carapace length. Carr et al. (1966) give the average incubation time for 13 nests as 58.6 days. The eggs are spherical in shape and are 36 to 41 mm in diameter. Hirth and Carr (1970), however, found that seven nesting females in South Yemen ranged from 25 to 28.5 inches carapace length as compared to means of 33.1 inches and 32.72 inches for Shell Beach, Guyana, and Costa Rica, respectively. John Schmidt (1916) described the hawksbill as being the most prolific breeder among turtles in the Danish West Indies.

LOGGERHEAD TURTLES

These turtles are known to breed as far north as North Carolina and Virginia during June and July (Coker, 1906). Caldwell, Berry, Carr, and Ragotzkie (1959) report that the loggerhead nests on beaches of all coastal south Atlantic and Gulf states from North Carolina to Texas. It concentrates in rookeries at Hutchinson Island, Florida; Jekyll Island and Little Cumberland Island near Brunswick, Georgia; and Cape Romain, South Carolina. According to Caldwell (1959a), 600 nests a season were on Cape Romain beaches around 1940, the largest number anywhere on the Carolina coast. In April and May the turtles appear most frequently in the bays and creeks behind the island, and mating couples are common. Laying begins in mid-May and continues to August.

True (1884) reports egg laying on the sandy shoals on the south side of Florida. Mast (1911) describes nesting at dusk on a Florida beach about 50 feet from the water. According to Routa (1967), loggerhead nesting occurs from the first week in May to the last week in August at Hutchinson Island, Florida. He estimated that over 5,000 nests were made in 1967. John Schmidt (1916) quotes Hooker (1908b) in giving the breeding season as April to June. Hooker describes two nests each season with 100 eggs each. Nesting on Sanibel Island and Captiva Island, Florida, occurs from May through August (Turtles with a new lease on life, 1970).

In Colombia, loggerhead turtles spawn from mid-April to mid-August east of Santa Marta on "wide-open beaches, on the average 25 to 30 m wide and ascending with a straight or smoothly sloping gradient up to the belt of vegetation" (Kaufmann, 1968, p. 45). In Tongaland, Natal, the season is from early November to late January with scattered nesting occurring a month before and after this period (Hughes, Bass, and Mentis, 1967). Hughes, Bass, and Mentis (1967, p. 13) state that although these turtles prefer sand of a finer texture than the leatherbacks that nest in the same area, this factor is secondary to the nature of the seabed directly off the beaches. They write that loggerheads "appeared to come ashore on beaches adjacent to reefs of rock which might or might not be exposed at lower tide levels." These littoral rocky reefs probably constitute a feeding ground for the adults, and a reasonable assumption is that the most heavily frequented nesting areas would be those in closest proximity to them. Caldwell (1959) found that nesting turtles on the eastern coast of the United States show a preference for beaches that are broken by dunes or vegetation and thereby present a dark and broken horizon to turtles in the water.

In a survey of beach types in relation to nesting preferences at Cape Romain, South Carolina, Baldwin and Lofton (Caldwell, 1959) noted that the most popular type was the wide sloping beach similar to that mentioned by Kaufmann. The turtles often made primary excavations and subsequently moved to another spot to nest. Baldwin and Lofton suggest that this occurs when the sand is packed too hard, the sand is too dry and soft, there are layers of oyster shells, or there is an abundance of tough vegetation roots. Primary excavations made too near the high tide mark may also be a reason for their abandonment.

The nesting behavior of the loggerhead turtle is similar to that of the green turtle. This has been described for the Atlantic subspecies by Caldwell, Carr, and Ogren (1959) and by Kaufmann (1968), and for the Pacific subspecies by Deraniyagala (1939a). The entire act from stranding to re-entering the surf takes about one hour (Kaufmann, 1968).

Apparently loggerhead turtles, like green turtles, breed every two or three years, and during the nesting season they may nest several times. The interval between nestings is given by Caldwell et al. (1959) as 12 to 15 days and by Hughes et al. (1967) as 16 to 17 days.

Comparative figures on the size of nesting females and clutch sizes are given in table 8.

Table 8. SIZE OF NESTING LOGGERHEAD FEMALES AND THEIR CLUTCHES

Location	Carapace length,* cm	Clutch size* (n = sample size)		Source
Cape Romain, S.C.	92.7 (84.5-102.5)	n = 18	126 (64-198) n = 71	Caldwell, 1959a
Jekyll Island, Ga.	95.9 (79.5-114.9)	n = 110		Caldwell, Carr, and Ogren, 1959
Tongaland, Natal	93.6† (4.6 SD)	n = 134	112 n = 98	Hughes, Bass, and Mentis, 1967
Tongaland, Natal	93.9† (4.3SD)	n = 156	118 n = 68	Hughes and Mentis, 1967
Colombia	87.5 (70.0-102.0)	n = 65	106 (58-163) n = 52	Kaufmann, 1968

*Bold numbers indicate mean; the range is given in parentheses; and SD is the standard deviation.
†Round shell measurements.

Fig. 15.   An adult loggerhead in comparison with a hatchling.

The eggs are round, between 1 5/8 and 2 inches in diameter, and weigh about 1 1/4 ounces each. Baldwin and Lofton (Caldwell, 1959) report incubation times ranging from 49 to 62 days, with an average of 55 days. In both McAllister, Bass, and van Schoor (1965) and Hughes and Mentis (1967) incubation times of Tongaland nests are close to 70 days. Two Florida nests took 57 and 68 days to hatch (Caldwell, Carr, and Hellier, Jr., 1956b). Schmidt (1962) lists a minimum incubation period of 45 days under artificial conditions in Florida. A fresh loggerhead turtle nest on Virginia Key, Florida, was discovered by Al Harris on the morning of 17 June 1971, and he and I carefully unearthed it on 29 July 1971. It contained 91 hatchlings, 1 dead embryo, and 3 infertile eggs. If we assume that the young turtles would have normally emerged the following night, the incubation period would have been 42 days. The average hatching success of 62 nests at Cape Romain, South Carolina, was 73.4% (Caldwell, 1959). Hughes and Mentis (1967) report 85.7% for 91 nests at Tongaland, Natal.

Newly hatched loggerheads range in color from a carapace of light brown to gray black. The plastron is usually white,

Fig. 16. Loggerhead hatchlings.

and the margins of the shell and the flippers are also white.
The hatchlings are about 1 4/5 inches long (carapace length)
and about 1 1/2 inches wide. They weigh about 3/5 of an
ounce.

RIDLEY TURTLES

Ridleys exhibit the strangest reproductive pattern of all the
sea turtles. The olive ridley nests in the Atlantic on the western coast of Africa and in the Guianas, and Kemp's ridley
nests on a stretch of shore north of Tampico, Mexico (Carr,
1963).

The breeding of the olive ridley in the Guianas has been
described by Pritchard (1969*a*). It nests in fair numbers on
Shell Beach, Guyana, and probably also on Waini Beach, Turtle Beach, and Dauntless Point, Leguan Island. He gives the
peak season at Shell Beach as May and June, with some nesting in August. Richard and Hughes (1972) found two large
nesting aggregations of *L. olivacea* on the Pacific coast of
Costa Rica. Between September and November over 100,000
turtles collect offshore at each of the two sites; smaller numbers are present as early as July and as late as November.

Pritchard (1969*d*) cites Schulz (1964) as recording 97 nesting emergencies at Bigi Santi, Surinam, between 29 April and
17 August 1964. A few turtles nest in April and May, but
more nest in June and July. Pritchard investigated a report of
mass nesting emergences at Elanti, Surinam, during early
June 1966. He estimates that during the nights of 7, 8, and 9
June 400, 100, and 300 turtles nested, respectively. He further mentions that another mass arrival comparable to the

earlier one occurred on 24 June, although he was unable to be there at that time. More intensive observation during the 1967 season established a 14-day periodicity to these peak nesting periods: "the mid-point of the first small wave on 30 May was followed by a major aggregation centering on 13 June, another on 11 July, and a small, tail-end peak centering around 25 July" (p. 103). A concomitant to this peak nesting was the presence of a fairly strong onshore wind.

According to Pritchard, the internesting interval for the olive ridley, as with the green turtle, is determined more by external factors than by internal ones. In Surinam the olive ridleys normally nest twice a season. The nesting process occurs at night and is similar to that of the green turtle. Most of the mature female ridleys measured by Pritchard were between 26 and 28 inches carapace length, although the range of 241 individuals was 24.5 inches to 29.125 inches. The largest female on record was from Ceylon; she was 31.1 inches long (Deraniyagala, 1939a).

The average clutch size for 928 nests at Surinam was 116.072 eggs. Incubation times for 22 nests ranged from 29 to 62 days, and Pritchard reports that the two nests he examined for hatching success showed strikingly high percentages of viable eggs. Eggs of the olive ridley from Guyana were 39 to 40 mm in diameter.

Pritchard (1969d), pp. 119-120) describes the coloration of the young thusly:

> The hatchling ridleys were uniform gray-black in color with a small white mark at each side at the supralabial scale, another on the hind part of the umbilical protruberance, and more where the ridges of the plastron cross the abdominal and femoral laminae. The extreme border of the carapace and a very thin line along the trailing edge of both fore and hind flippers were also white. This coloration is similar to that of hatchling *kempi* described by Carr and Caldwell (1958), except that *olivacea* lacks the thin white mark in the anal region.

The first record of a nesting Kemp's ridley (Padre Island, Texas) was published in 1951 (Werler). Fugler and Webb reported finding four juveniles in Veracruz in 1957, but the location of a major nesting area was not published until Carr (1963) and Hildebrand (1963). A film made in 1947, and unknown to the scientific community until 1961, of nesting ridleys at Rancho Nuevo, Mexico, was the basis for these reports. Carr estimates that 40,000 of these turtles were present during that filming. Like the olive ridley, which shows some aggregated nesting emergences, Kemp's ridley is unique in that it almost exclusively nests in these emergences, called *arribadas,* and in that it is the only sea turtle that nests primarily during daylight.

The subsequent work on the ridley population is summarized by Chavez, et al. (1967). Most of the nesting occurs within a small stretch of beach from Boca San Vicente to Barra Coma near Rancho Nuevo, Tamaulipas, Mexico. During the season studied, there were seven times of mass arrivals, with some solitary nesting: 3 and 4 May—200 females; 11 May—150 to 200; 28 May—100; 31 May—1,317; 4 June—20; 16 June—200; 23 June—25. These numbers apparently represent a drastic reduction in the numbers of laying females estimated to have used this area in the 1940s.

The average number of eggs per nest was 110 (n = 271, range: 54 to 185). The eggs ranged in size from 35 to 44.5 mm in diameter with an average of 38.9. The female takes less than an hour to nest, on the average, and the limited tagging data accumulated show renesting intervals ranging from 20 to 28 days. Incubation takes from 50 to 70 days.

Chavez et al. found that the turtle arrivals occurred when moderate to strong winds blew from the north, east, and southeast. The winds lower the air temperature, which may prevent dehydration in the turtles. Pritchard (1969a) notes that the presence of a moderately strong onshore wind is associated with mass arrivals in Surinam and Guerrero of *Lepidochelys olivacea* and in Tamaulipas of *Lepidochelys kempii.* He feels the most logical explanation for this association is the obliteration of nesting tracks by the wind. The track of a ridley turtle is so shallow it can be covered easily, and this erasure may have important survival value.

LEATHERBACK TURTLES

Until less than two decades ago leatherback turtles had rarely been observed breeding in the Mexican Gulf or the Caribbean. The little information available gave April as the nesting period (Pope, 1939).

The nesting period for leatherback turtles in Surinam and

Guyana is early May to early July (Pritchard, 1969a), close to the late April to mid-July season at Matina, Costa Rica (Carr and Ogren, 1959). At Silebache Beach in French Guiana, which has "possibly the largest breeding population of leatherbacks in the hemisphere" (Pritchard, 1969b), the nesting season is from early May to July and August (Pritchard, 1969a) and averages about 300 layings per night. Bacon (1970) lists March to August as the season in Trinidad. Pritchard (1971), reviewing the limited nesting records in Florida, gives this season as 15 April to 26 July.

John Schmidt (1916) gives the breeding season as March to May in the Danish West Indies, and he says that the eggs are laid well back from the water. He describes four laying periods at 15- to 17-day intervals, resulting in a total of 700 to 800 eggs.

Caldwell, Carr, and Hellier, Jr. (1956a) give American nesting records for the leatherback turtle in the following areas: Florida, Jamaica, Costa Rica, Trinidad, Tobago, St. Croix and Tortola, Honduras, Nicaragua, the Bahamas, and Brazil. Additional records are mentioned by Caldwell and Rathjen (1969): the Pedro and Morant cays, the Cayman Islands, Saint Kitts, Nevis, and Barbados. Kaufmann (1971) found seven nesting females and four other nests east of Santa Marta, Colombia, in 1970. Pritchard (1971) reviewed the breeding range and included Venezuela, Saint Thomas, Puerto Rico, Grenada, and Brazil. He adds that the leatherback appears to have a strong preference for mainland nesting.

A large breeding concentration of leatherbacks exists on the east coast of Malaya (Tweedie, 1953). According to Hendrickson and Winterflood (1961, p. 187), "North of the town of Dungun, Trengganu, as many as forty females have been counted in one night along five hundred yards of beach." These authors report the nesting season as extending from May to about the middle of September. Fitter (1961) estimated the adult female population in Malaya to be about 850, which he felt constituted the majority of the world population of females (1,000). This estimate now appears to be lower than the actual total. Pritchard's (1971) more realistic assessment puts the population of breeding females at between 29,000 and 40,000.

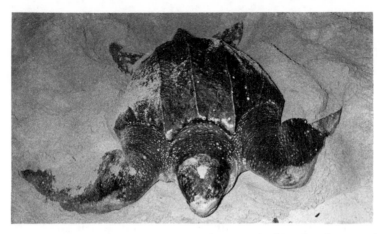

Fig. 17. The leatherback turtle is easily recognized by the absence of scutes, by the strongly tapering carapace, and by five to seven keels.

In Tongaland, Natal, the breeding season occurs from November to February with some nesting a month before and after these dates (Hughes, Bass, and Mentis, 1967). McAllister, Bass, and van Schoor (1965) observed that these turtles seemed to prefer beaches with coarse sand in contrast with loggerhead turtles that nest in the same area and favor beaches where the sand is of finer texture. As mentioned in the section on loggerhead nesting, this preference for a certain type of sand appears to be determined by the approach conditions of the beach. Hughes, Bass, and Mentis (1967) note that leatherbacks come ashore on stretches of beach that are most easily approached. They cite two probable reasons for this behavior:

(a) Leatherbacks, being so large, require plenty of room in which to maneuver and therefore shun rock-strewn areas where their movements may be restricted.

(b) The skin of the leatherback is tender and could easily tear or be damaged if the animal accidentally rubbed against or collided with the rocks.

Pritchard (1971, p. 17) found that leatherbacks in Malaya and the Guianas select beaches with "sufficient slope so that the climb to dry sand above the high tide mark would not involve a long overland trek."

In Ceylon the leatherback lays eggs three or four times during the year, particularly during the months of May and June. Nests are made at night, between 9:00 and 11:00 P.M., on exposed sandy beaches 50 to 60 feet from the water. From 90 to 150 eggs 50 to 54 mm in diameter are laid. The incubation period is about 60 days. Prior to nesting the males often follow the females into the littoral water, but they do not land (Deraniyagala, 1939a). West Africa, New Guinea, Thailand, Fiji, and the Pacific coast of Mexico are additional sites of leatherback nesting (Pritchard, 1971).

The nesting process is in all essential respects similar to that of the green turtle. It has been reported in detail by Deraniyagala (1939a), Carr and Ogren (1959), and Pritchard (1969d; 1971). The adult females exhibit a gait similar to that of the female green turtle; the leatherbacks use a simultaneous movement of all four limbs. This type of locomotion is presumably a factor of its large size and weight. At Matina, Costa Rica, nesting females make deep, primary excavations before digging the actual nest itself. These may be deep enough that the top of the carapace is level with the beach. In contrast, leatherbacks nesting at Bigi Santi, Surinam, do not excavate a deep body pit but instead start digging the egg cavity a few minutes after selecting the nest site. In either case the nest is generally deeper than that of the other sea turtles, and this factor, combined with the scattering of sand at the completion of nesting, makes locating the eggs later difficult.

Carr and Ogren (1959, p. 14) make the following observation regarding the egg complement: "A feature of the trunk-back egg complement . . . is the inclusion of a number of undersized, often misshapen, yolkless eggs. In the one case in which the position in the nest of these yolkless eggs was noticed they were at the top of the heap in the nest. It seems likely that they are usually laid last." This phenomenon appears to be universal to leatherback turtles throughout the world. Hughes, Bass, and Mentis (1967) examined 24 clutches of eggs at Tongaland. The mean number of yolked eggs per clutch was 106 (standard deviation of 22), and the mean number of yolkless eggs was 30 (standard deviation of 27). The number of normal eggs is slightly more than that found by Pritchard (1969d) in Surinam.

Hughes, Bass, and Mentis (1967) found that the average size of 26 adult leatherbacks was 164 cm carapace length (round shell measurement). Sixteen mature females from Surinam (Pritchard, 1969d) ranged in carapace length from 58 1/2 inches (149 cm) to 67 inches (170 cm). Twenty adult females in Trinidad (Bacon, 1970) had an average carapace length (round shell measurement) of 158 cm.

Pritchard (1969d) and Hughes, Bass, and Mentis (1967) found an internesting period for leatherbacks of 9 to 10 days. More extensive data on nesting by leatherbacks in Surinam show an average internesting interval of 10.5 days with the numbers of nestings during a season commonly being six, sometimes seven, and rarely eight or even nine times (Pritchard, 1971). Limited results suggest that these turtles do not breed every year but may nest in two- or three-year intervals.

The normal eggs of the leatherback are just over 2 inches in diameter. The incubation period is given by Pritchard (1969d) as 60 to 68 days, by Carr and Ogren (1959) as 51 to 74 days, by Hughes (1969) as 56 to 72 days, by Balasingam (1967) as 53 to 60, and by Pritchard (1971) (for Mexico) as 61 to 70 days. The newly hatched young are 2 3/8 to 2 3/4 inches long (carapace length), and they weigh about 2 ounces. Pritchard (1971, p. 28) describes the hatchlings.

The hatchlings are similar to the adults in appearance . . . but the fore flippers are proportionally even longer, and both shell and skin are covered with small scales. These flake off after a few weeks. No trace of the epidermal layer of mosaic bones is present at hatching; this develops during the first year or two of life. The hatchlings also possess striking white lines along each of the carapace ridges. These disappear well before maturity is reached, although their continuations along the skin of the neck remain.

MIGRATION

Early investigations into migration were made by John Schmidt (1916). He found little evidence of any extensive movement among green turtles. The greatest distance traversed by nine individuals tagged by him was fifty miles. Moorhouse snipped off the extensions of the pygal plates in order to mark 1,300 newly hatched young. They all swam toward deep water, and none are recorded as being later reported. Hornell (1927) states that hawksbill turtle populations are strongly localized.

At Tortuguero, Costa Rica, 3,205 adult green turtles were tagged by Carr (1965) over an eight year period. Most of the 129 returns came from the coast of Nicaragua, but others were distributed across the Caribbean, with distant returns as follows: one from Marquesas Keys off the tip of Florida; one from the northern tip of Cuba; four from the Gulf of Mexico off the Yucatán Peninsula; and two from the Gulf of Maracaibo in Venezuela. These returns, plus (1) no turtle has ever been found renesting elsewhere; (2) none has ever been caught at Tortuguero except during the nesting season; and (3) recovery times do not correlate with distance covered, suggesting a fixed travel schedule, support the theory that the green turtle does migrate.

The most impressive migration by any sea turtle is that suggested by tagging studies on the green turtle population on Ascension Island. These turtles travel 1,400 miles from this island, where they nest, to their feeding grounds on the coast of Brazil. The absence of grass beds around Ascension and the island's isolation from the mainland lend credence to recovery data since Ascension cannot be used for a feeding ground and accidental discovery by individual turtles is unlikely.

Koch, Carr, and Ehrenfeld (1969) believe the most tenable theory for the migratory mechanism of the turtles' travels from Ascension Island to Brazil is that of chemoreception. The authors rule out celestial navigation for three reasons: (1) lack of acuity in the turtle eye when it is out of water (Ehrenfeld and Koch, 1967); (2) a biological clock necessary for position finding would be reset by any shift in the external cycle of day and night; and (3) it is difficult to visualize the initial evolutionary process. They note that the diffusion of chemical substances from Ascension Island may render these chemicals only 100- to 1,000-fold lower in the vicinity of the Brazil coast, a "dilution factor which is not so great as to exclude chemical perception of an Ascension specific substance in the coastal waters of Brazil" (Koch et al., 1969, p. 175). Those persons interested in a complete discussion of possible mechanisms should refer to the paper cited at the beginning of this paragraph.

Carr (1965, p. 7) suggests that the behavior of a stranding female may be pertinent for a chemoreception theory. "In the course of coming ashore a female nearly always stops in the backwash of the surf and presses her snout deliberately against the sand, sometimes repeating the process as she moves up the wet lower beach. This behavior appears to be an olfactory assessment of the shore, although it could also be tactile." Koch, Carr, and Ehrenfeld (1969) think that the hatchlings may somehow be imprinted with some "sensible essence" of the beach from which they hatch. The detection of this essence could then guide them back to the same beach when they mature.

Carr and Caldwell (1956) tagged 43 immature green turtles and released them at 25(37) and 60(6) miles from their point of capture on the Gulf coast of peninsular Florida in the Cedar Keys—Crystal River region. An 18.6% recovery at the original area of capture (one was captured only hours after release and was heading in this direction), coupled with no recoveries in other areas, strongly suggests a homing tendency in green turtles. Only two recoveries from 25 immature ridleys tagged and released in a similar manner gave insufficient data to support similar tendencies in ridleys. Readers interested in accounts of green turtle homing as told by local inhabitants of the Caribbean should read Carr (1956a).

Caldwell, Carr, and Ogren (1959) found that loggerhead turtles can travel long distances. A female of 35 inches carapace length was tagged on 27 May 1957 at Hutchinson Island on the east coast of Florida. About 302 days later she was captured off the mouth of the Mississippi River, 1,000 shoreline miles from the place of tagging. Caldwell, Carr, and Hellier, Jr. (1956b) reported another female, tagged at Fort Pierce, Florida, that was recaptured three weeks later by a shrimp trawler off Daytona Beach, Florida, some 130 shoreline miles northward.

Recently *The Miami Herald* (19 July 1973) reported that a turtle tagged in Florida traveled 1,300 miles from Delray Beach, Florida to Aves Island. The 20-ounce turtle doubled its size and weight during the 12-month journey. This is the farthest distance a turtle tagged by the Department of Natural Resources in Jensen Beach has been reported to have traveled.

The green turtle, *Chelonia mydas,* has thus far been shown to be the most regular long-distance migrant. The ridley turtles, with their mass arrivals or *arribidas* for nesting, must also regularly return to the nesting site. The extent to which scattering and long distance movement occurs after the nesting season, however, is still not clear. If the immature ridley turtles in the Cedar Key—Crystal River area of Florida (Carr and Caldwell, 1956) do return to Rancho Nuevo to nest after maturity and are not simply waifs, they must travel a considerable distance.

Hornell (1927) stated that hawksbill turtle populations are strongly localized. These turtles travel less than other sea turtles, but there may be some movement by individual turtles.

Although loggerhead turtles are known to travel long distances, no evidence exists yet that they regularly migrate long

Fig. 18. An immature leatherback.

distances. The leatherback turtle, *Dermochelys coriacea,* is the greatest wanderer, reaching high latitudes more frequently than any other species of sea turtle. To what extent, if any, they make regular migrations is unknown, but Pritchard (1972) notes that their occurrence in Nova Scotia coincides with the final weeks of nesting at points 2,000 miles to the south.

PHYSIOLOGY AND BEHAVIOR

Like other reptiles, turtles are poikilothermal, and their body activity is dependent upon the temperature of the environment. They are indigenous to tropical areas and are found with only rare exception in the warmer seas of the world.

McGinnis (1968) found that the respiration rate in the Pacific green turtle, measured by radiotelemetry, is directly proportional to the degree of activity and the body temperature. He reports that the green turtle is eurythermal, that is, able to withstand changes in temperature. McGinnis observed that the turtles were more active in water with temperatures between 18°C and 22°C and that they assume a torpid state at temperatures between 26°C to 30°C. From his research, McGinnis found that the shell of the turtle appears to partially insulate the turtle from extreme heat and cold. Hirth (1962) gave limited data on cloacal temperatures of nesting females which showed their temperature to be slightly higher than that of the water, but his data were not conclusive. Mrosovsky and Pritchard (1971), however, substantiated this variance. They determined deep body temperatures of nesting *Dermochelys coriacea, Chelonia mydas,* and *Lepidochelys olivacea* by taking the temperatures of the eggs at laying. There was a significant difference between the ambient temperature and all three species as well as a significant gradation among species. Ridleys had the least elevation of body temperature, and leatherbacks had the most (about 3.0°C in the summer in the Guianas). The authors suggest that the large size and fatty insulation of *Dermochelys* as well as greater oxygen consumption may account for the higher elevation. The body temperature elevation in higher latitudes may reach 10°C or more and may account for the apparent well-being of leatherbacks in water of 12°C or less.

Being aquatic, sea turtles are assumed to have evolved an auxiliary mechanism as an adjunct to the lungs for interchanging oxygen and carbon dioxide with surrounding media. This adaptation has been accomplished by extensive capillary vascularization of the anus and cloacal region and the buccal cavity. While submerged, a sea turtle can circulate water in these cavities to some extent and thus prolong the time beneath the surface.

Pritchard (1969a) suggests that a papillose structure in the leatherback's throat may serve as an oxygen exchanger and enable the turtle to remain "at great depths at all times except when breeding." Bleakney (1965), however, believes this structure prevents jellyfish from sliding back up the turtle's throat.

A not inconsiderable problem confronts sea turtles when they attempt to breathe on land. Their body structure is adapted to the bouyant support of the water. When they crawl about on beaches, their entire weight is thrown onto the ventral surface, and breathing is accomplished only with difficulty. In order to expand the thoracic cavity, the great bulk of the animal must be forced upward.

It is well known, as Banks (1937) points out, that a heavier mortality occurs in green turtles being transported if they are not turned over on their backs. It is probably true that the luth is structurally more prone to asphyxiation on land, and the great bulk of this species makes breathing for them more difficult than for other turtles. The loggerhead is stronger in this respect.

In the presence of an overabundance of oxygen, no oxygen poisoning is likely to result at lower temperatures (Faulkner and Binger, 1927), although when 37.5°C is reached the symptoms are the same as for mammals suffering from oxygen poisoning; i.e., loss of appetite, rapid breathing, death. Hemorrhagic extravasations of lungs are found at autopsy.

Fig. 19. Turtles sometimes wedge themselves under rocks while resting.

Since these results were obtained with freshwater turtles, further work is needed to determine if these findings apply throughout the order Testudinata.

Shaw and Baldwin (1935) studied the breathing habits of freshwater turtles and found that a constant, strong inspiration is followed by a slow, interrupted expiration. Frequent pauses in the expiration allow the air to escape intermittently. Berkson (1966) found that Pacific green turtles in captivity follow a general sequence of long submergence, lasting from 15 to 50 minutes, followed by several short dives, lasting from 20 seconds to 2 or 3 minutes. McGinnis (1968) noted that long dives of these turtles in the wild were followed by a single breach. Closure of the nostrils by blood inflation of spongy tissue has been observed in resting loggerhead, green, and ridley turtles. It is presumed that this mechanism is used during the periods when the glottis might open reflexively to stimulus or during periods of low muscle tonus (Walker, 1959).

Berkson's (1966) studies on the Pacific green turtle show that they, and probably other sea turtles, make several physiological adjustments to diving that are common to other air-breathing vertebrates in aquatic habitats. Bradycardia (slow-ing of heart rate) develops slowly, but is broken when the animal struggles, and peripheral vasoconstriction occurs. Berkson's tests further suggested that metabolic rate decreases, thereby lowering oxygen demand. Oxygen content of tracheal air and carotid arterial blood dropped to less than 1% in about an hour following submergence. The turtles tested survived in this condition from 40 minutes to 5 hours before breathing again.

Belkin (1963) gives an anoxia tolerance for Cheloniidae breathing pure nitrogen of about 2 hours. He suggests this is achieved by slow metabolism, anaerobic glycolysis, and perhaps other "more exotic metabolic mechanisms." Experiments with freshwater turtles subjected to stagnant anoxia (Beldin, 1968) revealed the importance of blood circulation in the turtles' anoxia tolerance. Their lowered tolerance during stagnant anoxia is attributable to an inability to transfer substances between the blood and the central nervous system. Belkin (1968, p. 1088) states that "anaerobic glycolysis thus seems primarily responsible for maintaining the activity of the CNS [central nervous system] under anoxic conditions."

Because loggerhead turtles have been caught on red snapper banks by fishermen we can deduce that the turtles can withstand the pressures at 30 to 40 fathoms. Stomachs of green turtles kept under natural conditions are able to empty themselves of algae within 12 hours. When the turtles are kept out of water, however, the undigested food is still present in the stomach at the end of four days (Deraniyagala).

The secretion of copious tears by nesting sea turtles has been attributed to many causes, but the primary function of the tears appears to be osmoregulatory. Schmidt-Nielsen and Fange (1958) described a salt-excreting gland in the orbit of each eye in loggerhead sea turtles, similar to that previously noted in green turtles. This was confirmed by Holmes and McBean (1964), who found that the primary route of sodium and potassium excretion was through this gland, which is at least partially under the control of the adrenal cortex. Each gland consists of approximately 100 lobules that are filled with myriad, closely packed secretory tubules. Ellis and Abel (1964) examined glands from two loggerheads and four greens and found that they differed structurally from salt-secreting glands in marine birds but contained similar high concentrations of mitochondria and an intercellular system of agranular membranes that may participate directly in the secretion of electrolytes. A mucopolysaccharide fills the intercellular channels and may act as an ion trap to facilitate concentration of electrolytes. Those readers interested in the definitive structure of these glands and their enzymatic activities should refer to Abel and Ellis (1966).

The behavior of turtles has been observed for the most part during mating, egg laying, and immediately after hatching, since during these periods the turtles are most easily observed. Mating and nesting behavior are described in preceding sections.

The newly hatched turtles react very strongly to light and in a positive manner, as shown originally by Moorhouse, Hornell, and Deraniyagala and later confirmed by Daniel and Smith (1947). Mrosovsky and Carr (1967) found that the young green turtles show a preference for light and shorter wavelengths (blue and green versus red). Studies on both adults and hatchlings as they find their way to the sea indicate that the quality of the sky above the ocean is the primary stimulus for orientation. Even turtles who lack a direct view of the water have shown sea-finding ability except in cases of overcast skies or when blinded. Mrosovsky and Shettleworth (1968, p. 250) comment that "a brightness preference; a tropotactic reaction to light and the almost invariable association of the open horizon with seaward direction will explain the sea finding performance of hatchling green turtles on the Tortuguero beaches." Fischer (1964) demonstrated that hatchling green turtles possessed a sun compass sense but that loggerhead hatchlings did not have this sense of direction.

Within six days after hatching the hatchlings' reaction to light becomes very weak, and at the end of three weeks it may be completely reversed so that the young turtles avoid strong light (Daniel and Smith, 1947). The sea-finding ability, however, is not lost in either the adult males or females (Caldwell and Caldwell, 1962).

All young turtles are very active. They respond to vibra-

Fig. 20. Green hatchlings heading for the ocean.

tions in the water (rather than to sound) by diving. Some begin feeding the second day after hatching, but they cannot dive more than a few centimeters when first hatched. They are very sensitive to dirty water.

The first year of a turtle's life is called the "lost year" because no one really knows where the turtles spend this period of their life. Directly after entering the water for the first time, the hatchlings swim frantically out to sea. Continued swimming might take them out to the open ocean, where scattered evidence indicates they may be associated with raft communities. Caldwell (1969) reports that commercial fishermen in Mexico catch the young a good distance offshore and later sell them. Nine young loggerhead turtles were taken from one raft of sargassum weed in the Gulf Stream off Florida (Carr, 1967a). One neonate, about 11 weeks old, was taken in a 1-meter ring net along with sargassum weed and juvenile fish typical of a sargassum community. W. G. Smith (1968) and Caldwell (1968) report that encrustations on young loggerheads washed ashore provide additional evidence that the turtles associate with sargassum weed in their early life.

Experiments have shown that hatching success is at least

partially dependent upon clutch size. Clutches of less than 10 eggs have difficulty after hatching in reaching the surface. Carr and Hirth (1961) have described the social facilitation in green turtle siblings that helps them escape successfully from their nest. The hatchlings perform more or less three distinct functions: those on top scratch down the ceiling, those on the sides undercut the walls, and those on the bottom trample and compact the sand. The young on the bottom further act as a receptor-motor device when, during periods of quiescence, the weight of the other turtles stimulates them to activity, thereby inducing activity in the others.

Young green turtles while on shore walk like any four-footed beast, leaving an open track in the sand. Adults, however, advance by a series of heaves. Both fore flippers are brought forward to pull while the hind ones push. Derani-yagala claims that green turtles are able to travel at a rate of 10 meters per second in water.

FISHING METHODS

In the early days of Bermuda (1610) sea turtles were sufficiently abundant that fishermen could make a good haul by
going off the coast in small boats, finding the sea turtles, and
hitting them with iron bars or goads. William Strachey
(personal communication), who gives us this information,
also states that at other times, during the spring months, the
animals were caught as they climbed the beaches to lay.
Catching egg-laying turtles is widespread today, although the
practice is illegal in many parts of the Caribbean.

In some parts of the world a small fish called a remora,
Echeneis naucrates is attached to a line. The fish seeks out
turtles and attaches itself to one of them by its sucking de-
vices. The fishermen in some areas may attach two or three
other remoras and play the turtle as one would a fish; in
other areas the fishermen may follow the line to the turtle's
hiding place. For a comprehensive discussion of this unusual
fishing method, see James Parsons (1962).

The most efficient method of catching turtles and the one
used in the most productive parts of the Caribbean consists
of a mesh net constructed of a cotton line of about 33 thread
with a mesh varying from 8 to 12 inches knot to knot. The
net may be up to 200 feet long and from 20 to 40 feet deep.
It is supported by wooden floats and frequently is supplied
with wooden decoys shaped and painted like turtles. These
decoys, called mounting boards, range from very crude struc-

tures to very realistic imitations and are reportedly of value in luring males into the nest area. The net is set in water up to 12 fathoms or more and checked in the morning. Turtles are usually enmeshed when they come to the surface to breathe during the night. Unless they are removed, they may be attacked by sharks, which not only destroy the turtles but also damage the net.

Another method of capture uses a 5-foot iron ring with a strong, coarse mesh net, similar to a large dip net. This net is dipped from a boat over the turtle, which then becomes entangled. To some extent, usually when turtles are encountered casually, grains, harpoons, and spears are used. The methods most in vogue in different parts of the Caribbean are mentioned in the section on Value and Administration of the Fishery.

Turtles are frequently transported considerable distances, as from Nicaragua and Costa Rica to Florida. Some were landed from schooners at Key West, Florida, where they were kept in saltwater pens (kraals) until a sufficient number were ready for butchering. There is evidence that appreciable loss of weight occurs under these conditions. John Schmidt (1916) records a turtle weighing 34 1/2 pounds when shipped from the West Indies. When landed in Copenhagen about four weeks later, the turtle had decreased in weight by 20%.

Since they are unable to support the weight of the carapace properly when lying out of water, turtles transported alive are almost always turned over on their backs. In this position, with their flippers tied, they are unable to escape and are safe from suffocation.

TURTLE PRODUCTS

GREEN TURTLES

Although green turtles are captured primarily for their meat, their eggs are used often for food. Hendrickson (1958, p. 456) reports that in Malaya and Sarawak "some millions of *Chelonia mydas* eggs are marketed each year, contributing valuable fats and proteins to the local diet."

The flesh of the green turtle includes the muscles of the body and flippers. It constitutes about 40% of the entire

Table 9. WEIGHT DISTRIBUTION OF GREEN TURTLES, IN PERCENT

Total live weight	Male, 261 lb.	Female, 212 lb.	Female, 187 lb.	Female, 150 lb.	Female, 100 lb.
Head	2.0	2.4	2.4	2.3	3.0
Tail	1.4	0.24	0.25	0.09	0.06
Flippers and meat	47.0	52.0	47.0	46.0	57.0
Neck	1.9	1.7	2.6	3.3	3.5
Kidney	0.12	0.23	0.15	0.17	0.25
Liver	2.7	2.3	2.6	2.5	2.0
Heart	0.3	0.24	0.3	0.3	0.3
Calipee	7.0	6.7	6.2	6.7	7.5
Carapace	15.0	15.5	15.4	17.3	17.0
Entrails	8.5	10.5	8.1	8.0	6.5

Note: The author is indebted to Mr. Gerald Leanse for the data upon which these figures are based.

body weight. Covering the flesh and under the surface of the exoskeleton is a layer of rather gelatinous fat, which is particularly valuable for making soup. The dorsal fat and that of the flippers are characteristically green in color and are referred to as calipash. The fat from the ventral surface of the body is more yellowish in color and is called calipee. The word calipee is often used today to include all the fat. The carapace itself is said to make excellent soup.

In Ceylon the ends of the flippers, the plastron, the neck, and green fat are used for making turtle curry.

The North American and European markets for turtle meat are mainly for turtle soup, either canned or fresh. Most of the green turtle meat and soup that goes into cans is processed in the New York area or in London, although some soup is made in Key West, where canned green turtle soup has long been produced. The following turtle products are made by one London firm (James Parsons, 1962): several types of soup, a meat extract, tinned turtle steaks in Madeira sauce, tinned calipee, a cosmetic oil for soap and face cream, and even stick shaving soap with a turtle oil base.

In the last few years two other turtle products have become prominent—turtle oil and turtle leather. The oil has been promoted as an ingredient in cosmetic lotions, and the leather is being used to replace alligator and crocodile hides for expensive shoes and womens' handbags. Only the skin of the neck and upper forequarters is used as leather (Carr, 1970).

Richard and Nguyen (1961) give the composition of a sea turtle egg as: white = 8.75 grams (28.38%); yolk = 20.75 grams (67.30%); and shell = 1.33 grams (4.31%). The white is 97.33% water, but the yolk consists of 16.75% protein, 13.18% total lipids, 0.2% phosphorus, 0.08% lipid phosphorus, 2.08% lecithin, 0.33% cholesterol, and the rest is water. The egg has 39 calories compared to a chicken egg of 39.33 grams with 55 calories. Shell makeup includes 33.48% protein, which accounts for its elasticity.

HAWKSBILL TURTLES

These turtles are valued chiefly for their shells, although the flesh and eggs are occasionally eaten. The inhabitants of Cay-

Fig. 21. The scutes of the carapace overlap strongly in all but the very oldest hawksbills.

man Brac, San Andrés, and Old Providence Islands are said to prefer hawksbills to the green turtle (Carr, 1956a). Tamil fishermen of Ceylon regularly eat the flesh, but cases of death from poisoning are reported. Experienced fishermen remove the liver first and feed it to crows as a test to avoid being poisoned. The symptoms of poisoning are vomiting, limb pains, weals or a rash, and in severe cases coma followed by death. It is believed in Ceylon that the occasionally poisonous nature of the flesh is a result of the turtle eating some unspecified seaweed (Deraniyagala, 1939) or, in American waters, some poisonous invertebrates or plants. The flavor of the meat varies depending on the dietary regimen of the animal (Carr, 1956a).

The shell of the hawksbill turtle consists of scutes or scales that overlap at first but that become juxtaposed in large specimens. The shell is most valuable before juxtaposition occurs.

A turtle of about 30 inches long provides about 8 pounds of shell. The second and third costals are the largest, but the marginal plates are most prized for their thickness. The yellow plastral scutes are of special value for inlaying. Clear and light colored rather than dark colored shell has the greatest market value. The shell, readily softened by immersion in hot water, may be welded by means of heat or pressure.

The aboriginal tribes of the southwest Pacific are reported to have suspended living turtles over hot embers. The softened scutes then became loosened and were easily removed. These people believed that on subsequent liberation the turtle would regenerate the lost shell. Some evidence exists that such regeneration does, in fact, take place, but this cruel practice appears to have been largely abolished (Deraniyagala).

At the present time the shields are removed from the shell of the freshly killed turtle by immersion in boiling water. Turtle shell is worked in a manner similar to horn, but with greater care. The plates are first flattened by heat and pressure. Undue heat tends to darken the shell. The shell has a variety of uses for jewelry and for inlay work on toilet accessories, knife handles, and similar objects.

RIDLEY TURTLES

Ridley turtle meat is often sold as loggerhead turtle meat on the west coast of Florida. The eggs of both species of *Lepidochelys* are eaten by the local people.

LEATHERBACK TURTLES

Ray and Coates (1958) commented that, although not used commercially, the flesh eaten from a leatherback captured in the Gulf of Maine tasted like sirloin, "but with a touch of the gaminess of venison." Halstead (1956) reports that the leatherback may be poisonous.

CULTIVATION OF TURTLES

The breeding, hatching, and cultivation of turtles have frequently attracted persons concerned with the welfare of the industry. There is little information in the literature on sea turtle culture, however, and in this respect the most elaborate and successful attempts at cultivation have been with the diamondback terrapin. Although these animals are not strictly within the scope of this study, a review of the cultivation methods may have some application. We should remember, however, that these animals are brackish-water forms and that methods of propagating sea turtles would necessarily involve modifications of the terrapin methods.

Diamondback turtles or terrapins have been successfully reared for decades. In 1902 the U.S. Bureau of Fisheries undertook the study of the life history of terrapins, and by 1909 the methods had been advanced sufficiently to make artificial propagation feasible. Since that time, as many as 16,425 young have been hatched annually at the U.S. Fishery Biological Laboratory at Beaufort, N.C. By 1946, 241,013 young terrapins had been produced. Most of these were distributed in the coastal waters from Chesapeake Bay to Florida after they had been reared and protected for 8 to 12 months. Several small groups were reared to maturity in captivity to demonstrate the ease with which they could be cultivated.

The studies at Beaufort showed that the pens or kraals

must be especially well constructed to prevent the escape of the animals. Of great importance were the walls, the lower edges of which were sunk well below the surface of the ground. A projection of shelf, both inward and outward along the top, helped to keep the terrapins in and the rats out. The latter are great predators on the eggs and the young of all turtles and are mentioned as serious pests for sea turtles by several workers.

Concrete is preferable to lumber for terrapin pens, especially where marine borers (ship worms and *Limnoria*) are prevalent. Pens may be built anywhere along the shore, on hard clay or sand if such are available, but mud provides a poor bottom. A clean, unpolluted supply of brackish water should be available. A small arm of an estuary or a part of a bay is ideal.

A small-mouthed bay with a concrete wall or stone and pile fence across the mouth and a fence on land to enclose the area completely would be a highly practical place to raise marine turtles. A much more expensive arrangement would be fencing in an area of straight shoreline some distance from the water's edge. A location experiencing high tides would require stronger and higher protection, and construction of a pen would be more expensive here.

If possible, the pens should be flushed by the tide. Free circulation of water by some means is highly desirable if only by gates or pipes. These water passage areas can be closed to turtles by gates or screens. It has been calculated that for each diamondback 1.5 square feet of space within the pen will be needed, assuming adequate clean water. Young turtles require less space depending upon their size.

Sand beds are constructed for the laying of eggs. When young terrapins are ready to feed, usually about a month after hatching, they are given finely chopped fish, crab meat, minced oysters or clams, or a mixture of any of these. The young terrapins will eat chopped beef and liver, but best results are not obtained from these foods. We might mention that baby loggerheads, raised from hatching in Key West, Florida, thrive on chopped barracuda.

At Beaufort the young were kept in a rearing house during most of the first year because growth was greater and mortality lower than if the young were allowed freedom. In the rearing houses were wooden tanks with space for the young turtles to crawl out of the water. During hibernation the turtles were covered with straw that was occasionally dampened to keep it from drying out.

During the fall and spring feeding periods, great care was taken to keep the containers in which the terrapins were held clean and sanitary. For this at least three washings and six changes of water were necessary each week. The best procedure was to keep the young in freshwater for two days a week and in seawater for the balance of the time, with careful washing of the tanks after each triweekly feeding period.

Rearing tanks were constructed of cypress in groups of four, each 24 inches long, 18 inches wide, and 5 inches deep with a 2-inch overlapping strip on top to keep the animal from climbing out. From 75 to 100 were accommodated in each tank. A piece of copper screen, 2 inches square, was kept in each tank at all times to ward off "sore tail" and "soft shell," diseases that are capable of destroying great numbers of young. Copper is an excellent preventative against most of the fungus diseases. Weaker specimens generally die during the first year or two of life, or before they reach a length of 2 to 2.5 inches. In the case of sea turtles the length would be closer to 8 inches. Thereafter the deaths from natural causes are negligible. The high rate of terrapin survival compares favorably with that of chickens.

The only enemy of importance at Beaufort was the common Norwegian house rat. This predator not only ate the eggs but killed the young if it could reach them. A single rat has been known to kill three dozen young terrapin in a single night. Generally the rats gnaw a hole through the carapace in the region of the heart and, after taking the blood made available, leave the body of the victim without further molestation. It follows that any turtle-rearing establishment should nòt only be at some distance from rat-infested areas but that proper precaution should be taken against these predators in any case.

For terrapins the sex ratio is favorable: one male to six females. This relationship pertains in nature, apparently, just as under artificial conditions, and ensures a high degree of fertility. It is not known to what extent this ratio is present in sea turtles.

The chief difficulty in terrapin farming is the slow growth of the animals and the long time before returns may be expected; however, the rapid growth of sea turtles to some extent eliminates this unfavorable feature, although the cost of feeding would increase.

JAPANESE TURTLES

The "suppon," *Trionyx japonicus,* which occupies the same position in the Japanese market as the green turtle holds in the Occident, has been cultivated successfully and on a large scale since 1866. In that year a Mr. Hattori caught the first breeding stock. By 1875 he had a breeding stock of 50 animals. Mr. Hattori's "farm" consisted of a pond of 1,296 square feet with an island in the center. Adequately fenced and tended, it provided a place to raise over one hundred young turtles the first year, even though the adults preyed heavily on the babies.

SEA TURTLES

In his studies on the Great Barrier Reef Moorhouse made many valuable contributions to our knowledge of the cultivation of sea turtles. He planted eggs of *Chelonia mydas* obtained from two different sources: (1) from the oviducts of animals killed for soup making; (2) from nests made by females. His results are tabulated in table 10 for those eggs taken at the slaughterhouse.

Table 10. HATCHING OF GREEN TURTLE EGGS FROM SLAUGHTERED FEMALES

Nest	No. of eggs	Young hatched	Percent hatched
1	122	12	10
2	88	9	10
3	107		
4	98	25	24
5	95	Not hatched at close of experiment	

The low percentages of hatchings are not as serious as they at first appear. For instance, eight eggs from nest number 1 were taken at various intervals to note progress. Inasmuch as each of these embryos was developing normally, we can assume that if it had been allowed to continue its development it would have hatched. These eight eggs would have brought the hatch to 16%. Nest number 2 was disturbed by a loggerhead, and several eggs were thrown away. Moorhouse believes that this tragedy occurs frequently in nature. Nest number 3 consisted of eggs picked up from the floor of the factory where they were floating around in the water that is freely used during the killing and cleaning of the animals. Some eggs had not been removed from the section of oviduct that contained them. The poor showing of this group points up the need for removal of all offal from eggs procured from slaughtered females. Although this experiment was clumsily handled, the fact that eggs removed from killed turtles and planted will hatch has been demonstrated.

In not one instance did eggs taken from nests and replanted develop fully. All were opened and showed that the embryo had stopped growing and subsequently died. Moorhouse believed that the failure to hatch was due to injury during transplanting. Handling eggs after the first day from laying normally results in high mortality.

The information dealing with eleven nests of the first laying which were not disturbed and from which hatchings resulted is shown in table 11.

It will be seen that the number of eggs produced, the

Table 11. HATCHING OF TURTLE EGGS FROM UNDISTURBED NESTS

Animal number	Eggs	Young produced	Percentage hatch	Date of laying in Nov.	Date of hatching in Jan.	Incubation period Weeks	Days
1	85	50	59	4th	10th	9	4
10	139	67	50	13th	17th	9	2
13	68*	89	?	14th	18th	9	2
16	106*	77	@ 72	16th	27th	10	2
19	152	77	50	15th	25th	10	1
20	119	63	53	16th	26th	10	1
24	119	66	55	16th	27th	10	2
25	113	58	51	17th	25th	9	6
31	105*	68	@ 65	18th	26th	9	6
33	90	37	41	19th	26th	9	5
48	141	123	86	23rd	30th	9	5
†	150	83	55	17th	24th	9	5

*The animal had commenced laying when observed so that the number of eggs was greater than shown.
†In the above list is a loggerhead turtle that was observed in order to compare with the green turtle.

percentage hatch, and the incubation period for the logger-head follow closely those seen for the green turtle and that since two other marked nests were destroyed the losses in the nests of these animals are as great as are those in the green turtle.

It is noticeable that the mortality among these undisturbed eggs, naturally laid, was much lower than in the previously described experimental batches.

Moorhouse tried keeping young green turtles in freshwater with no success. The animals so treated remained out of water and on the bank most of the time, and although they appeared to be healthy, the mortality rate was excessively high. Eighty-three young loggerheads kept in a freshwater pool for five weeks were in perfect health. In groups kept in salt water for the same length of time only one death occurred.

It was noted that in the saltwater pools the young often remain motionless on the surface for long periods with their limbs stretched to the full extent.

Realizing that the first months of a sea turtle's life are extremely critical, Moorhouse not only recommended the culture of young but actually experimented in that direction. Coops of small meshed wire netting with 2-foot sides and covered-in tops were erected over nests of eggs. They were built to ensure that the sides were 6 inches under the surface of the sand surrounding the nest so that no young could escape.

The cages were examined each evening until the young appeared and for some days after the first appearance to ensure that late arrivals would be procured. The young were removed and placed in pools made above the high water mark or in floating cages of wire netting surrounding a wooden frame which were anchored out in the water of a protected place.

The pools were all straight-sided to keep the young turtles within bounds and were enclosed by a fence of wire netting with a small path at the sides. The tops were covered to keep out heron and gulls. Moorhouse found it a mistake to impound the turtles in straight-sided pools since the turtles enjoy a walk, and, by their continued efforts to crawl up the straight sides, they wore away the little horny toes of the

Fig. 22. Young pen-reared green turtles.

flippers. After this was noticed, ramps up which the young scrambled on their way out of the water were added to the four corners of the pools. When the young had sufficient time out of the water they dropped back of their own accord.

Moorhouse recommends that pools for the young turtles be so constructed that their long axes are parallel to the beach and that the side nearest to the beach slopes gradually down, giving a scooplike depression. The turtles, when they come out of the water, should be supplied with shade, because the hot sun tends to desiccate them. In torrid conditions the shields fall off and blindness often follows, resulting in death.

The food of young turtles is fish, although after they have been on this diet for some time they seem to relish seaweed. Any of the seaweeds found growing on the reef flat were eaten in very small quantities. Other food was suspended by cords at distances sufficient to allow room for several animals to eat at each point. Small fish, such as "hardy heads" (*Hepsetia pinguis*), were found by Moorhouse to be greedily eaten, but cooked fish was just as readily taken. Floating cages were not successful because in rough weather the turtles were tossed about and drowned. Moorhouse's observations, similar to those discovered by diamondback terrapin raisers in Beaufort, N.C., stress such factors as frequent changes of water and protected bays for the best locales. He also mentions protecting the turtles from predator birds by erecting nets or by other means.

Outside of experimental pilot operations, the only commercial sea turtle culture operation presently operating is that by Mariculture Ltd. in Grand Cayman, British West Indies. In October 1970 Dr. Robert E. Schroeder was kind enough to send me the following information on Mariculture Ltd.

> Our stock inventory is classified, but I can say that we have well over 30,000 animals, all sizes, in captivity.
>
> Growth rates will permit us to market turtles at an age of 2 1/2 to 4 years, depending on market size. Obviously as long as the turtles continue to convert feed efficiently, it pays us to feed them. We will market when the growth curve breaks, or before if other factors render it feasible.
>
> Although we have released about 5,000 turtles in Cayman waters, and open-range ranching appears eminently feasible, we will rear turtles entirely in battery, in land-based tanks. This eliminates the need to police large areas of shallows, and roundups for which techniques have not been developed. Initial costs, of course, are much higher.

According to Heffington (1970), the cultivated turtles are raised in round plastic tanks and later moved to large concrete tanks. Montalbano (1973) puts the number of green turtles being raised at around 70,000. *The Miami Herald* (25 Oct. 1973) reports the number of turtles has increased to 100,000. Since the eggs are collected from the wild (under permit), Mariculture Ltd. releases 1% of the yearling turtles to offset the depletion of natural resources.

A 1973 harvest of 17,000 turtles, each weighing 100 pounds and averaging three years of age, will yield about $118 per turtle, according to Montalbano (1973). He gives the average yield as 16 pounds of steak ($3.60 per pound retail in the United States) and 36 pounds of meat for soup, stew, and "turtleburgers." In addition (Montalbano 1973, p. 24):

> The by-products include seven pounds of calipee . . . ; 11 pounds of fat which is rendered for oil for the cosmetic industry; two pounds of leather for such things as handbags, gloves and shoes; and a 15-pound shell, which is cured and worked for jewelry or is sold as an artifact to people who admire turtle shells.

Since Schroeder furnished the information previously quoted, the Grand Cayman operation has had difficulties with epidermal infections, mortalities above a desirable level, and water quality. Solving these problems is essential for eventual success of the venture. Dr. Bustard, an Australian biologist, is hopeful that successful turtle culture farms can be established in the Torres Strait Islands, Australia, but this venture still requires more research (Turtles with a new lease on life, 1970).

The prospects for successful turtle farms have caused concern among conservationists. They stress that such farms can change a luxury market for turtle products into a broader based market by stabilizing supply and thereby increasing demand. In addition, the use of wild eggs rather than a brood stock puts further pressure on wild populations.

The report of the spawning of a green turtle in captivity and its subsequent laying of eggs a year later (Witham, 1971), even though many of the eggs were malformed and none hatched, coupled with research by the Caribbean Conservation Corporation, makes it seem possible that the ability to maintain a brood stock, at least for hatchery purposes, may come in the near future. It is anticipated that for many years any turtle culture operation would rely on wild eggs only.

VALUE AND ADMINISTRATION
OF THE FISHERY

The figures that have been compiled from numerous scattered sources are far from complete and in all cases give a low estimate of production. They may serve, however, as a rough guide to the relative importance of various areas and the general trend in time. The use of turtles and eggs for local domestic consumption is not estimated because the circumstances are such as to give no basis for calculations. Reports for Florida and the Gulf states of the United States are more numerous and more detailed than for the Caribbean countries, but are still woefully inadequate. Furthermore, a considerable quantity of the Caribbean production in the 1940s and 1950s was landed in the United States and was included in figures for Florida production. For these reasons the paragraphs relating to Florida are somewhat fuller than for the other areas.

FLORIDA

A brief recapitulation of past statistics will show how much the value of the turtle fishery has decreased in Florida and in other maritime states of the southeastern United States and Gulf coast.

Charles Parke, quoted by Wilcox (1896), stated that in 1886 he was able to catch 2,500 turtles with eight nets. In 1895 he was only able to land 60 animals using six nets. His location was in the Indian River district, where a small-scale turtle fishing industry was operated.

A total of 738 turtles weighing 36,900 pounds and valued at $2,722 were landed at Indian River in 1890. This number was caught by 24 men using 168 turtle nets.

By 1895 the output had dropped to 519 turtles (18,900 pounds). The take was worth $1,320 (about $0.07 per pound). Fifty-one of the creatures were captured in gill nets that had been set out for fish.

In addition to man's depredations, the weather has apparently contributed to some of the decline of the turtle population from time to time. It is recorded that in the winter of 1894-95 the Indian River region experienced an unusual cold period that killed many turtles. Several hundred were found floating in a numb and dazed condition.

Capital investment for turtle fishing was apparently never very large in the Lake Worth area. Brice (1896) reports that in 1894 only 24 turtle nets valued at $240 were in use here. These nets caught 3,407 pounds of turtles valued at $238. In 1895 in Biscayne Bay, 425 hawksbills and greens were landed, total value of which was reported at $3,076, $1,295 of which was for 436 pounds of tortoiseshell. In Key West during the same year and during what Brice terms a "depleted" period, 76 persons were engaged in turtle fishing, 27 of them on registered vessels, and 49 on sailboats. They used 29 boats and 54 nets.

Table 12. PRODUCTION OF TURTLE
IN KEY WEST, 1895

	Pounds	Value, $
Green turtle	337,400	16,780
Loggerhead	25,000	200
Hawksbill	40,280	403
Tortoiseshell	712	1,674
Eggs	6,750	810
Total	410,142	19,957

In Tampa, although the industry had been lively in 1890, it was nearly dead by 1895 (Brice, 1896). During 1895 three vessels using four nets caught 9,375 pounds of turtles (55 animals) valued at $563.

Table 13. SEA TURTLES LANDED IN FLORIDA, 1880-1947

Year	Pounds	Values, $	Year	Pounds
1880	180,000	7,200	1938	9,000
1884	300,000	10,500	1939	87,070
1890	468,256	20,972*	1940	31,883
1895	410,000		1941	66,711
1896	520,000	28,500	1942	48,260
1897	634,616	22,736	1943	50,086
1918	72,220	4,831	1944	58,450
1925	54,200	3,705	1945	91,027
1936	18,700		1946	40,847
1937	10,000		1947	60,536

Note: Principally green turtles.
*Fourth of value of fisheries in the state.

Table 14. GREEN TURTLE LANDINGS IN FLORIDA

Year	East coast Pounds	Value, $	West coast Pounds	Value, $	Total Pounds	Value, $
1950	3,000	300	6,800	680	9,800	980
1951	300	30	6,000	600	6,300	630
1952	1,048	157	88,213	13,232	89,261	13,389
1953			12,368	1,855	12,368	1,855
1954			1,745	262	1,745	262
1955	55	8	1,286	193	1,341	201
1956	202	30	646	97	848	127
1957	348	52	4,475	671	4,823	723
1958	268	43	4,565	730	4,833	773
1959			6,620	993	6,620	993
1960	952	143	19,876	2,981	20,828	3,124
1961	200	30	30,206	4,531	30,406	4,561
1962	835	125	26,615	4,168	27,450	4,293
1963	480	120	51,487	9,117	51,976	9,237
1964			29,639	4,274	29,639	4,274
1965			24,915	3,668	24,915	3,668
1966	210	42	28,511	5,200	28,721	5,242
1967			151,643	25,401	151,643	25,401
1968	100	10	62,855	14,319	62,955	14,329
1969	145	51	12,218	2,956	12,363	3,007
1970	8,380	7,301	410,455	90,562	418,835	91,863
1971	5,162	1,290	120,542	30,137	125,704	31,427

Table 15. LOGGERHEAD TURTLE LANDINGS IN FLORIDA

Year	East coast Pounds	East coast Value, $	West coast Pounds	West coast Value, $	Total Pounds	Total Value, $
1951	100	8	4,100	336	4,200	344
1952	941	122	26,319	3,421	27,260	3,543
1953			8,390	1,091	8,390	1,091
1954			500	50	500	50
1955			211	21	211	21
1956	696	70	1,059	106	1,755	176
1957			5,105	510	5,105	510
1958						
1959	4,015	602	100	15	4,115	617
1960	2,640	396	7,204	1,081	9,844	1,477
1961	1,005	151	2,655	398	3,660	549
1962	1,525	229	6,641	701	8,166	930
1963			8,057	1,026	8,057	1,026
1964			1,124	112	1,124	112
1965	2,200	330	1,200	120	3,400	450
1966	3,854	386	114	11	3,968	397
1967	2,010	201			2,010	201
1968	844	73	1,906	178	2,750	251
1969			673	37	673	37
1970	3,722	563	22,167	2,623	25,889	3,186
1971	9,699	2,469	15,906	1,709	25,605	4,178

Note: Figures also include ridley turtles sold as loggerheads.

In Cedar Key in 1890 113 nets caught 89,958 pounds valued at $6,297. By 1895 the number of nets had decreased to 43. In that year 42 men using 28 boats were occupied with turtle fishing. They brought in 2,651 animals weighing 107,610 pounds and valued at $6,981.

In table 13 no distinction is made between turtles caught in Florida and those imported from the Caribbean area, since they are not separated in official returns. During the period covered, turtles were imported into Florida in steadily increasing amounts. By 1947 few turtles were actually caught for the market in Florida, so that the figures for the more recent years in the table reflect the imports from Costa Rican and Nicaraguan waters.

Catches in tables 14 and 15 represent locally caught turtles. Pounds are given in round weight, that is, back calculated from meat weight reported by retailers. The values reflect only those turtles sold commercially and not those used for personal consumption. Since ridley turtles are often sold

Fig. 23. Turtles arriving by schooner in Key West. The turtles are kept on their backs during transport.

as loggerhead meat, they have been reported as loggerheads, and although they represent less of an input than loggerhead turtles, it is impossible to discern what fraction of the total catch they constitute.

Catches of immature green turtles (12 to 115 pounds) in the Cedar Key—Crystal River area of Florida were estimated by Carr and Caldwell (1956) to be about 1,000 individuals per year. About 300 immature ridleys (7 to 59 pounds) are caught per year in the same area.

Laws in Florida regulating the taking of turtles originally were only applicable during the months of May, June, July, and August, the months which are believed to be the breeding season. During this period it was forbidden to destroy or capture sea turtles while they were on the beach or out of the water. Eggs and hatchlings were also protected. Additionally,

Fig. 24.   Unloading turtles in Key West.

by rule a size limit on green turtles of 41 inches carapace length was instituted for the 1971 season.

Ingle (1972) evaluated Florida's turtle industry just prior

Table 16. CATCH OF TURTLES,
PRIMARILY GREEN, IN FLORIDA, 1970

Area	Value, $	Weight, lb.	No.	Av. wt., lb.	Av. carapace lgth., in.	Best season
Levy-Citrus region						
Crystal River area	1,000	4,000	125	35	20	June, July
Homosassa	2,919		325	30	15	April, July, Oct.
Cedar Key	4,700	18,800	345	65	25	May-Oct.
Total above	8,619		795	43	20	
Keys	90,000		1,800*	225	35	April-Oct.

Source: Figures are rough estimates from interviews.
*Only about 150 produced in Florida, rest were harvested in Caribbean.

Table 17. CATCH OF TURTLES BY STATE

Year	Pounds	Value, $	Year	Pounds	Value, $
	Georgia			North Carolina	
1897	1,000	20	1897	24,000	1,920
1918	11,250	100	1918	8,400	77
			Louisiana*		
1880	30,000	1,200	1954	1,400	210
1890	90,793	2,335	1955	200	20
1918	4,360	218	1956	4,300	598
1925	8,650	173	1957	200	20
1932	6,450†	129	1958	3,500	286
1933	145,000	6,000	1959	4,600	250
1936	3,500*	70	1960	6,200	415
1948	11,600	1,740	1961	6,300	813
1949	5,800	630	1962	3,300	199
1950	4,800	466	1963	2,200	223
1951	2,800	280	1964	3,000	420
1952	10,500	1,311	1965		
1953	2,600	263	1966	3,300	407
			Texas		
1880	24,000	720	1918	6,671	447
1889	82,800	1,409	1925	2,550	204
1890	83,000	1,390			
			Virginia*		
1948	2,800	156	1956	4,400	44
1949	600	18	1957	1,600	16
1950	6,900	138	1958	1,200	88
1951	1,200	22	1959	2,200	22
1952	6,900	169	1960	1,600	16
1953	6,400	128	1961	1,100	11
1954	5,100	51	1962	600	6
1955	2,600	52			
	Mississippi				
1918	337	20			

*Principally green turtle.
†Loggerhead only.

to the 1971 restrictions. He found estimation difficult, primarily due to the segmented, localized nature of the fishery. Operations are restricted to two main areas: (1) on the west coast of Florida—Levy and Citrus counties and (2) the keys

Table 18. TERRAPIN AND TURTLE MEAT, SOUP, AND STEW CANNED IN THE UNITED STATES

Year	Number of plants	Cases	Pounds	Value, $
1948	4	940	45,120	30,899
1949	3	946	45,408	25,164
1950	8	25,074	1,203,552	279,674
1951	10	26,127	1,254,096	279,195
1952	8	24,160	1,159,680	258,568
1953	8	18,923	908,304	255,180
1954	8	8,879	426,192	144,684
1955	9	9,983	479,184	126,768
1956	9	10,927	524,496	160,995
1957	7	16,613	797,424	295,099
1958	6	12,610	605,280	226,316
1959	5	15,037	721,776	244,216
1960	6	12,610	605,280	226,316
1961	10	26,928	1,292,544	390,729
1962	8	18,755	900,240	301,140
1963	7	14,333	687,984	262,622
1964	9	17,043	818,064	271,155
1965	8	15,910	763,680	276,034
1966	6	14,190	681,120	273,004
1967	6	7,945	381,360	201,546
1968	6	8,593	412,464	243,388
1969	4	10,799	518,352	297,461

Table 19. IMPORTS OF LIVE TURTLES TO THE UNITED STATES

Year	Pounds	Value, $	Year	Pounds	Value, $
1948	794,429	56,933	1959	659,000	47,000
1949	1,047,521	54,119	1960	471,000	41,000
1950	1,276,863	64,316	1961	778,000	74,000
1951	1,491,899	84,729	1962	783,000	50,000
1952	1,384,165	79,897	1963	489,000	101,000
1953	1,171,857	66,790	1964	398,000	47,000
1954	974,000	55,000	1965	520,000	56,000
1955	913,000	44,000	1966	199,000	36,000
1956	695,000	34,000	1967	353,000	154,000
1957	1,033,000	56,000	1968	444,000	324,000
1958	886,000	64,000	1969	213,000	236,000

section of Monroe County. The 1971 rule was replaced by a statute in June 1971, which is described in the following paragraph.

On the east coast of Florida (from the Georgia state line through and including Dade County) it is unlawful to destroy or capture green turtles or their eggs at any time; the other species of sea turtles are protected from May through August. On the west coast of Florida between the Monroe-Collier county line and the western boundary of the state, all species of sea turtles have a size limit of a 26 inch carapace length. Capture while on land is strictly forbidden; egg taking is also prohibited. In Monroe County green turtles are protected by a 41 inch carapace length size limit.

BERMUDA

The best season for turtle fishing is late July or August. As far back as 1609 turtles were caught here with nets, with spears, and by overturning on the beach. An anonymous writer of that date is quoted by Garman (1884) as reporting that two boats in a single day caught 40 turtles.

Later information is provided by Mowbray (personal communication, 1949) and James Burnett-Herkes (personal communication, 1970). Mowbray related that turtles had been fished at that time by only two groups of men. Their catch averaged 60 turtles of an average weight of 70 pounds. The largest green turtle caught during the 1930s and 1940s weighed 183 pounds, and the largest hawksbill weighed 125 pounds. The best catch was 6 in one day. Other sources give the 1931 catch as 18 green and 2 hawksbill turtles. This estimate is considered low. One boat operated in 1948 and brought in 22 green turtles. Loggerhead turtles are not taken here; they are considered inedible.

Five boats are now engaged in turtle fishing on a part-time basis. Each is manned by two men who use tangle nets for capturing the turtles. All the catch is consumed locally, but there is no shell industry. (The catch is estimated to be 90% green and 10% hawksbill.)

Burnett-Herkes states that no records are presently kept but that a survey of "turtle fishermen" in 1970 indicated that 26 turtles were taken (all greens), having a total weight of about 2,500 pounds or an average weight of 96 pounds.

The weights ranged from 55 pounds to 167 pounds. This survey is probably typical for all years, with 25 to 30 turtles having an average weight of about 100 pounds being taken annually. Only one mature female turtle (green) has been taken within memory, about 20 years ago.

In 1884 the meat brought 4 to 10 cents per pound alive and 12 to 18 cents dressed. Immediately prior to 1940 prices were 20 cents per pound alive and 30 cents dressed, and they have been 60 cents per pound live weight since 1949.

Although early writers claimed that turtles breed in Bermuda, none of those killed contained ripe eggs. James Burnett-Herkes believes that the last known attempt at nesting was by a loggerhead in 1963. This turtle was turned before laying, however, and later escaped.

The fishery is regulated by a minimum size limit of 40 pounds. Under consideration is a regulation that will make it possible to place a closed season on turtles at any time; this would be put into effect should mature specimens be observed in the area or taken by fishermen.

Since 1966, hatchling green turtles from Costa Rica have been released in Bermuda annually. No results have yet been obtained from this stocking. Some hatchlings are being raised to two years old and tagged before release, and caught specimens are also being tagged.

BAHAMAS

Catesby (1731-43) reports that turtles were harpooned and exported to the Carolinas. Green turtles are not believed to breed here.

Reliable records for turtle meat are not available until 1944 and then only for Grand Bahama Island. These recorded weights from 1944 are (1) for June: loggerheads, 22,851 pounds; hawksbills, 5,232 pounds; and greens, 676 pounds and (2) for July: loggerheads, 4,807 pounds; hawksbills, 637 pounds, and greens, 63 pounds. The total for loggerheads was 27,658 pounds; for hawksbills, 5,869 pounds, and for greens, 739 pounds.

All turtle shell sold in the Bahamas is reported to the government. Table 20 is compiled from government records of shell exports.

Table 20. EXPORTS OF TURTLE SHELL FROM THE BAHAMAS

Year	Weight, lb.	Price per pound, £ S D	Value, £
1940	600	0.18.6	555
1941			
1942			
1943	400	1.18.0	760
1944	1600	1.0.4	1630
1945	400	0.17.6	351
1946	3200	1.11.0	4926
1947	1300	2.2.0	2755
1948	500	1.8.0	700

Turtle meat is eaten throughout the Bahamas, and the local consumption must be high compared to the amount exported.

Strict rules regulate the landing of turtles for sale, both in New Providence and the Out Islands. The main laws of interest are: (1) taking or capturing turtles on any beach is an offense; (2) the taking, buying, and selling of turtle eggs is an offense; and (3) there is a closed season on the taking of loggerhead turtles from 1 April to 30 June inclusive. The minimum size limits for the hawksbill turtles are 17 inches from the neck scales to the tail pieces and for the green turtle, 15 inches from the neck scales to the tail pieces.

TURKS and CAICOS ISLANDS

The information that follows was supplied by T. M. Nicholl (personal communication). Turtles are generally scarce in these islands; those taken are incidental catches by fishermen when they see them. The hawksbill is the only species that nests with any regularity here, and their eggs are taken during the nesting season from March to May. The eggs, along with the meat from hawksbills, greens, and loggerheads, are consumed locally. A small amount of shell is exported.

The fishery is regulated by size limits of 17 inches for the hawksbill and 15 inches for the green turtle. Taking of turtles on any beach and possession of eggs are prohibited.

CUBA

Turtles are relatively plentiful on the south coast of Cuba, but they are generally not highly esteemed. Most of the Cuban production is for local consumption. The following official figures are quoted by J. L. Martinez (1948):

Table 21. ANNUAL PRODUCTION OF TURTLES
IN CUBA

Year	Meat, lb.	No. of eggs	No. of bloodcakes	No. of roe
1937-41 (aver.)	17,000		172	169
1942	65,000	12,000	80	0
1943	20,000	48,000	42	0
1944	8,000	0	0	0
1945	23,000	0	0	0

Caldwell, Carr, and Hellier (1956b) mention a commercial hawksbill fishery at Gibara. Production for 1958 was 39,997 pounds (Cuba's fishing industry 1958, 1959).

JAMAICA

In 1731, according to Catesby, turtle flesh was the principal meat eaten in Jamaica. At that time 40 sloops from Port Royal were engaged in the industry. Duerden reports the export in 1900 of green turtles to the value of £1,693. At that time shell was valued between 10 shillings and 20 shillings per pound.

In 1900 green turtles valued at £7,248 and hawksbills valued at £1,693 were landed or exported from Jamaica. In 1929 1,834 green turtles valued at £3,668 and 1,880 hawksbills valued at £5,962 are recorded. In 1934, 348 green turtles were landed or exported.

The catching of turtles is prohibited from April to September. Eggs may not be taken and turtles may not be captured while on the beaches.

Since a high proportion of the turtles sold in Jamaica are produced by Cayman Islanders working not only in the Jamaica Cays but also in the cays nearer to the mainland, the statistics are not reliable. (See paragraph on Cayman Islands.)

CAYMAN ISLANDS

Practically all the green turtles landed in these islands are caught on the banks and shoals of Nicaragua, Honduras, and Costa Rica, since the turtles are greatly depleted in the Caymans. Nevertheless, the quantity landed has been relatively large, and the Caymans have been the principal center of the whole industry.

The last few years have seen a decline in the Cayman industry. Apparently restrictions by other countries, as well as increased interest in the turtle trade by their nationals, has shifted production to these countries.

The weather is a prime factor in determining the turtle season, but usually it lasts from January to March and from July to September. During the 1940s, 12 to 17 schooners with an average of 10 men each were employed in the industry. Today there are less. The nets used are of 30- to 33-thread cotton line with meshes 10 inches knot to knot. Wooden decoys accompany the nets. The shorter nets are 12 fathoms long by about 4 fathoms deep. Longer nets 30 fathoms long and 8 fathoms deep are also used. The nets are set at night (E. F. Thompson, 1947).

About 200 turtles are taken by each boat during the sea-

Table 22. EXPORT OF GREEN TURTLES FROM THE CAYMAN ISLANDS, 1929-1939

Year	Number	Value, £	Average value, shillings
1929	1,834	3,670	40
1930	2,214	4,428	40
1931	2,298	4,552	40
1932	1,004*	1,049*	20
1933	966	966	20
1934	1,504	1,504	20
1935	1,673	2,059	24
1936	3,161	4,979	32
1937	2,921	2,865	20
1938	3,489	4,684	26
1939	2,685	2,665	20

*Grand Cayman only.

Table 23. EXPORT OF TURTLE SHELL FROM
THE CAYMAN ISLANDS, 1929-1939

Year	Number	Value, £	Average value, shillings
1929	4,590	5,962	26
1930	3,000	1,975	13
1931	4,150	2,160	10/6
1932	619*	306*	10
1933	1,990	1,115	11
1934	9,883	5,960	11
1935	5,302	2,593	10
1936	6,789	2,984	9
1937	6,650	3,728	11
1938	3,211	1,281	8
1939	2,995	1,108	7/6

*Grand Cayman only.

son, their weight ranging from 80 to 200 pounds and averaging about 155 pounds. There is a 10% loss in transit during the passage from the mainland to the Caymans and about 5% during subsequent shipment to the United States.

Hawksbill turtles are scarce in the Caymans and are principally taken in Colombia, near San Andrés and the Serrana and Seranilla banks and the outermost Mosquito Cays. Some are fished on the Jamaica Cays, and on Pedro, Morants, and Rosalind banks. The seasons are similar to those of the green turtle. Five-foot iron-ring nets are used for trapping the hawksbills. They are butchered on the spot, and only the shell is retained. They appear to limit their movements to cleaner beaches than the green turtle and will not lay in captivity (E. F. Thompson, 1947).

James Parsons (1962) reports that 4,109 green turtles (live) were exported in 1956 and were valued at £20,000. Twenty-four thousand pounds of turtle skin, valued at £18,000, were also exported that year.

The Cayman Brac Islanders, traditionally the hawksbill hunters in the Cayman Islands, provided large quantities of tortoiseshell until synthetic plastic products caused this market to collapse. In the last decade, however, there has been a revolution against imitation tortoiseshell products by the consumer, and the hawksbill is again being fished for this export.

HAITI

A maximum of 2,000 pounds of hawksbill turtle shell is reported to be produced each year. Very little additional information is available, but it appears certain that no great quantity is produced.

PUERTO RICO

A small production for local consumption is reported; the catches are incidental to other fishing operations. Hawksbill turtles are the most frequently caught; green turtles usually are heavier although second in numbers. Loggerheads rank third in the catch, and leatherbacks are rare and only occasionally caught, according to Rolf Juhl (personal communication). Juhl reports the catch of all species in 1969 to have been 19,114 pounds. J. L. Dibbs (personal communication) gives the catch from 1 January 1968 to 30 June 1969 as 24,108 pounds with a value of $2,900. Some eggs are taken illegally from hawksbill and leatherback nests, the only two species that nest here.

Law GE-11 of 12 April 1949 states: "It is prohibited to destroy, take, possess or sell the eggs of any tortoise or turtle, or to kill or capture any tortoise or turtle found on the shore or laying eggs in the sand."

Restocking of hatchling green turtles from Costa Rica has been in progress for the last few years, so far without apparent results.

BRITISH VIRGIN ISLANDS

Most of the captured turtles are caught with tangle nets; others are turned on the beach when they come to lay. Four species are caught, green, loggerhead, hawksbill, and leatherback, and about a quarter of the green and hawksbill turtle meat is exported to the U.S. Virgin Islands. A closed season on all turtles is in effect from 1 July to 31 August. Swingle, Dammann, and Yntema (1969) list the 1967 catch as 5,880 pounds valued at $4,140.

U.S. VIRGIN ISLANDS

Natives catch some turtles on the beaches and in short, set nets. All turtles are consumed locally, including turtles sometimes brought to the Charlotte Amalie harbor from other islands in the Lesser Antilles. Swingle et al. (1969) lists the 1967 production as 11,280 pounds valued at $17,160 and Dibbs in personal communication estimated the 1968 catch to have been 17,200 pounds.

SAINT KITTS – NEVIS

There is no organized industry, and statistics are not available. Turtles and eggs are protected from 1 June to 30 September.

ANTIGUA

The production is stated to have declined greatly during the history of the colony. Hawksbill and green turtles are caught in nets year round, and a few are turned when they nest. Eggs of these two species are also taken. All products are for local consumption.

A size limit of 20 pounds or 10 inches in length is imposed. Turtles and eggs are protected from 1 June to 30 September. Some figures for turtles landed in Antigua in the 1940s are 1943, 40; 1944, 79; 1945, 68; 1946, 46; 1947, 116; and 1948, 53.

MONSERRATE

The industry is irregular. Twelve nets were used in the northern district and four at Plymouth during 1948. Fishing is carried out from April to November, the calm-weather months.

Seventy turtles were landed at Plymouth during 1948, but no statistics are available for the northern district. Shell valued at $96, representing about 100 pounds, was exported to the Leeward Islands.

MARTINIQUE and GUADELOUPE

No statistics are available.

SAINT VINCENT

The following information is from personal communication

with L. Errol Ollivierre. The fishing season lasts for eight months. During the closed season (May through August), catching turtles and removing eggs are prohibited. Green and hawksbill turtles are the only species on which the fishery is based; other species are rarely caught.

Hawksbill shell (about 1,500 pounds annually) is exported to Saint Lucia, but no market is available for any of the other species. No statistics have been kept.

No fishermen are engaged in the turtle fishery on a full-time basis, so estimating the number of individuals involved is difficult. Most of the turtles are caught with tangle nets, but some hawksbills are turned while nesting. About 65 to 70% of the total catch comes from the island of Bequia. In addition to the closed season, there is a minimum size limit of 20 pounds.

SAINT LUCIA

During the months of May to August, about 300 turtles weighing approximately 45,000 pounds are caught on Aves Island and taken to Saint Lucia by a local schooner. About 30% of the meat is exported to the U.S. Virgin Islands and to England. About 600 pounds of dried turtle meat and calipee and calipash are exported annually to each of two countries, England and Germany. The fishery takes place from September to April, and greens, hawksbills, and leatherbacks are captured. Landing estimates for 1969 are given by Cyril Matthew (personal communication) as 37,500 pounds of green turtle and 24,000 pounds of hawksbill turtle. A closed season is in effect from 1 May to 31 August, but it does not

Table 24. HAWKSBILL TURTLES LANDED
IN DOMINICA

Year	Pounds	Year	Pounds
1959	749	1964	
1960	1,029	1965	497
1961	595	1966	
1962	245	1967	
1963	375	1968	986

Source: L. M. Sorhaindo.

apply to animals taken outside territorial waters. Large quantities of turtles are taken from Aves Island during the closed season.

Turtles are caught in nets and when they come ashore to lay eggs, although the latter practice is illegal. Both the nesting females and their eggs are protected by law, but this regulation is not enforced.

BARBADOS

Fishing is mainly for hawksbill for meat and shell, although a few green turtles are taken. Fifty to sixty men operate nets on the inshore reefs from March to July. The export demand for shell has diminished. Turtles are imported alive from Grenada. No turtles or eggs may be taken on shore nor may nets be set within 100 yards of a beach.

One-third of the production shown in table 25 is shell production.

Table 25. PRODUCTION OF TURTLES IN BARBADOS

Year	Number	Value, $
1945	92	2,760
1946	128	3,850
1947	160	5,000
1948	165	5,250

GRENADA

Around 1949, 8 to 10 boats with 32 nets and 92 men fished principally from October to December and to a lesser extent in April. During 1948, 694 green turtles, 279 hawksbills, and 2 loggerheads were exported from Grenada to Barbados and Trinidad. Today about 20 boats, averaging two men each, fish for sea turtles on a part-time basis from October through May. Over three-fourths of the turtles are caught with nets; the remainder are harpooned or turned on the beach. Green turtles are found up to 300 pounds; they lay eggs here from June to September. Both the loggerhead and the hawksbill have a similar nesting season.

The eggs are considered a delicacy locally. Prior to World

War II an export trade in live turtles existed with London. About 180 turtles from 80 pounds upward in weight were shipped in troughs at a freight rate of £15 per ton and were watered and fed while en route. Approximately 25 pounds of turtle shell are exported annually to Barbados and Trinidad each.

Duerden reports production of shell valued at £400 during 1900.

No turtles may be taken on land nor may eggs be taken. The closed season is May to September inclusive.

With regard to present-day turtle production, N. M. Greaves (personal communication) states:

> The fishery division has no statistics on the amount of turtles caught, but we have just completed a survey which revealed that there are 61 turtle nets [in operation], . . . they should catch approximately 10 turtles each during the open season, and each turtle should give 60 lbs. of meat. . . . Turtle turning is practiced during the closed season, which is illegal, and I assume no less than 100 are caught this way . . . for the year 1969 [estimated] turtles caught in Grenada and Carriacou equaled 710 live, weight — 71,000 lbs.; 42,600 lbs. of meat.

J. L. Dibbs (personal communication) estimated that the landings for 1964, 1965, and 1967 were 25,000, 27,500, and 30,000 pounds, respectively.

The closed season is from June to September inclusive, and nesting females and their eggs are protected. No turtle under 25 pounds may be taken.

TRINIDAD and TOBAGO

The industry in Tobago was started by French settlers in 1776 in the southwestern part of the island. By 1950 only a few turtles were being taken from Buccoo Reef for food and shell. Nearly half of the green turtles taken at Matelot, Trinidad, on the north coast during 1947 were half-grown. In this area during 1946 one man in a boat caught 10,000 pounds valued at nearly $1,000, providing a return of $0.89 per man hour. No statistics are available for that era, but a partial volume of the trade is given by the weight of turtles sold in the Port of Spain market. In 1947 this amount was 60,000 pounds.

Today the turtle industry at Trinidad and Tobago is a small one, a part-time enterprise for the persons involved. About half the turtles (green, loggerhead, and leatherback) are caught with nets, about one-quarter with harpoons, and the rest by turtle turning or as incidental catches in other fishing. Green, hawksbill, loggerhead, and leatherback turtles nest from April to September here, according to the senior fisheries officer, and some eggs are taken illegally. He gives the landings of all species as 11,747 pounds in 1969, the first year for which statistics were kept. Bacon (1970) estimates that in 1968 there were 23 leatherbacks killed, mainly by local villagers in Matura Bay. In 1969, 13 were slaughtered on the north section alone. Because poachers hide the carcasses, the true figure may be higher, and Bacon feels that 20 to 30% of the nesting leatherback population is being killed each year.

Green turtle hatchlings have been stocked here from Costa Rica, but no results are noticeable as yet. The possession and/or sale of turtle eggs during the closed season, 1 June to 30 September, is forbidden by law. Female turtles are protected within a thousand yards from shore and within any reef; it is unlawful to possess or sell any turtle between 1 June and 30 September. All these offenses are punishable by a fine of $48 or two months imprisonment.

GUYANA

The principal nesting area, Shell Beach, is beset with parties of hunters who camp there for a few days, collect all the eggs they can find, and usually carry off one or more of the nesting females (Pritchard, 1969d, p. 137): "Apparently a live adult hawksbill sells for only $5 ($3 US) in the North-West District but will fetch $15 in the Pomeroon, where an adult green sells for $35-40. The higher price of the green turtle merely reflects the greater amount of meat obtainable from it; no preference for the flavor of the green turtle was expressed." Pritchard gives the market value of eggs as one cent to five cents (BWI) each, according to demand.

The fisheries officer reported that in December 1967 an amendment to the fisheries regulations was published forbidding the capture of turtles, among other things, except under license. The fee is $10 (Guyana). The fine for breach of the regulations is a maximum of 6 months in jail or $240. However, these regulations are difficult to enforce. The officer thinks that the majority of the people who catch turtles are probably not aware that the regulations exist.

FRENCH GUIANA

Leatherback turtles are killed for shark bait. Pritchard (1969d) reports that a local fisherman he talked to caught about one leatherback per day during offshore shark fishing over the two- to three-month season. These he cut up for bait and for any shelled eggs they might contain. Eggs are also collected from Silebache Beach.

In 1969 French Guiana passed a law creating a closed season for eggs and turtles between 1 May and 30 July. Sale, purchase, display in markets, transport, destruction, and collection are all prohibited.

SURINAM

Between 1940 and 1964 Schulz (1969) estimates that 50 to 80% of all eggs laid at Bigi Santi and Galibi nesting grounds were harvested; in 1964 80 to 90% of the eggs of *Chelonia* and *Lepidochelys* laid at Galibi beaches were collected and sold in the capital and coastal district at wholesale prices of about $1.60 per 100. It is now illegal to take eggs anywhere in the Wia-Wia Nature Reserve, which includes Bigi Santi, an important nesting beach for the green turtle and the leatherback. Since 1964, the killing of turtles anywhere has been completely prohibited, but the taking of eggs is permitted from 1 May to 1 September.

Pritchard (1969d) gives the following account of this activity:

Egg taking is legal on beaches near the Marowijne River, and the Indians in this region resent any attempt to interfere with their rights to this resource. The Indians can predict quite accurately when the massive aggregations of nesting ridleys are due to arrive on the beach at Eilanti. They move down to the beach and endure two or three sleepless nights in order to collect as many eggs as possible, and very few escape them. The exploitation is highly organized, and the village captain allots each man a small section of the beach on which to collect eggs. Huge piles of turtle eggs accumulate in the Indians' huts on these *arribada* nights; they are taken to Paramaribo by boat and sold wholesale for approximately 15 guilders (ca. $8.50 US) per thousand. The retail price in Paramaribo is about one guilder for 30.

In 1967 and 1968, about one-half million ridley eggs were bought and replanted in an effort to conserve this resource (Schulz, 1969).

PANAMA

Both meat and eggs of the green turtle and the hawksbill turtle are taken for local consumption. A majority of the shell is exported to Colombia. Arquimedes Franqueza (personal communication, December 1970) writes that Panama, Costa Rica, and Nicaragua signed a treaty to prohibit the fishing of *Chelonia mydas* for a period of three years. Turtle shell exports from Panama in 1942 were 81 pounds valued at $81 and in 1945 were 3,852 pounds valued at $6,684.

VENEZUELA

Mr. Tania Coba de Barany of the Fundación Científica los Roques (personal communication) supplied the information that follows unless otherwise noted. At the present time there is no control of the fishery because research necessary to implement proper regulations has not been completed. Until recently a permit was necessary to fish for sea turtles. At the present time the permits are not being issued, but the fishery continues at the Archipelago of the Roques throughout the whole year.

The fishery is conducted in small vessels of approximately 25 feet, and the product is sold to larger vessels that take it to La Guaira. These larger vessels have boxes for the transport of fish and other products. The number of boats that spend most of their time fishing for turtles is approximately the same as the number of lobster boats, but none fishes for turtles exclusively. The vessels that transport the turtles to La Guaira are the ones that report to the Fishery Inspection Office of el Gran Roque, giving the weight in kilos (size and individual weight is not taken into account).

Table 26. 1948-1969 CATCH OF SEA TURTLES
IN VENEZUELA

Year	Catch, kilograms	Value, Bolivares
1948	3,600	
1949	25,944	29,743
1950	7,406	7,750
1951	10,907	12,425
1952	9,951	9,378
1953	157,802	57,968
1954	49,750	25,894
1955	6,665	6,198
1956	9,747	8,481
1957	13,260	11,654
1958	13,812	13,220
1959	16,722	15,409
1960	20,038	22,798
1961	4,852	4,747
1962	3,216	3,780
1963	19,687	20,446
1964	34,002	31,381
1965	38,259	30,898
1966	51,321	46,526
1967	51,991	44,902
1968	55,975	54,578
1969	46,550	40,021

Source: From Venezuelan National Fisheries Office as supplied by Ulpiano Nascimento of FAO.

The fishermen use gill nets, which are set every other day. Three species of turtles are caught: *Chelonia mydas, Caretta caretta,* and *Eretmochelys imbricata;* the latter two are fished for local consumption only. Eggs are extracted and either sold or used for personal consumption. A minimum weight of 20 kilograms is in effect for all sea turtles. The weights in kilograms for the reported turtle landings in 1970 as recorded by the Fishery Inspection Office at Los Rogues, and of those turtles transported to La Guaira are:

January: 1,138
February: 6,052
March: 2,704
April:1,715
May: 2,199
June: 1,610
July: 2,436
August: 160
September: 2,500
October: no data
November: 2,000
December: 680
January (1971): 1,300

COSTA RICA

Twenty-five men were engaged in the fishery during 1948 catching turtles on the beach after they nested between 10 June and 10 September. Carr (1954a) commented on this practice.

To support the export trade in Green Turtles the beach is rented in sections to contractors, who employ "veladores" among the local people to patrol mile long strips and turn every turtle that

Table 27.   EXPORT OF TURTLES FROM COSTA RICA

Year	Weight, kilos	Value, $
1933	35,232	1,741
1934	75,840	3,565
1935	70,160	2,582
1936	77,450	3,030
1937	161,600	9,161
1938	108,800	6,482
1939	162,893	8,578
1940	113,400	3,759
1941	176,500	6,301
1942	5,000	900
1943	20,700	1,054
1944	23,840	1,561
1945	148,300	7,979
1946	126,550	5,072
1947	78,600	3,790

comes up to lay. Periodically, a launch coasts along from Puerto Limon and picks up the accumulated catch. The females are not allowed to lay before being turned, despite the existence of a Costa Rican law requiring this, because the delay in waiting the half-hour or more of [sic] the laying process would cut down the number of turtles that could be taken at night. All turtles not used locally along the thinly settled shore are carried to Puerto Limon for transshipment.

It has been illegal for some years to take eggs or to molest the animals on shore. Carr (1969b) estimated that the commercial take of green turtles by harpoon and net off the Tortuguero nesting ground before the turtles were protected averaged between 4,000 and 5,000 individuals. Since 1969 the legal limit for harpooning has been moved to five kilometers offshore (Carr, 1970).

Turtle and turtle products are exported principally to the United States, Holland, and Japan, according to Eduardo Bravo P. (personal communication). He estimates that about 90% of the green turtles and about 80% of the hawksbills that are captured are exported.

NICARAGUA

In the 1940s turtles were caught in nets of 10- to 12-inch mesh, mainly from December to May and from July to September. The nets were spread by catboats carried on the vessels. Today only about one-quarter of the turtles are caught this way; most are harpooned, although a few are turned on the beaches and others are sometimes caught incidental to another fishery. The fishery takes place year round on a part-time basis, except for the green turtle, which is protected by a closed season from 15 May through 15 July.

Eggs of the three species that nest in Nicaragua (green, hawksbill, and loggerhead) are taken for local consumption. Hawksbill shell and green turtle steaks, fillets, and fins are exported to the United States. Nesting females are protected, and the minimum legal weight for the green turtle is 55 kilograms.

Prior to 1948 some figures for the exportation of turtles from Nicaragua and their value at that time are: 1938—2,054 ($12,078); 1939—1,728 ($8,481); 1940—1,578 ($8,065); 1941—1,239 ($6,645); 1942—1,638 ($8,101); 1943—1,374

($6,875); 1944—1,603 ($8,015); 1945—2,593 ($12,955); 1946—3,661 ($15,826); 1947—2,906 ($14,530); and in 1948—1,975 ($9,758).

Antonio Flores commented (personal communication) as follows on the post-1948 years. He believes turtle processing for export only started during 1970. The exploitation of turtles along the Atlantic coast, chiefly by the Mesquito [Indians], has been a traditional activity for many years, as has been the fishery in the Mesquito Keys by Cayman Islanders. The government understands the need for conservation, but lacks the means to enforce any measures, especially since the exploitation occurs in remote areas of the country.

BRITISH HONDURAS

Approximately 75% of the green, hawksbill, and loggerhead turtles are caught in nets, about 25% are harpooned, and a few are turned on the beaches. Craig (1966) believes that not more than a dozen turtle fishermen still remain. According to him, the meat of a large loggerhead brings the fisherman about $25; the calipee is no longer saved. In conjunction with their nets the fishermen use decoys, which they believe to be effective. Gil Rosado (personal communication) estimates local consumption of turtles as: green—1,000 pounds per year; hawksbill—2,500 pounds per year; loggerhead—5,000 pounds per year. About 800 pounds of loggerhead meat was exported to the United States in 1969 and again in 1970. A closed season on all sea turtles exists from 1 June through 31 August. The minimum weight restrictions are 30 pounds for the green, 50 pounds for the hawksbill, and 20 pounds for the loggerhead. Egg taking is prohibited.

The exportation of hawksbill shell was once a fairly substantial enterprise, with nearly all the shell being exported to England. In 1937, 2,576 pounds ($5,318) were exported; in 1938, 1,457 pounds ($2,919); in 1939, 1,211 pounds ($2,078); in 1940, 319 pounds ($482); and in 1941, 850 pounds ($1,131). During 1945 4,346 pounds of green turtle, 7,131 pounds of loggerhead turtle, and 1,110 pounds of hawksbill turtle were sold within the colony.

COLOMBIA

Dr. Reinhard Kaufmann provided the information on Colombia. Four species (*Chelonia mydas, Caretta caretta, Eretmochelys imbricata,* and *Dermochelys coriacea*) nest in Colombia, and eggs are taken from all, but mainly from loggerheads and leatherbacks. The turtles are caught by turning when they come ashore to lay and are used for local consumption.

Kaufmann comments:

> There is nobody who has any information and statistics about sea turtle fishing. With the exception of a 7.5 km long beach, which could be protected this year [1970] by a sort of beach guard, all turtles coming to nest are turned and slaughtered, and all eggs are collected by the "tortugeros," belonging to the poor coast-population.
>
> As I know from the peninsula La Guajira in the far north-east of Colombia, the Guajira-indians are fishing turtles by nets in offshore waters. This agrees with my own observations, that the coast is not suited for a nesting beach there.

Bill Rainey reports that hawksbills are fished extensively around the Caribbean banks of Colombia (Providence Island fishermen go to Quita Sueño, Serrano, and Bocador). The shell is sent to England through Panama and brings 132 Colombian pesos per kilogram. Turtle meat sells for 6.60 pesos per kilogram.

NETHERLAND ANTILLES

H. Girigorie (personal communication) comments that there are no specific turtle fisheries in the Netherland Antilles, and consequently no statistics are available. The few turtles caught are either speared by sports fishermen or turned. Green turtles are imported from Venezuela and Colombia.

Dr. Ingvar Kristensen, reporting in personal communication on Curaçao, Aruba, and Bonaire, states that eggs are taken for local consumption from the three species that nest —green, hawksbill, and loggerhead. Turtles are captured by tangle nets and as incidental catches in other fisheries and are used locally, except for the hawksbill shell. Thirty-four percent of the shell is exported. Egg taking on Bonaire is prohibited.

Table 28. CATCH OF TURTLES IN CURAÇAO

Year	Number	Year	Number	Year	Number
1949	232	1956	117	1963	72
1950	160	1957	104	1964	54
1951	133	1958	100	1965	24
1952	152	1959	105	1966	32
1953	143	1960	88	1967	86
1954	140	1961	64	1968	77
1955	117	1962	58	1969	17

Source: Dr. Ingvar Kristensen.
Note: Ninety-nine percent green and 1% hawksbill.

MEXICO

Except where otherwise noted, the information in this section was supplied by Juan Luis Cifuentes L. (personal communication) and covers only the Gulf of Mexico and the Caribbean area.

Turtles are taken by harpoon, tangle nets, and as incidental catches in other fisheries. Loggerhead and green turtle meat (frozen) is exported to the United States (in 1968 10,200 kilograms were exported) as well as consumed locally. Carranza (1967) reports that 200 kilograms of tortoiseshell are produced yearly in Yucatán, and green turtles are captured there almost exclusively to fill the U.S. demand.

Egg taking is prohibited, and nesting females are protected. It is illegal to capture leatherback turtles year round and to capture green, loggerhead, ridley, and hawksbill turtles from May through August. The minimum legal size of the loggerhead is 60 cm and of the hawksbill 45 cm.

Turtle camps have been installed for the protection of female *Lepidochelys kempii* turtles that nest on Tamaulipas State coasts and for the protection of female *Caretta caretta* and *Chelonia mydas* in Isla Mujures, Yucatán. In both places the eggs are incubated, and the hatchlings are released in the sea.

Table 29. CATCH OF TURTLES IN MEXICO
(CARIBBEAN AND GULF OF MEXICO AREA), KG

Year	Green	Hawksbill	Loggerhead
1949	293,909		
1950	347,518		900
1951	261,591		1,500
1952	286,810		
1953	160,121	190	350
1954	159,275	2,816	
1955	160,147	2,034	
1956	65,017		420
1957	119,733		300
1958	48,540		410
1959	107,646		47,188
1960	494,338		103,424
1961	39,963		204,808
1962	295,734		182,280
1963	63,792		51,623
1964	156,771		134,086
1965	181,669		54,480
1966	62,000		10,000
1967	108,000		9,000
1968	134,619		7,136
1969	99,775		5,214

DISCUSSION
AND RECOMMENDATION

The few scattered statistics of early catches show that the yield of sea turtles has dropped considerably since the earliest days of exploitation and, to a smaller extent, during the last three decades. The first considerable drop from the yield of almost virgin fishery to a steady, smaller annual return was inevitable because the early fishermen were drawing their catch from a turtle pool representing age groups spread over at least ten to twenty years. Thus the catch would be many times optimum yearly crop.

The fluctuations in the demand for turtle products (especially tortoiseshell) during the past 20 years have lessened the fishing pressure for brief intervals, but the resurgence of old product demand and the new uses of turtle leather as a fashion commodity and of turtle oil for cosmetics have revived the luxury trade and its concomitant profits for the fisherman or the poacher.

Areas that have historically been large producers of turtles and turtle products exhibit severe depletion of the species fished. Carr (1969a and b and 1970) points out the over-exploitation of the green turtle in Costa Rica, even with a government at least partially sympathetic to the problem. Carr et al. (1966) mention that the prevailing market, even in 1966, allowed a fisherman to realize as much as $14 for a few pounds of easily prepared and transported products from a single hawksbill.

There can be no doubt that the practice of taking eggs and of capturing turtles during the vulnerable nesting process has done far more harm to the stock than could possibly have been caused by heavy fishing alone. In addition, the use of wild eggs to stock farming operations would represent further hazards to the populations of sea turtles if the farming becomes popular and widespread. Fortunately, there appears to be little likelihood that this will happen. Formidable problems appear at this time to doom most enterprises economically.

Since the yield of turtles has never been great enough to satisfy modern markets dependent upon large volumes of a uniform product, the trade is based on small-volume luxury items. The relatively high returns for small catches of turtles encourage both heavy legal exploitation and poaching. The latter is usually accompanied by much wastage since very little of the turtle is removed and sold.

From a conservation standpoint, it would seem more desirable to encourage domestic consumption and interisland trade than to continue a luxury or semiluxury trade with the United States or Great Britain, particularly in view of the current heavy imports of protein food into the Caribbean area. The demand does exist, however, and its satisfaction provides undeniable dollar credits. It is advisable that any export of turtle products should be restricted for the most part to items not used for local consumption (tortoiseshell, turtle leather, etc.) and that such products should only be derived from turtles slaughtered within the limits of a reasonable conservation system. It is best to encourage in every way possible the domestic manufacture of costume jewelry and ornaments and the decoration of toilet accessories with turtle shell, rather than shipping the raw shell. Such local use would allow the country of origin to retain the economic benefit of the production. This domestic manufacture should appeal to foreign importers because of the lower cost of native handicraft labor.

Administration of the fishery calls for rigid prohibition of egg taking and of turtle catching on the beaches at all times of the year. Compared with other marine resources, the breeding potential is low, and there seems to be no doubt regarding the high mortality of newly hatched turtles. These factors render the protection of the eggs and of the vulnerable breeding female of major importance.

The migratory habits of the green turtle and, to a lesser extent, of the other species of sea turtles, suggest the necessity of both uniform regulations throughout the Caribbean and cooperative research. Rigid restrictions on the nesting beaches will be far less effective if wholesale slaughter occurs at the feeding grounds. It is not difficult to understand a country's reluctance to restrict fishing for its own citizens and to expend money for enforcement of laws if these measures save the turtles for other peoples' profit. Nevertheless, continued reticence on the part of individual governments will result in the loss of a potentially productive resource.

The enforcement of a size limit is important from a conservation viewpoint. Since it is effective both in maintaining the breeding potential and also in preventing overfishing, the minimum-size regulation is a valuable safeguard. The size at which sexual maturity is attained varies between species and even slightly within species from one area to another. The actual size limits, therefore, should be determined on a regional basis.

In certain localities the gradual encroachment of mankind upon the nesting beaches must certainly have interfered with the normal nesting habits and thus have cut down recruitment in the turtle population of that area. Although little may be done to counteract this advancing encroachment, it should not be ignored as a potent factor in the declining population.

Interference with the breeding potential by egg taking and the capture of nesting females is probably the most serious cause of decline in production. It is equally probable that increasing the breeding potential by care of the breeding females and hatchlings would lead to an increase in production. The amount of increased production might not justify these measures economically; nevertheless, they should be done if the catastrophic depredations are to be halted. Any proposal for private turtle cultivation or farming for profit should be carefully investigated from the viewpoint of financial cost compared with the probable increased production.

Several proposals for turtle hatcheries or farms have been suggested, particularly by Thompson. Earlier attempts, including those of Moorhouse, are described in the appropriate section. Culture proposals should be viewed with careful scrutiny, and the use of wild eggs as a source of animals should be carefully managed. It should also be noted that a reliable supply of turtle products from such farms might add impetus to the demand for these products and thus create even further pressure on wild stocks.

Transplantation of hatchlings to restore a breeding population remains of doubtful benefit since experiments conducted along these lines have so far yielded no positive results. The high mortalities of hatchlings both on the beach and the first few days in the water suggests that protection of the young from natural nests may be an effective conservation measure. Collection of the young after hatching and care for the first few months before release should reduce this mortality. Since sea turtles have low fecundity in comparison with most other marine animals, a reduction in mortality during the early stages can have a significant effect on production.

In setting up regulations for closed seasons and minimum sizes it is important to have accurate scientific data regarding growth rate, age of maturity, and duration of breeding season. This and equally desirable information regarding suitable sites for breeding or cultivation should be sought by the local fishery officers. Now lacking for many areas, information regarding the average weight, numbers produced, and similar statistics is very valuable in judging the trend of the industry, the possibility of overfishing, and the presence and extent of a decline. Every effort should be made to collect such data and to make it available at least in mimeographed form. As an aid to enforcement it is highly desirable that regulations throughout the Caribbean be as uniform as possible.

The enforcement of regulations and the collection of information are greatly aided by educational activities that enlist the interest, understanding, and sympathy of the fishermen. A brief, well-illustrated, and simply worded pamphlet, distributed through local officials, school teachers, justices of the peace, and constables could bring about a considerable change in the attitude of the fishermen and go far toward enlisting their support in protection of the industry as well as their aid in collecting information.

BIBLIOGRAPHY

ABBOTT, W. L. 1894. Notes on the natural history of Aldabra, Assumption and Gloriosa Islands, Indian Ocean. Proc. U.S. Nat. Mus. 16: 759-764.

   Aldabra: 220 mi. NW of Madagascar. 22 mi. long and 8 wide. Coral formation. Giant land tortoises similar to those of Galapagos are indigenous. Aldabra is one of the Seychelles group. Many species of land tortoises once lived on Seychelles. Rats eat young. Thousands of sea turtles ascend the beaches annually to lay eggs. Sea turtles overfished, especially hawksbill. Other islands of the group similar to Aldabra.

ABEL, JOHN H., JR., and RICHARD A. ELLIS. 1966. Histochemical and electron microscopic observations on the salt secreting lacrymal glands of marine turtles. Amer. J. Anat. 118(2): 337-357.

   Unusual features of the turtle salt gland and common characteristics it shares with similar marine vertebrates elaborated. Fine structure of secretory cells described.

ABERSON, A. A. 1947. Proposals transmitted to the Chairman, Caribbean Research Council by the Caribbean Coordination Commission Netherlands by letter dated 30 October 1947.

   Points out the need for inter-Caribbean protection of the sea turtles.

ACKMAN, R. C., and R. D. BURGHER. 1965. Cod liver oil fatty acids as secondary reference standards in the gas liquid chromatography (GLC) of polyunsaturated fatty acids of animal origin: analysis of a dermal oil of the Atlantic leatherback turtle. J. Amer. Oil Chem. Soc. 42(1): 38-42.

   Oil is a low iodine value oil but different from most marine lipid

---

Publications without authors are listed under the titles of the reports. Scientific names have been spelled as they appear in the publication cited.

systems in that it has a high proportion of polyunsaturated fatty acids of "linoleic" type. Absence of polyunsaturated C_{16} acids. Fat may be primarily used for buoyancy. Presence of dodecanoic acid and of a high percentage of tetradecanoic acid is noteworthy.

ADAMS, LEVERETT ALLEN. 1947. Introduction to the vertebrates. John Wiley & Sons, New York.
Comparative anatomy.

ADAMS, W. E. 1962. The carotid sinus-carotid body problem in the Chelonia (with a note on a foramen of Panizza in *Dermochelys*). Arch. Int. Pharmacodyn 139(1-2): 25-37.

AGASSIZ, ALEXANDER. 1888. Three cruises of the U.S. Coast and Geodetic Survey steamer *Blake*. Bull. Mus. Comp. Zool. 14.
This is a leisurely written account of the voyage of the *Blake*. Since the mission was primarily for the study of the geological and hydrographical aspects of the Caribbean, the notes on turtles are scarce. An interesting ecological background is provided, however, for the study of any animal indigenous to this region, including sea turtles.

AGASSIZ, L. 1857a. Embryology of the turtle. Contr. Nat. Hist. U.S. 1 and 2. Boston.
Quoted by many other workers. Excellent descriptive embryology with many useful plates depicting stages in embryology.

AGASSIZ, L. 1857b. North American Testudinata. Contr. Nat. Hist. U.S. 1 and 2. Boston.

AGASSIZ, L., and E. D. COPE. 1871. Proc. Amer. Assoc. Adv. Sci. 19: 235.
Mentioned by Cope (1875) with Gray as source for family (*Chelonidae*) 1823.

AGUAYO, C. G. 1953. La tortuga bastarda (*Lepidochelys olivacea kempii*) en Cuba. Mem. Soc. Cubana Hist. Nat. 21(2): 211-219.
Some turtles previously misidentified found to be *Lepidochelys kempii*. (Later examination has shown this identification to be incorrect). Key given to families and species of Cuban turtles.

AHRENFELDT, ROBERT H. 1954. Identification of the amphibians and reptiles recorded in Jamaica by Hans Sloan (1688-89). Copeia 1954(2): 105-111.
Includes *Chelonia mydas*, *Caretta caretta*, and *Eretmochelys imbricata*, with short comments on nomenclature.

ALBERT I, Prince of Monaco. 1898. Sur le développement des tortues (*T. caretta*) Soc. Biologie Paris, 5: 10-11.

ALEXANDER, A. B. 1902a. Statistics of the fisheries of the South Atlantic States. Rept. Comm., U.S. Comm. Fish Fish. 29:343-410.
Raw data on production and values. A few notes on methods and gear employed.

ALEXANDER. A. B. 1902b. Statistics of the fisheries of the Gulf States. Rept. U.S. Comm. Fish Fish. 29: 411-482.
Raw data on production and values. Some notes on methods and gear.

ALLEN, E. ROSS, and W. T. NEILL. 1953. Know your reptiles: the
green turtle. Fla. Wildlife 7(4): 19, 32.
Very brief review of life history and habits.
ALLEN, E. ROSS, and W. T. NEILL. 1957. Another record of the
Atlantic leatherback, *Dermochelys c. coriacea*, nesting on the Flor-
ida coast. Copeia 1957(2): 143-144.
Second record of leatherback nesting in the state in 100 years.
Hatchlings discovered on Miami Beach. Tail rudderlike, rounded
below but with a high, thin keel above; this feature not observed
in specimens of 5 inches carapace length or more.
AMERICAN ASSOCIATION OF ANATOMISTS. 1932. Abstracts of
papers presented at 48th annual session. Anat. Rec. 52 (Supp. Feb.):
1-81.
The cerebellum of Chelonians is dealt with briefly.
Amphibious land and water tortoises, their care in captivity. 1938.
Marshall Press Ltd., London.
ANDERSON, A. W., and C. E. PETERSON. 1952. Fishery statistics of
the U.S. 1949. U.S. Fish Wildlife Ser., Stat. Dig. 25. 278 pp.
ANDERSON, A. W., and C. E. PETERSON. 1953. Fishery statistics of
the U.S. 1950. U.S. Fish Wildlife Ser., Stat. Dig. 27. 492 pp.
ANDERSON, A. W., and C. E. PETERSON. 1954. Fishery statistics of
the U.S. 1951. U.S. Fish Wildlife Ser., Stat. Dig. 30. 341 pp.
ANDERSON, A. W., and E. A. POWER. 1948. Fisheries statistics of the
U.S. 1944. U.S. Fish Wildlife Ser., Stat. Dig. 16.
377,032 pounds of "turtles" imported. The value of these was
$33,495. Louisiana production of green turtle was 500 pounds
with a value of $10. Florida production of green turtle was
41,600 pounds with a value of $4,546.
ANDERSON, A. W., and E. A. POWER. 1951. Fishery statistics of the
U.S. 1948. U.S. Fish Wildlife Ser., Stat. Dig. 22. 305 pp.
ANDERSON, A. W., and E. A. POWER. 1955. Fishery statistics of the
U.S. 1952. U.S. Fish Wildlife Ser., Stat. Dig. 34. 345 pp.
ANDERSON, A. W., and E. A. POWER. 1956a. Fishery statistics of the
U.S. 1953. U.S. Fish Wildlife Ser., Stat. Dig. 36. 338 pp.
ANDERSON, A. W., and E. A. POWER. 1956b. Fishery statistics of the
U.S. 1954. U.S. Fish Wildlife Ser., Stat. Dig. 39. 374 pp.
ANDERSON, A. W., and E. A. POWER. 1957. Fishery statistics of the
U.S. 1955. U.S. Fish Wildlife Ser., Stat. Dig. 41. 446 pp.
ANGEL, FERNAND. 1946. Reptiles and Amphibians. Faune de
France, 45. Feder. Fran. Soc. Sci. Nat.
Good taxonomic source material. Lists of publications of early
descriptions of all species of sea turtles. Species listed: *Eret-
mochelys imbricata, Colpochelys kempii, Caretta caretta, Der-
mochelys coriacea.* Some natural history notes are also included.
ANNANDALE, N. 1915. Notes on some Indian Chelonia. Rec. Ind.
Mus. 11(11): 184-196.
Sea turtles not mentioned.
ANNUAL SUMMARIES. 1953. Imports and exports of fishery prod-

ucts 1949-1953. U.S. Dept. Int., Fish Wildlife Ser., Bur. Comm. Fish., CFS No. 1003. 7 pp.
ANNUAL SUMMARIES. 1957. Imports and exports of fishery products 1953-1957. U.S. Dept. Int., Fish Wildlife Ser., Bur. Comm. Fish., CFS No. 1839. 11 pp.
ANNUAL SUMMARIES. 1962. Imports and exports of fishery products 1958-1962. U.S. Dept. Int., Fish Wildlife Ser., Bur. Comm. Fish., CFS No. 3185. 11 pp.
ANNUAL SUMMARIES. 1963. Imports and exports of fishery products 1962-1963. U.S. Dept. Int., Fish Wildlife Ser., Bur. Comm. Fish., CFS No. 3671. 12 pp.
ANNUAL SUMMARIES. 1965. Imports and exports of fishery products 1964-1965. U.S. Dept. Int., Fish Wildlife Ser., Bur. Comm. Fish., CFS No. 4185. 9 pp.
ANNUAL SUMMARIES. 1967. Imports and exports of fishery products 1966-1967. U.S. Dept. Int., Fish Wildlife Ser., Bur. Comm. Fish., CFS No. 4743. 9 pp.
ANNUAL SUMMARIES. 1969. Imports and exports of fishery products 1968-1969. U.S. Dept. Int., Fish Wildlife Ser., Bur. Comm. Fish., CFS No. 5295. 9 pp.
ANNUAL SUMMARY. 1950, 1952-1962. Florida landings. U.S. Dept. Int., Bur. Comm. Fish., Fla. St. Bd. Conserv., Mar. Lab., U. Miami, CFS Nos. 681: 3 pp., 971: 9 pp., 1016: 9 pp., 1170: 9 pp., 1331: 9 pp., 1592: 9 pp., 1817 (revised): 9 pp., 2001: 10 pp., 2250: 10 pp., 2557: 13 pp., 2886: 13 pp., 3236: 13 pp.
ANNUAL SUMMARY. 1963-1968. Florida landings. U.S. Dept. Int., Fish Wildlife Ser., Bur. Comm. Fish., Fla. St. Bd. Conserv., CFS Nos. 3602: 15 pp., 3795: 12 pp., 4123: 18 pp., 4416: 18 pp., 4660: 18 pp., 4966: 19 pp.
ANNUAL SUMMARY. 1969. Florida landings. U.S. Dept. Int., Fish Wildlife Ser., Bur. Comm. Fish., Fla. Dept. Nat. Resources, CFS No. 5269: 19 pp.
ANNUAL SUMMARY. 1970-1971. Florida commercial marine landings. Fla. Dept. Nat. Res. 61 pp., 64 pp.
ATWATER, W. O. 1888. The chemical composition and nutritive values of food-fishes and aquatic invertebrates. Report U.S. Comm. Fish Fish., pp. 697-868.
    Excellent tabulations of protein, fat, and mineral content of muscle tissue of *Chelonia mydas* from Key West, Florida.
AUDUBON, JOHN JAMES. 1834. The turtlers. *In* Ornithological biography. Vol. II. Edinburgh: Adam & Charles Black, pp. 370-376.
BABCOCK, H. L. 1919. The turtles of New England. Mem. Boston Soc. Nat. Hist. 8: 323-431.
BABCOCK, H. L. 1930*a*. Variation in the number of costal shields in *Caretta*. Amer. Nat. 64(690): 95-96.
BABCOCK, H. L. 1930*b*. *Caretta kempii*. Copeia 1:21.
BABCOCK, H. L. 1931. Notes on *Dermochelys*. Copeia 3:142.
BABCOCK, H. L. 1938. The sea turtles of the Bermuda Islands, with a

survey of the present state of the turtle fishing industry. Proc. Zool. Soc. London, A. 107(4): 595-601.

    1. *Dermochelys coriacea* (Linne). Leatherneck. Rare.

    2. *Chelonia mydas* (Linné).

    3. *Eretmochelys imbricata* (Linné). Eats ascidians, Physalia.

    4. *Caretta caretta* (Linné). Sedentary, depleted. 1500 to 1600 pounds. Perhaps also *Caretta kempii* (Garman). Statistics.

BACON, PETER R. 1967. Leatherback turtles. J. Trinidad Field Natur. Club 1967: 2-3.

    Interim report of study of *Dermochelys* in Trinidad.

BACON, PETER R. 1969. The leatherback turtle project, progress report 1967-1968, and recommendations. J. Trinidad Field Natur. Club 1969: 8-9.

BACON, PETER R. 1970. Studies on the leatherback turtle, *Dermochelys coriacea* (L.), in Trinidad, West Indies. Biol. Cons. 2(3): 213-217.

    Gives some details of the breeding biology of the leatherback in Trinidad from data collected between May 1965 and July 1969. Estimated population size of nesting females between 150 and 200 each year; season from at least March to August. Green and hawksbill turtles known to nest in Trinidad but rarely seen during study, possibly because of different beach preferences. Main natural causes of egg destruction: oviposition too near the sea and beach erosion. Slaughter of adults (20 to 30% of nesting population every year) needs to be controlled.

BALASINGAM, E. 1969. Marine turtles in West Malaysia. *In* Marine turtles. Proc. Work. Meet. Mar. Turtle Special. IUCN Morges, Switzerland.

    Species and nesting areas listed. Exploitation, conservation, research, and national requirements covered.

BANKS, E. 1937. The breeding of the edible turtle (*Chelonia mydas*). Sarawak Mus. J. 4(4): 523-32.

    Mostly green turtle, few visits by hawksbill. Die if not turned on backs. Sizes, 3 ft. 6 in. to 4 ft. Copulate again on reaching the sea. Each female lays at least three times at about 14-day intervals. *Caretta* rare here. Turtles lay all year but mostly from May to September. Eggs important, not the meat. Illegal to kill adults. Great range in number picked up—1,790,370 in 1934 and 503,526 in 1935. Numbers vary in the various islands. Eggs are collected each night, dried in the sun, and shipped. The biggest year, 1927, grossed $23,000. It is estimated that only 2 to 3% of those labeled grow up. Turtles double size in six months. At 28 months are 18 inches long. It takes at least seven years to reach 4-foot stage.

BARBOUR, THOMAS. 1908. Some new reptiles and amphibians. Bull. Mus. Comp. Zool. 51(12): 315-325.

    Sea turtles not mentioned.

BARBOUR, THOMAS. 1912. A contribution to the zoogeography of the East Indian Islands. Mem. Mus. Comp. Zool. 44(1).

Sea turtles not mentioned.

BARBOUR, THOMAS. 1914. A contribution to the zoogeography of the West Indies, with special reference to amphibians and reptiles. Mem. Mus. Comp. Zool. 44(2).

Sea turtles not mentioned.

BARBOUR, THOMAS. 1926. Reptiles and amphibians. Their habits and adaptations. Houghton Mifflin Company, pp. 1-125.

BARNEY, R. L. 1922. Further notes on natural history and artificial propagation of Diamond Back Terrapin. Bull. U.S. Bur. Fish. 38: 91-112.

Facts included in this article could have a bearing on sea turtle propagation. Gives growth rates, mortality figures. Barney favors selecting the most vigorous young for cultivation. Various types of feeding described, and results given for each.

BARTH, EDVARD K. 1965. Notes on the common loggerhead *Caretta caretta* (L.). NYTT Mag. Zool. (Oslo) 12:10-13.

Dead female, 562 mm carapace length, given to museum in May 1962. Carapace width of 500 mm; growth in 3 1/2 years from 5 kilograms to 30.5 kilograms. Maxillary bones of skull have long median contact line anterior to vomer. Number of laminae not diagnostic for *Caretta caretta*. Number of marginals, inframarginals, and several measurements of seven individuals of the same species in the museum collection listed.

BARTH, RUDOLF. 1962a. Beobachtungen an einer verstuemmelten Schildkroete, *Chelonia mydas* L. An. Acad. Brasil Cienc. 34(3): 411-413.

Female preparing to lay eggs observed with hind leg partially amputated and a portion of posterior rim of carapace damaged. Nature of the wounds, rather fresh, suggested attack by a sperm or killer whale.

BARTH, RUDOLF. 1962b. Observacoes sobre a grande tartaruga marinha *Chelonia mydas* L., feitas na ilha de Trinidade. An. Acad. Brasil Cienc. 34(3): 405-409.

Describes conditions the green turtle faces on annual nesting visit to the island. Turtles nest on sloping beaches formed by volcanic eruption. Difference in locomotion on land by young and swimming mechanisms by adults indicate some modification of the reflexes controlling locomotion in order to develop the swimming reaction.

BASS, A. J., and H. J. McALLISTER. 1964. Turtles breeding on the Natal coast. S. Afr. J. Sci. 60(9): 287-288.

Dermochelys coriacea coriacea and *Caretta caretta caretta* breeding along the coast between Oro Point and Saint Mary's Hill. Estimated 170 leatherback females and 370 loggerhead females breeding between September and March.

BAUR, G. 1887. On the morphogeny of the carapace in Testudinata. Amer. Nat. 21: 89.

BAUR, G. 1888. Osteologische Notizen über Reptilien. Anat. Aug. pp. 423-4.

BAUR, G. 1888. Osteologische Notizen über Reptilien. Zoologischer Anzeiger 2: 417-424.

BAUR, G. 1890. On the classification of the Testudinata. Amer. Nat. 24: 530-536.

BEAUFORT and R. COKER. 1910. Diversity of scutes of *Chelonia*. J. Morph. 21.

BEEBE, WILLIAM. 1924. Galapagos; World's End. G. P. Putnam's Sons. New York.

BELKIN, D. A. 1963. Anoxia: tolerance in reptiles. Science 139: 492-493.

> Sea turtles (Cheloniidae—species not stated) have a minimum anoxic anoxia tolerance of about two hours, lower than other turtles and higher than lizards, snakes, and crocodilians tested. Suggested that turtles use mechanisms in addition to anaerobic glycolysis to attain their higher level of tolerance than other reptiles.

BELKIN, D. A. 1968. Anaerobic brain function; effects of stagnant and anoxic anoxia on persistence of breathing in reptiles. Science 162: 1017-1018.

> Turtles (no Cheloniidae tested) showed lower tolerance to stagnant anoxia than other reptiles tested. Their difference in relative tolerance to stagnant and anoxic anoxia (Belkin, 1963) strengthens the assumption of anaerobic glycolysis as the prime mechanism.

BELL, T. 1827-28. Characters of the order, families, and genera of the Testudinata. J. Zool. Soc. London. 3:513-516.

BEMMELEN, J. F. van. 1896. Bemerkungen zur Phylogenie der Schildkröten. C. R. 3. Congr. Internat. Zool. Leyde, pp. 322-335.

BEMMELEN, J. F. van. 1928. Animaux disparus. (Animals that have disappeared.) Palaeobiologica (Vienna) 1(1): 281-294.

> A review of various phases of evolution, partly from the standpoint of fossils. Contains references to Chelonians.

BENEDICT, FRANCIS GANO. 1932. The physiology of large reptiles with special reference to the heat production of snakes, tortoises, lizards, and alligators. Carnegie Inst. Wash. Pub. 425.

> Much of the material on tortoises applicable to sea turtles. Bibliography extensive, in form of footnotes.

BERKSON, H. 1966. Physiological adjustments to prolonged diving in the Pacific green turtle (*Chelonia mydas agassizii*). Comp. Biochem. Physiol. 18(1): 101-119.

> Turtles observed in captivity followed a regime of long dives (15 to 20 min.) followed by several short dives. Pacific green turtle found to be similar to other air-breathing vertebrates in its physiological adjustments to diving. Prolonged diving accompanied by bradycardia, peripheral vasoconstriction, and reduction of metabolic rate. Aspects peculiar to the turtle (versus other vertebrates

previously studied): its ability to endure extreme depletion of its oxygen depots; bradycardia is extreme, but it is frequently slow to set in or breaks any time the animal moves or struggles; selective ischemia breaks down in the latter part of a prolonged dive.

BEVENS, MICHAEL H. 1956. The book of reptiles and amphibians. Garden City Books: Garden City, New York. 62 pp.

BIERDRAGER, J. 1936. Een geval van massale schildpadver giftiging in New Guinea. Geneesk. Tijdschr. Nederland-Indie 76: (31).

Poisoning of 52 people with 9 deaths caused by eating turtle (*Chelonia imbricata*). Illness characterized by symptoms of acute poisoning with sleepiness or a semicomatose condition, with an infection of mouth and throat. At autopsy toxic and degenerative alterations found. Prognosis depended on loss of consciousness. Still uncertain whether the species of turtle in question is poisonous, or whether some temporary condition produced this result.

BLEAKNEY, J. SHERMAN. 1955. Four records of the Atlantic ridley turtle, *Lepidochelys kempi*, from Nova Scotian waters. Copeia 1955(2): 137.

Four individuals previously misidentified as *Caretta caretta*, leaving only one record of the loggerhead for Canadian Atlantic waters.

BLEAKNEY, J. SHERMAN. 1965. Reports of marine turtles from New England and Eastern Canada. Can. Field. Natur. 79(2): 120-128.

Covering the period from 1824 to 1964, 112 records compiled from the literature, newspaper reports, correspondence, and personal observations. Occurrence of marine turtles an annual event in these waters; behavior of turtles indicates that water temperatures of 55 ° to 65°F do not benumb them. Feeding habits of the leatherback indicates they exist chiefly on jellyfish and their parasites and symbionts. Good source of turtle sightings from this area.

BLEAKNEY, J. SHERMAN. 1967a. Food items in two loggerhead sea turtles, *Caretta caretta caretta* (L.) from Nova Scotia. Can. Field. Natur. 81(4): 269-272.

Fish, algae, invertebrates in stomach contents described.

BLEAKNEY, J. SHERMAN. 1967b. Marine turtles as introductory material to basic biology. Turtox News 45(3): 82-86.

Suggestions given for using the skeletons of leatherback turtles in teaching homology and comparative anatomy.

BOCOURT, M. 1868. Description de quelques chéloniens nouveaux appartenant a la faune Mexicaine. Ann. Sci. Nat. 5, Zool. 10(1-3).

Taxonomy. *Chelonia agassizii* mentioned as coming from Mexico. Species of *Emys* and *Emysaurus* reported from salt water.

BOEKE, J. 1907. Rapport betreffende een voorloopig onderzoek naar den toestand von de Visscherii en de Industrie van Zeeprudukten in de Kolonie Curacao, 1: 121. Haag.

An account of the turtle fishery of Curaçao with a description of a method of raising young turtles in small ponds.

BOJANUS, L. H. 1819-21. Anatome Testudinis Europae. Vilnae. Vols. 1 and 2.

BOULENGER, G. A. 1889. Catalogue of Chelonians, Rhynchocephalians, and Crocodilians in the British Museum.
Descriptions refer mainly to the osteology.

BOWEN, J. DAVID. 1960. To save the green turtle. Americas 12(12): 14-17.
Short review of historical green turtle exploitation. Account of Carr's conservation efforts begun in 1959 on Costa Rican coast.

BRACHET, A. 1935. Traité d'embryologie des vertébrés. Paris.
Deals in detail with the fundamental problems of morphogenesis. Includes turtles and all general classifications of reptiles.

BRATTSTROM, B. H. 1955. Notes on the herpetology of the Revillagigedo Islands, Mexico. Amer. Midland Nat. 54(1): 219-229.
Islands located approximately 210 miles southwest of tip of Baja California, Mexico. Sea turtles listed: *Chelonia mydas agassizi, Caretta caretta gigas* (new record).

BRAUN, M. 1899. Trematoden der Dahlschen Sammlung aus Neu-Guinea nebst Bemerkungen über endoparasitische Trematoden der Cheloniden. Zentralbl. Bakt. Parasit. 25: 714-725.
Parasites from all sea turtles mentioned. No bibliography.

BRAVO, RAMON. 1970. Reprieve for the turtles of Rancho Nuevo. Oceans Mag. 3(5): 42-47.
One day every year during the second half of May thousands of parrot turtles (*Lepidochelys olivacea kempi*) come out of the water and nest from about 9 A.M. to sunset. Surrounding inhabitants collect eggs and sell them at high profit, thus endangering species. Department of Fisheries of the Mexican government declared area a game preserve and protects it with marines, much to the dislike of the local people. Females tagged by biologists, and their nests and young protected from predators. Conservation program in effect for four years.

BRICE, JOHN J. 1896a. Rept. Comm. Fish Fish. 22: 132. Statistics.

BRICE, JOHN J. 1969b. The fish and fisheries of the coastal waters of Florida. Rept. U.S. Comm. Fish Fish. 22: 263-342.
Brief notes on breeding habits.

BROCKERHOFF, H., P. C. HWANG, R. J. HOYLE, and CARTER LITCHFIELD. 1968. Positional distribution of fatty acids in depot triglycerides of aquatic animals. Lipids 3(1): 24-29.
Stereospecific triglyderide analyses performed on fat of five aquatic invertebrates, five freshwater fish, six marine fish, three marine birds, two amphibians, two seals, a whale, and the dermal fat of a speciman of *Dermochelys coriacea* from the Nova Scotian coast. Polyenoic acids of turtle fat prefer position 2 (fatty acid composition is positions 1,2, and 3 — 1,2,3-triacyl-L-glycerol — were determined); saturated acids, 16:0 and 18:0, position 1; longer acids, position 3. Accumulation of 12:0 and 14:0 in alpha positions peculiar for turtle fat.

BRONGERSMA, L. D. 1961. Notes upon some sea turtles. Zoologische Verhandelingen 51: 1-46.

Specimens from various museums examined and literature reviewed with notes on variations in individual cases and locality records. Discussion of nomenclatural problems raised by Deraniyagala and Wermuth.

BRONGERSMA, L. D. 1967a. British turtles — guide for the identification of stranded turtles on British coasts. Brit. Mus. (Nat. Hist.) Pub. No. 659. 23 pp.

Key to identification of sea turtles commonly found stranded on British beaches, with notes on turtle biology. Very clear and concise; recommended for the layman.

BRONGERSMA, L. D. 1967b. What you should do if you see or catch a turtle. Fish. News (Nov. 3) No. 2839: 7,8.

BRONGERSMA, L. D. 1968a. Miscellaneous notes on turtles. I. Kon. Ned. Akad. Wetensch. Proc. Ser. C Biol. Med. Sci. 71: 439-442.

Lepidochelys kempi. Nests on west shores of Gulf of Mexico. Recorded north as far as Nova Scotia with records in eastern Atlantic from Eire (5), Scotland (2), Wales (3), England (7), Netherlands (1), Channel Islands (1), Azores (1), Madeira (1), and France (1). Length, weight, and other data given on 111 specimens.

Lepidochelys olivacea. Four specimens discussed; three hatchlings (one from Ceylon, two from Indian Ocean). Two have fourth inframarginal separated from abdominal and femoral.

Caretta caretta. Juvenile from Bay of Biscay, only four costal scutes on left side; carapace length 184.5 mm.

BRONGERSMA, L. D. 1968b. The Soay beast. Beaufortia Ser. Misc. Publ. Zool. Mus. 15(184): 33-46.

The Soay beast, sighted 13 September 1959 near Soay, Scotland subject of speculation by several individuals. Reviews theories and eyewitness accounts and convincingly argues that it was a large leatherback turtle.

BRONGERSMA, L. D. 1968c. Turtles. Mar. Observ. 38: 18-34.

Distribution of sea turtles, especially in the Atlantic, discussed. Reports of sightings by ships, whether of individuals or of mass migrations, would be helpful. Key to six species known from Atlantic.

BRONGERSMA, L. D. 1968d. The great sea serpent and the leathery turtle. I. Kon. Ned. Akad. Wetensch. Proc. Ser. C Biol. Med. Sci. 71(3): 209-218.

Synonyms, accounts of possible mistaken identity.

BRONGERSMA, L. D. 1968e. The great sea serpent and the leathery turtle. II. Kon. Ned. Akad. Wetensch. Proc. Ser. C Biol. Med. Sci. 71(3): 219-228.

BRONGERSMA, L. D. 1968f. Notes upon some turtles from Surinam. Kon. Ned. Akad. Wetensch. Proc. Ser. C Biol. Med. Sci. 71(2): 114-127.

Five species of sea turtles exist in Surinam. Discussion of historical taxonomy. Specimens examined: *Chelonia mydas* (15); *Lepidochelys olivacea* (3); *Caretta caretta* (3). *Lepidochelys kempi* should be called Kemp's ridley; *L. olivacea* should be called the olive ridley.

BRONGERSMA, L. D. 1968g. Notes upon some turtles from the Canary Islands and from Madeira. Kon. Ned. Akad. Wetensch. Proc. Ser. C Biol. Med. Sci. 71(2): 128-136.

Counts and measurements on the following—Canary Islands: two juvenile loggerheads; Madeira: seven loggerheads, three Kemp's ridleys, one green turtle, two hawksbills, one leatherback. Comments on distribution and abundance included.

BRONGERSMA, L. D. 1969. Miscellaneous notes on turtles. II A and B. Kon. Ned. Akad. Wetensch. Proc. Ser. C Biol. Med. Sci. 72: 76-102.

Specimens and sightings of a few leatherback turtles reviewed, along with the literature on leatherback food habits. Entozoa of the leatherback discussed.

BRONGERSMA, L. D. 1972. European Atlantic turtles. Zoologische Verhandelingen. Uitgegeven Door het rijksmuseum van natuurlijke historie te Leiden, No. 121. 318 pp.

Comprehensive discussion and listing of European Atlantic turtle records. Extensive references.

BROOM, R. 1934. On the fossil remains associated with *Australopithecus africanus*. S. African J. Sci. 31: 471-480.

A bone breccia from the floor of the cave in which the skull of *A. africanus* was found includes many skulls, all of them broken, a fact that leaves no reasonable doubt that they were broken by the ape for food. *Chelonia* represented.

BROWN, H. H. 1946. The fisheries of the Windward and Leeward Islands. Development and Welfare Bulletin No. 20. Bridgetown, Barbados.

Brief notes on conservation laws. Mentions great decrease in numbers since 1774.

BRUCE, J. R., J. S. COLMAN, and N. S. JONES (Eds.). 1963. Marine fauna of the Isle of Man and its surrounding seas. University Press, Liverpool. 307 pp.

BRUHL, LUDWIG. 1930. Schildkrötenzucht in Japan. (Turtle breeding in Japan.) Naturforscher (Berlin). 7(1): 1-8.

The author describes this industry and the establishments used in conducting it. The species concerned is *Trionyx japonicus*, and its life history sketched. The possibility of introducing the industry in Germany discussed.

BURDON, JONES C. 1961. Atlantic leatherback turtle in Wales. Natur. Wales 7: 39-42.

BURNE, R. H. 1905. On the musculature and visceral anatomy of the leathery turtle (*Dermochelys coriacea*). Proc. Zool. Soc. London.

BURT, CHARLES E., and MAY D. BURT. 1932. Herpetological results of the Whitney South Sea Expedition 6. Bull. Amer. Mus. Nat. Hist. 63(5): 461-597.

Technical paper with full bibliography of articles on individual islands.

BUSTARD, H. ROBERT. 1966. Turtle biology at Heron Island. Australian Natur. Hist. 15(8): 262-264.

Review of studies on ecology and behavior of sea turtles since 1964 on Heron Island. *Chelonia mydas* and *Caretta caretta* nest during summer months. Nesting periodicity similar to other areas; clutch size of green turtle averages about 110.

BUSTARD, H. ROBERT. 1967. Mechanism of nocturnal emergence from the nest in green turtle hatchlings (*Chelonia mydas*). Nature 214(5085): 317.

Of 5,287 hatchlings at the hatchery at Heron Island only 161 (3%) emerged during the day. Mechanism to control the time of emergence presumably enhances survival by limiting effects of predators and high temperatures. Observations have shown that turtles emerging in sunlight will remain in an inactive state while only the head or upper regions protrude above the surface. Suggested that individuals at the top have a dampening effect on siblings below and act as a "cork" to prevent exit from the nest until after sundown.

BUSTARD, H. ROBERT. 1968. Protection for a rookery: Bundaberg sea turtles. Wildlife Australia 5(2): 43-44.

Mon Repos Beach near Bundaberg, Australia only mainland beach that is an import rookery. *Caretta caretta, Chelonia mydas,* and *Chelonia depressa* nest there. People visting the beach destroy nests and scare nesting females in contrast to the orderly tourists at Heron Island rookery. Bundaberg rookery supports population of well over a thousand adult loggerheads; its uniqueness in this respect has tourist potential; rookery should be managed.

BUSTARD, H. ROBERT. 1969*a*. Queensland protects sea turtles. Oryx 10(1): 23-24.

In 1968 Queensland protected sea turtles along coastline and the whole Great Barrier Reef. History of turtle protection in Queensland and Bustard's population studies discussed.

BUSTARD, H. ROBERT. 1969*b*. Marine turtles in Queensland, Australia. *In* Marine turtles. IUCN Publ. New Ser., Suppl. Paper No. 20: 80-87.

Status, exploitation, conservation, research, and national requirements. Brief comments on other Australian areas.

BUSTARD, H. ROBERT. 1970. The adaptive significance of coloration in hatchling green sea turtles. Herpetologica 26(2): 224-227.

Hatchlings have black above and white below. This coloring disadvantageous during crawl to the sea over light sand, but helpful camouflage in the sea. Solar radiation, accented by the dark color, lethal to hatchlings during the day on the beach. Experiments show that a marked "heating effect" results from solar radiation, which presumably increases metabolism and therefore food assimilation and growth, allowing hatchlings to pass through "critical stage" more quickly.

BUSTARD, H. ROBERT, and P. M. GREENHAM. 1968. Physical and chemical factors affecting hatching in the green sea turtle, *Chelonia mydas* (L.). Ecology 49: 269-276.

Work done on Heron Island, Queensland. Found temperature rise of approximately 6°C within the egg mass during later stages of incubation. Construction of successful nests requires sufficient moisture and/or tree rootlets. Chlorinity values of natural nests very low — average 50 mg Cl/kg.; experimental incubation achieved hatching at chlorine values much higher than those found within all nests not covered by seawater at some time. Eggs must be adapted to withstand an 8°C temperature range (2° climatic variation and 6° from metabolic heating). Sixty percent incubation success at 27°C and 32°C. Incubation time varied from 80 days at 27°C to 47 to 49 days at 32°C. Calcium for ossification of the embryo may be obtained externally from metabolism of the egg mass.

BUSTARD, H. ROBERT, and P. M. GREENHAM. 1969. Nesting behavior of the green sea turtle on a Great Barrier Reef island. Herpetologica 25(2): 93-102.

Nesting behavior divided into nine stages based on detailed observations of "several thousand" nesting turtles. Contrary to Costa Rican observations, the turtles did not "smell" the beach during their ascent. Other differences included minor details of the digging activity and a longer excavating time.

BUSTARD, H. ROBERT, and COLIN LIMPUS. 1969. Observations on the flatback turtle, *Chelonia depressa* Garman. Herpetologica 25: 29-34.

Chelonia depressa is a separate taxon from *Chelonia mydas*. Distinctive characteristics: strongly depressed carapace, upward curve along edge of carapace, the presence of small scales along the middle of the upper surface of front flippers, three postoculars, large head, wrinkled skin on flippers, coloration differences. Rookery at Mon Repos Beach in Southeast Queensland described. Data given on incubated eggs; hatchlings larger than *C. mydas*. Enemies of nests are foxes (*Vulpes vulpes*) and monitor lizards (*Varanus* spp.).

BUSTARD, H. ROBERT., K. SIMKISS, and N. K. JENKINS. 1969. Some analyses of artificially incubated eggs and hatchlings of green and loggerhead sea turtles. J. Zool. 158(3): 311-315.

Eggs incubated in coral sand or silica sand moistened with distilled water. Eggs and hatchlings analyzed for calcium, magnesium, and phosphorus. Major influx of calcium in the egg contents during development comes from the eggshell. Loggerheads showed greater efficiency in the incorporation of yolk and materials during development.

BUSTARD, H. ROBERT., and K. P. TOGNETTE. 1969. Green sea turtles: a discrete simulation of density-dependent population regulation. Science 163: 939-941.

Field data from the Great Barrier Reef used to construct a stochastic model. Nest destruction by turtles is density dependent and serves to stabilize a natural nesting population.

CABALLERO y CABALLERO, EDUARDO. 1959. Trematodos de las tortugas de Mexico VII. Descripción de un trematodo digeneo que parasita a tortugas marinas comestibles del Puerto de Acapulco, Guerrero. An. Inst. Biol. Univ. Mexico 30(1/2): 159-166.

Cymatocarpus undulatus from small intestine of *Chelonia mydas*.

CABALLERO y CABALLERO, EDUARDO. 1962. Trematodos de las tortugas de Mexico X. Presencia de *Occhidasma amphiorchis* (Braun, 1899) Loose, 1900 en una tortuga marina, *Chelone mydas*, de las costas de Estado de Tamaulipas, Mexico. An. Inst. Biol. Univ. Mexico 33(1/2): 47-55.

O. amphiorchis redescribed. Previously found only in *Caretta caretta caretta* captured at Tortugas, Florida. List of trematodes found in sea turtles of the Gulf of Mexico included.

CADENAT, J. 1954. Notes sur les tortues des côtes du Senegal. Bull. Inst. Français d'Afrique Noire 11(1-2): 16-35.

At least five species of sea turtles found on the coast of Senegal: *Sphargis coriacea (Dermochelys coriacea), Eretmochelys imbricata, Chelonia mydas, Caretta caretta gigas* (Probably *C. c. caretta*), and *Caretta olivacea (Lepidochelys olivacea). Chelonia mydas* most common of the five. No systematic fishery for sea turtles exists in Senegal; some are taken at sea by harpoon, others on the beach during egg laying. Most taken incidental to the shark fishery.

CAGLE, FRED R. 1939. A system of marking turtles for future identification. Copeia 3: 170-173.

Description of method by which turtles can be released and later identified. Notches are filed on marginal plates, and toes are clipped.

CALDWELL, DAVID K. (Ed.). 1959a. The loggerhead turtles of Cape Romain, S.C. Bull. Fla. St. Mus. 4(10): 319-348.

Manuscript written in 1940 by William P. Baldwin, Jr. and John P. Lofton, Jr., abridged and annotated by Caldwell to complement other articles in publication. No correlation between nesting activity and the stage of the moon, tide, or weather conditions. Description of nesting and factors affecting selection of nesting sites. Data on incubation, hatching success, egg and hatchling sizes, as well as adults. Enemies of eggs and young discussed.

CALDWELL, DAVID K. 1959b. On the status of the Atlantic leatherback turtle, *Dermochelys coriacea coriacea*, as a visitant to Florida nesting beaches, with natural history notes. Quart. J. Fla. Acad. Sci. 21(3): 285-291.

Eleven nesting records of the leatherback on the south Atlantic coast of Florida in 1957 show it comes regularly to nest. Two individuals laid 127 and 129 eggs. Attemps to keep the young in captivity failed.

CALDWELL, DAVID K. 1960. Sea turtles of the United States. Fish Wildlife Serv. Fish. Leaf. 492.

Review of general biology, nesting habits, and the fishery, with comments on conservation.

CALDWELL, DAVID K. 1961. The ecology and systematics of the shore fishes of Jamaica. Yr. Book Amer. Phil. Soc.: 275-277.

Two collecting trips to Jamaica allowed Caldwell to make the following observations on sea turtles: Four of the five species of western Atlantic sea turtles are known to fishermen—leatherback, green, hawksbill, and loggerhead; reports of limited summer nesting by green and hawksbill turtles on the north coast of Jamaica.

CALDWELL, DAVID K. 1962a. Comments on the nesting behavior of Atlantic loggerhead sea turtles, based primarily on tagging returns. Quart. J. Fla. Acad. Sci. 25(4): 287-302.

Land development on Jekyll Island, Georgia, has caused a shift of nesting females to adjacent Little Cumberland Island. Tag returns show two- and three-year nesting cycles as well as multiple nesting at intervals of 12 to 15 days during the season. Grouping in season and after still seems a tenable theory for loggerheads. Unusual nesting behavior reported for a few females; the author suggests inexperience as the causative factor.

CALDWELL, DAVID K. 1962b. Carapace length-body weight relationship and size and sex ratio of the northeastern Pacific green turtle, *Chelonia mydas carrinegra*. Los Angeles County Mus., Contr. Sci. 62. 27 pp.

Empirical values listed for 323 green turtles caught in central Gulf of California and landed at Bahia de Los Angoles. The equation describing the relation is log $W = -2.14 + 2.60$ log L. Tendency for males to be lighter than females, but individual variation within each sex overshadows intersexual variation. Females caught about twice as often as males.

CALDWELL, DAVID K. 1962c. Growth measurements of young captive Atlantic sea turtles in temperate waters. Los Angeles County Mus., Contr. Sci. 50. 8 pp.

Growth averages given for *Chelonia mydas mydas* and *Eretmochelys imbricata imbricata;* limited growth data on *Caretta caretta caretta* and *Lepidochelys kempii.* Author suggests that time to maturity varies between subtropical and tropical waters, the latter being the shorter time.

CALDWELL, DAVID K. 1962d. Sea turtles in Baja California waters (with special reference to those of the Gulf of California), and a description of a new sub-species of northeastern Pacific green turtle. Los Angeles County Mus., Contr. Sci. 61. 31 pp.

New subspecies, *Chelonia mydas carrinegra*, described. All five genera of sea turtles occur in outside waters of Baja California and within Gulf of California. Distribution and abundance of turtles along the California coast and nesting in the Gulf of California discussed.

CALDWELL, DAVID K. 1963a. Second record of the loggerhead sea turtle, *Caretta caretta gigas*, from the Gulf of California. Copeia 1963(3): 508-509.

Female, 37 inches carapace length, captured 4 February 1963 near Isla Angel de la Guarda in the central Gulf of California, Mexico.

CALDWELL, DAVID K. 1963b. The sea turtle fishery of Baja California, Mexico. Calif. Fish Game 49(3): 140-151.

Surveys historical background, present fishery, biological information, and conservation practices. Turtles (green most common) caught mostly by harpooning, but a few caught in entangling nets or large seines. Steps needed to prevent harvesting nesting females when the nesting grounds are discovered.

CALDWELL, DAVID K. 1966. A nesting report on the American ridley. Int. Turt. Tort. Soc. J. 1(1): 10-13, 30.

Author suggests that main eastern Pacific ridley nesting sites lie in the Mexican state of Guerrero; main nesting site of the Atlantic ridley is Rancho Nuevo, Mexico. Restricted nesting area endangered by egg takers. Some conservationists transporting eggs to Padre Island. Protection of 15 km stretch of beach between Barra de Calabazas and Barra de la Coma in the Mexican state of Tamaulipas by the government started 15 April 1966.

CALDWELL, DAVID K. 1968. Baby loggerhead turtles associated with sargassum weed. Quart. J. Fla. Acad. Sci. 31(4): 271-272.

Several baby loggerheads that washed ashore on the Atlantic beaches of northeastern Florida in October 1968 had encrustations of bryozoans and worm tubes typical of sargassum weed communities.

CALDWELL, DAVID K. 1969. Hatchling green sea turtles, *Chelonia mydas*, at sea in the northeastern Pacific Ocean. Bull. S. Calif. Acad. Sci. 68(2): 113-114.

Substantial numbers of hatchling or just posthatchling green turtles captured by fishermen near the Revilla Gigedo Islands. Others captured about 50 miles southeast of Manzanillo, Mexico, about 10 miles offshore. These turtles presumed to come from rookeries in the Revilla Gigedo Islands and on the coast of the Mexican state of Michoacán. First reported catch of large numbers of turtles of this size after turtles have left the nesting beach.

CALDWELL, DAVID K., FREDERICK H. BERRY, ARCHIE CARR, and ROBERT A. RAGOTZKIE. 1959. Multiple and group nesting by the Atlantic loggerhead turtle. Bull. Fla. State Mus. 4(10): 309-318.

Tagging results suggest group adherence of individuals in multiple emergences; eggs of a season laid in two or more batches. Counts and measurements of unlaid eggs included.

CALDWELL, DAVID K., and MELBA C. CALDWELL. 1962. The black "steer" of the Gulf of California. Quart. Los Angeles County Mus., Sci. Hist. 1(1): 14-17.

Report on darkly pigmented green turtle of Gulf of California whose meat is preferred to beef locally. Caught with harpoon and nets, mostly at night. Over 1,000 of both sexes have been examined and measured, ranging from 20 to 275 pounds, data not included. Experiments show adults retain sea-finding ability, presumably through visual mechanisms.

CALDWELL, DAVID K., and MELBA C. CALDWELL. 1969. Addition of the leatherback sea turtle to the known prey of the killer whale, *Orcinus orca*. J. Mammalogy 50(3): 636.

Dissection of three killer whales taken May 1968 showed leatherback remains in all three.

CALDWELL, DAVID K., and ARCHIE CARR. 1957. Status of the sea turtle fishery in Florida. Trans. 22nd N. Amer. Wildlife Conv., March 4, 5, 6, 1957: 457-463.

Ridley, loggerhead, and green are only ones of commercial value today. Impossible to evaluate depletion accurately. Although 1898 freeze may have been a factor, turtle turners and egg robbers constitute the past and present real threat to the species. Recommendations include stopping egg collecting and killing of nesting females from North Carolina to Texas and establishing a restocking, management, or farming program.

CALDWELL, DAVID K., ARCHIE CARR, and THOMAS R. HELLIER, JR. 1956a. A nest of the Atlantic leatherback turtle, *Dermochelys coriacea coriacea* (Linnaeus), on the Atlantic coast of Florida, with a summary of American nesting records. Quart. J. Fla. Acad. Sci. 18(4): 279-284.

Only the second reliable report of a leatherback nesting on North American mainland beaches in the last 100 years. Nested on Hutchinson Island in mid-July, 1955.

CALDWELL, DAVID K., ARCHIE CARR, and THOMAS R. HELLIER, JR. 1956b. Natural history notes on the Atlantic loggerhead turtle, *Caretta caretta caretta*. Quart. J. Fla. Acad. Sci. 18(4): 292-302.

Thirty-seven loggerheads marked in 1953, 1954, and 1955 on the coast of Florida. Tendency to clump during emergences noted. Measurements given for the growth of two juveniles over a two-week period and carapace length, carapace width, and weight for 57 hatchlings and the very young. Comments on length to weight relation of adults.

CALDWELL, DAVID K., ARCHIE CARR, and LARRY H. OGREN. 1959. Nesting and migration of the Atlantic loggerhead turtle. Bull. Fla. State Mus. 4(10): 295-308.

Account of observations of nesting and of results of tagging operations on the coasts of Georgia and Florida. Known rookeries listed and nesting behavior described.

CALDWELL, DAVID K., and RICHARD S. CASEBEER. 1964. A note on the nesting of the eastern Pacific ridley sea turtle, *Lepidochelys olivacea*. Herpetologica 20(3): 213.

> Nesting observed on 27 January 1963; turtle laid approximately 75 whole, somewhat ovoid, soft leathery eggs on Pacific beach in Costa Rica.

CALDWELL, DAVID K., and DONALD S. ERDMAN. 1969. Pacific ridley sea turtle, *Lepidochelys olivacea*, in Puerto Rico. Bull. S. Calif. Acad. Sci. 68(2): 112.

> Ridley, 48 cm carapace length, captured about three miles west of San Juan Harbor, Puerto Rico, in October 1967 by charter fishing boat.

CALDWELL, DAVID K., and W. F. RATHJEN. 1969. Unrecorded West Indian nesting sites for the leatherback and hawksbill sea turtles, *Dermochelys coriacea* and *Eretmochelys i. imbricata*. Copeia 1969(3): 622-623.

> New records reported for Saint Kitts, Nevis, Barbados (northeast coast) for leatherback and Aves Island for the Hawksbill. Good listing of nesting sites in the North Atlantic.

CALDWELL, DAVID K., W. F. RATHJEN, and B. C. C. HSU. 1969. Surinam ridleys at sea. Int. Turt. Tort. Soc. J. 3: 4-5, 23.

> In western North Atlantic *Lepidochelys kempi* is found mostly in the Gulf of Mexico. *Lepidochelys olivacea* has been taken as far north as Cuba and Puerto Rico, but usual range is northeastern coast of South America, adjacent islands, and surrounding waters. Notes given on ridleys captured in trawls by FAO exploratory fishing vessel *R/V Calamar*. Authors suggest information given indicates either a resident population of Indo-Pacific ridleys off northeast South America and in the Antilles, or a constant recruitment from Africa via the north-south equatorial currents, or a movement by the turtles not totally at the will of the current flow.

CALDWELL, MELBA C., and DAVID K. CALDWELL. 1962. Factors in the ability of the northeastern Pacific green turtle to orient toward the sea from land, a possible coordinate in long-range navigation. Los Angeles County Mus., Contr. Sci. 60.

> Individuals studied were both females and males ranging from 20 to 275 pounds. Tests of seaward orientation both in enclosures and on the beach showed definite photic responses. The degree of crawling response and activity showed four levels: (1) visual contact with water during daylight hours—strongly motivated; (2) behind barriers on clear nights—response to relative brightness, crawling slow but steady with periods of "peering"; (3) behind barriers in daylight—no activity to weakly motivated crawling; (4) all visual stimuli removed—orientation circles, head raising with peering or looking about. Literature on subject reviewed.

CALDWELL, NORMAN W. 1951. The turtle hunters. Walkabout (Sydney) 17(7): 29-32.

Account of green turtle fishing at Cossack, northwestern Australia. Includes observation of shark attack on a large male green turtle. Fishermen in boats chase turtles and catch them by hand in the water.

CAPOCACCIA, LILIA. 1968. La *Dermochelys coriacea* (L.) nel Mediterraneo (Reptilia, Testudinata). Atti. Accad. Ligure. Sci. Lett. 24: 318-327.

Leatherback more frequent in western and central Mediterranean and chiefly near Marseille, in the Ligurian and Tyrrhenian seas, and in Tunisian waters. Seasonality of capture in regard to seasonal movements and the possibility of breeding in the Mediterranean discussed.

Captively reared green turtle spawns. 1969*a*. Fla. Conserv. News 5(2): 5.

Two green turtles, raised in captivity, observed mating in 1968. In June of 1969 the female started laying eggs. Attempts to hatch eggs in artificial nests failed, probably because eggs were exposed to seawater.

CARR, A. F. 1942. Notes on sea turtles. Proc. New Eng. Zool. Club 21: 1-116.

In describing *Lepidochelys kempii*, Carr states that it is irascible but that loggerheads and green turtles may be handled with comparative (the latter with complete) impunity. He refers to *Caretta caretta caretta* as "Loggerheads."

CARR, ARCHIE F. 1952. Handbook of turtles: The turtles of the United States, Canada and Baja, California. Comstock Publishing Associates, Ithaca, N. Y. 542 pp.

CARR, ARCHIE F. 1954*a*. The zoogeography and migrations of sea turtles. Yr. Book Amer. Phil. Soc., pp. 138-140.

Résumé of Carr's fieldwork in the Caribbean.

CARR, ARCHIE F. 1954*b*. The passing of the fleet. Bull. Amer. Inst. Biol. Sci. 4: 17-19.

Editorial condensation of Dr. Carr's address to AIBS convention. Discusses importance of green turtle to Caribbean history, its decline, fishing pressure, methods, possible migratory movement, and conservation. Concern expressed over turtle-turning operations at Tortuguero, Costa Rica.

CARR, ARCHIE F. 1955. The riddle of the ridley. Animal Kingdom 58(5): 146-156.

Condensed chapter one of *The Windward Road* by Carr (1956). Examines uncertainties of Atlantic ridley (*Lepidochelys kempi*) life history at that time.

CARR, ARCHIE F. 1956*a*. The windward road. Alfred A. Knopf, Inc., New York. 258 pp.

Interesting and informative account of Carr's travels in the Caribbean.

CARR, ARCHIE F. 1956*b*. Don't give tag to baby. Fla. Wildlife Mag., April 1956, pp. 30-31.

Informational article for public on tagging program.

CARR, ARCHIE F. 1957. Notes on the zoogeography of the Atlantic sea turtles of the genus *Lepidochelys*. Rev. Biol. Trop. 5(1): 45-61.
Further study may prove genus to be one, far-ranging, reproductively continuous species. Nesting site for *L. kempi* in Florida no longer a tenable theory; evidence cited suggests a more distant nesting ground, possibly Spanish Sahara coast. Evidence of migratory travel of *L. kempi* examined.

CARR, ARCHIE F. 1961a. Pacific turtle problem. Nat. Hist. 70(8): 64-71.
On shores surrounding the Gulf of California only two regularly occurring kinds of sea turtles—*Lepidochelys* and *Chelonia*. No reports of loggerhead turtles. Fifty-three turtles examined. Black turtle occurs from March and April to October or November and represents a nonbreeding colony. Parallels to life cycles of *Chelonia* in Gulf of Mexico and Caribbean. Evidence indicating presence or absence of turtles in several localities mentioned.

CARR, ARCHIE F. 1961b. The ridley mystery today. Animal Kingdom 64: 7-12.
Examines knowledge that has accumulated since "The riddle of the ridley" (1955). Sighting of turtles in travels occurred not in groups or masses but by one or twos. Two Mazatlan turtles had nothing but tiny shrimp about 1 inch long in their stomachs. Author's explanation for lack of information: (1) scattered nesting emergences with no rookeries formed; (2) nesting range comprises inaccessible and little visited shores; (3) emergence trails easily obliterated; (4) nesting by daylight.

CARR, ARCHIE F. 1961c. Rätsel der Ridley-Schildkröten. Tier 12: 32-36.

CARR, ARCHIE F. 1962. Orientation problems in the high seas travel and terrestrial movements of marine turtles. Amer. Scient. 50(3): 354-374.
Brief account of migration studies at Tortuguero, Costa Rica and Ascension Island. Visual tracking unsatisfactory; telemetry should be used in the future because an adult female can carry apparatus and apparently will not exceed 20 to 30 miles a day in sustained migratory swimming. Current theories of sun orientation not applicable to turtles. Unpredictability of motivation promises to be the most important obstacle in short-range tracking studies with sea turtles. Sea findings of hatchlings involves a type of telotaxis, a tendency to move toward better-illuminated sky. Wet sand initiates swimming response in young. Relation of guidance mechanism, topography, and environmental conditions with respect to hatchling sea orientation discussed.

CARR, ARCHIE F. 1963. Panspecific reproductive convergence in *Lepidochelys kempii*. Ergebn. Biol. 26: 298-303.
Nesting site for American ridley is Rancho Nuevo, Mexico. Mass nesting emergence occurs sometime between April and June in

the daytime. Emergence repeated three times each season at ten-day intervals. Such mass nesting offers excellent opportunity for migratory studies.

CARR, ARCHIE F. 1964a. Transoceanic migrations of the green turtle. BioScience 14(8): 49-52.

Results of tagging program in 1960 indicate that green turtles nesting at Ascension Island migrate from Brazil and show periodicity in nesting. Problems of studying migration discussed and author suggests assays of fat deposition as helpful in migratory studies.

CARR, ARCHIE F. 1964b. Transoceanic migrations of the green turtle. Naval Res. Rev. 17(10): 12-18.

Reprint of Carr 1964a.

CARR, ARCHIE F. 1965. The navigation of the green turtle. Sci. Amer. 212(5): 79-86.

Over 8 years 129 recoveries from 3,205 tags indicate migratory sequence and pattern of green turtle to Tortuguero to nest. Fourteen recoveries of 206 tags indicate migration of over 1,400 miles from Brazil to Ascension Island for nesting. Distribution of green turtles given: includes nesting beaches and principle feeding grounds. Females go ashore three to seven times to lay eggs during a season. Fertilization for next season may occur during the present season. Mechanisms of migration discussed include olfactory or tactile assessment of shore; solar navigation, olfaction or current detection, and visual recognition.

CARR, ARCHIE F. 1967a. So excellent a fishe. The Natural History Press, Garden City, N.Y. 248 pp.

Well-written and highly informative account of the author's experience with sea turtles in the Caribbean. Notable sections on migration and conservation.

CARR, ARCHIE F. 1967b. Caribbean green turtle. Imperiled gift of the sea. Nat. Geo. Soc. 131(6): 876-890.

Entertaining and informational article revolving around Carr's work with the green turtle in the Caribbean.

CARR, ARCHIE F. 1967c. Adaptive aspects of the scheduled travel of *Chelonia*. *In* Robert M. Storm (ed.) Animal orientation and navigation, pp. 33-55. Oregon State Univ. Press, Corvallis.

Review of Tortuguero and Ascension Island tagging results. Thirty-eight drift bottles released at Tortuguero recovered at green turtle feeding grounds, thus lending credence to the theory of passive transport of hatchlings and active migration of adults. Open-sea migration of *Chelonia* between Ascension Island and Brazil coast discussed. Experiments with telemetry have been unsuccessful. Mechanisms of migration discussed: olfactory, visual cues, celestial, magnetic guidance, phototaxis, and light compass sense. Evolution of island finding (Ascension) postulated.

CARR, ARCHIE F. 1967d. 100 turtle eggs. Natur. Hist. 76(7): 47-54.

Discussion of factors involved in setting the size of the egg complement: predation, synchrony of hatchling, other social advantages, egg and hatchling size, and size of nest.

CARR, ARCHIE F. 1967*e*. No one knows where the turtles go. Part II: 100 turtle eggs. Natur. Hist. 76(8): 40-43, 52-54, 58-59.

Article relating details of his work and his colleagues' work on the sea-finding orientation of hatchling green turtles and their habitat for the first year of their life. Until more is known about this first year no one can explain the reason a turtle lays 100 eggs.

CARR, ARCHIE F. 1969*a*. Sea turtle resources of the Caribbean and Gulf of Mexico. IUCN Bull. 2(10): 74-83.

Covers the five genera of sea turtles found in these areas, the increasing pressures from man, Costa Rican advancements in conservation, and a program for conservation of these resources.

CARR, ARCHIE F. 1969*b*. Survival outlook of the West-Caribbean green turtle colony. *In* Marine turtles. IUCN New Publ. Ser. Suppl. Paper No. 20: 13-16.

Vulnerability in nesting ashore combined with increased market demand has increased danger. Two important nesting grounds of Caribbean *Chelonia:* Aves Island (only protection is natural isolation) and Costa Rica. Heavy predation occurs offshore in Costa Rica by net and harpoon. Author recommends severe restriction of turtling efforts and cooperation between Caribbean countries. A program of research and international trade restriction given.

CARR, ARCHIE F. 1970. Green sea turtles in peril. Nat. Parks Conserv. Mag. 44(271): 19-24.

Resurgence of old markets and addition of turtle leather as a fashion commodity and turtle oil for use in face cream have increased danger to sea turtles. Fluctuations at the Tortuguero rookery discussed as well as Costa Rica's conservation attempts. International cooperation needed, and turtle farms need scrupulous control. Author proposes international program to protect and maintain sea turtle populations in the Caribbean.

CARR, ARCHIE F., and DAVID K. CALDWELL. 1956. The ecology and migrations of sea turtles: 1. Results of field work in Florida, 1955. Amer. Mus. Nov. 1793.

Data given on green and ridley turtles in the Cedar Key-Crystal River area of the Gulf coast of peninsular Florida. Commercial fishing by tangle nets 100 to 200 yards long, 8 to 10 feet deep, and with an 8- to 12-inch bar mesh; estimated catch about 1,000 individuals per year.

Green: local population composed almost entirely of nonbreeding juveniles; suggested that the greens consist of strays from the main Caribbean population and that they are forever lost to that population. Eight recoveries of 43 tags indicated movement to the original point of capture from the release points. The size of the population is roughly 5,600. Data on growth is insufficient.

Empirical data on 208 greens gave a length to weight relation of log $W = -2.195 + 2.87 \log L$. Most were between 12 and 115 pounds. Postocular scale counts of 205 turtles varied from 3 to 5 on either side.

Ridley: Florida population comprises only sexually immature individuals, strongly seasonal in occurrence. Ninety-six individuals examined yielded a length to weight relation of log $W = -1.69 + 2.49 \log L$. A report of a ridley of 93 pounds with eggs (yolks but no whites) butchered in October 1955 and of another "ridley with eggs" in 1953. Only two recoveries of 25 tags. Estimate of population size is 3,750. Estimate of yearly catch is 300. Lateral laminae counts were 5-5 except for one individual of 6-5 count.

CARR, ARCHIE F., and DAVID K. CALDWELL. 1958. The problem of the Atlantic ridley turtle in 1958. Rev. Biol. Trop. 6(2): 245-262.

Adults show sexual dimorphism. Some evidence of nesting on the Atlantic shores of Veracruz. Counts and measurements included on four very young ridleys from Veracruz. Lower limit of breeding size is 25 inches carapace length. Early summer is nesting season. Suggested that the ridley may be endemic to the Gulf of Mexico, and records for the Atlantic coast of North America, Bermuda, and Europe are of strays.

CARR, ARCHIE F., and MARGORIE H. CARR. 1970. Modulated reproductive periodicity in *Chelonia*. Ecology 51(2): 335-337.

Fifteen years of tagging at Tortuguero, Costa Rica confirm nesting periodicity of two and three years, with the latter more common. Modulation between these and a possible four-year cycle occur, and authors suggest that this may be due to ecological factors.

CARR, ARCHIE F., and LEONARD GIOVANNOLI. 1957. The ecology and migrations of sea turtles, 2. Results of field work in Costa Rica, 1955. Amer. Mus. Nov. 1835.

Recoveries of tagged individuals (1) lend evidence for multiple nesting at 10- to 14-day intervals; (2) show long-distance individual movement and possible migration to feeding grounds in Panama (three returns) and Miskito Bank (seven returns). Attempts to morphometrically separate schools on the basis of postocular counts failed. Seasonal trends in shell length occurred, but their significance uncertain. Contains the first account of the nesting of the Atlantic green turtle in the literature; nesting discussed in relation to the behavior of *Lepidochelys olivacea*, *Caretta*, and Pacific *Chelonia*. Site tenacity and recognition covered.

CARR, ARCHIE F., and COLEMAN GOIN. 1955. Guide to the reptiles, amphibians, and fresh water fishes of Florida. Univ. of Florida Press, Gainesville. 341 pp.

Key, descriptions, and ranges given for *Chelonia mydas mydas*, *Eretmochelys imbricata imbricata*, *Caretta caretta caretta*, *Lepidochelys kempii*, and *Dermochelys coriacea*.

CARR, ARCHIE F., and DONALD GOODMAN. 1970. Ecological implications of size and growth in *Chelonia*. Copeia 1970(4): 783-786. Data of 15-year tagging program at Tortuguero (through 1969 season) showed no long-term reduction in maximum body length. Data further suggest that observed body sizes may be more strongly influenced by differential size on reaching maturity than by post-maturity growth rates (less than 0.1 inches/year carapace length). Differences in size of females at Costa Rica versus those at Ascension Island discussed with regard to ecological advantages.

CARR, ARCHIE F., and HAROLD HIRTH. 1961. Social facilitation in green turtle siblings. Animal Behavior 9(1, 2): 68-70.

Survival advantage of egg clutches over single eggs or small groups because of (1) rise in nest temperature (2.3°C over ambient), which may aid in incubation and (2) social facilitation of hatchlings in digging out of nest, i.e., those at the top scratch down the ceiling, those on the sides undercut the walls, and those on the bottom trample and compact the sand and add impetus to digging of those on top. Hatching of eggs also gives working space. May be an advantage in numbers in the trek to the sea.

CARR, ARCHIE F., and HAROLD HIRTH. 1962. The ecology and migrations of sea turtles, 5. Comparative features of isolated green turtle colonies. Amer. Mus. Nov. 2091. 42 pp.

CARR, ARCHIE F., HAROLD HIRTH, and LARRY OGREN. 1966. The ecology and migrations of sea turtles, 6. The hawksbill turtle in the Caribbean Sea. Amer. Mus. Nov. 2248. 29 pp.

Based on work at Tortuguero, Costa Rica incidental to green turtle work. Measurements of males, females, hatchlings, and eggs. Incubation time, nesting periodicity, and renesting discussed along with nesting behavior, orientation of hatchlings, migration, and survival status.

CARR, ARCHIE F., and ROBERT M. INGLE. 1959. The green turtle (*Chelonia mydas mydas*) in Florida. Bull. Mar. Sci. Gulf Car. 9(3): 315-320.

Two records of nesting in Florida included. Depletion of this species in Florida leads authors to suggest using Florida eggs to develop a nursery and to release the young at about one-half pound to minimize predation hazards.

CARR, ARCHIE F., and LARRY H. OGREN. 1959. The ecology and migrations of sea turtles, 3. *Dermochelys* in Costa Rica. Amer. Mus. Nov. 1958. 29 pp.

Summary of work in Costa Rica. No tagging done, but observations of nesting and eggs at Matina Beach reported. Orientation, hatchlings in captivity, and systematics discussed.

CARR, ARCHIE F., and LARRY H. OGREN. 1960. The ecology and migrations of sea turtles, 4. The green turtle in the Caribbean Sea. Bull. Amer. Mus. Nat. Hist. 121(1): 1-48.

Summary of work at Tortuguero through the 1959 season. Includes data on size of females, nesting periodicity, renesting frequency, incubation periods, observations on hatchling emergence, and nesting behavior. Tests of orientation capacity and flexibility in hatchlings and in females discussed. Evidence for migration and site tenacity presented.

CARR, ARCHIE F., and DONALD SWEAT. 1969. Long-range recovery of a tagged yearling *Chelonia* on the east coast of North America. Bio. Conserv. 1(4).

Turtle raised in captivity until one year of age and then released in the Florida Keys in October 1967. Captured off Cape Hatteras in November 1968. Authors suggest such viability of pen-reared turtles is important to conservation efforts through rearing of young turtles past the critical stage and to the problems of ecological geography of the first year of green turtles.

CARRANZA, J. 1967. Survey of the marine fisheries and fishery resources of the Yucatán Peninsula, Mexico. Thesis, Univ. of Michigan. 193 pp.

Sea turtle fishery one of the most important enterprises in the Yucatán. Production has been declining since 1950 (principally green). Methods of fishery and status of stocks. Green turtle landings from 1956 to 1959.

CATE, J. 1936. Rückenmarksreflexe bei Schildkröten. Act. Brevia Neerland 6(5-6): 63-64.

Almost all the reflexes known to the behavior of the frog and mammal can be elicited from the isolated lumbosacral cord of the turtle. Poor reflexes of the intact turtle probably due to the protective action related to the development of the carapace.

CATESBY, MARK. 1731-43. The natural history of Carolina, Florida, and the Bahama Islands. 2 vols. London.

Green turtle lays eggs three to four times a season with about 14 days between each laying. Does not breed in the Bahamas. Green turtle eggs most delectable. In Jamaica 40 sloops from Port Royal engaged in catching turtles. Markets are supplied with turtle meat just as butchers' markets in England are supplied with beef. Many are fished in the Bahamas and sold in the Carolinas. Goes by the name of *Testudo marina viridis* (Rochefort). In catching turtles in Cuba men go up and down the beaches turning them on their backs. Some are so bulky that three men are needed to turn them. In the Bahamas turtles are harpooned, struck with detachable metal point.

Hawksbill *Testudo caretta* (Rochefort). Eats a "fungus" known locally as "jews ears."

Loggerhead *Testudo marina caouana*. (Raij. Syn. guad. p. 25, Rochefort). Voracious, hardly edible. Feed on shellfish, particularly *Buccinum*.

Trunk turtle: (*Testudo arcuata*). Flesh not good, but is source of an oil. They are fished for this product.

CHANDRASEKHARAN, N. 1969. The Malaysian sea turtle eggs as a source of Vitamin A. Med. J. Malaya 23(3): 214-215.

Eggs from Trengganu, Malaya; species not stated. Average weight of 63.7 grams, 46% yolk. Turtle eggs [1363 international units (i.u.)] richer in vitamin A than hen (640 i.u.) or duck eggs (1100 i.u.).

CHARI, S. T. 1964. Marine turtle fishery of India. Indian Seafoods 2(1): 9-11.

CHAVEZ, HUMBERTO. 1966. Propositos y finalidades. Bol. Prog. Nac. Marcado Tortugas Mar. 1(1): 16 pp. (mimeo)

List of 287 female turtles marked by the fisheries biology station in Tampico. Includes location, carapace length, tag number, and date.

CHAVEZ, HUMBERTO. 1967. Nota preliminar sobre la recaptura de ejemplares marcados de tortuga lora, *Lepidochelys olivacea kempii*. Bol. Prog. Nac. Marcado Tortugas Mar. 1(6): 5 pp. (mimeo)

Marked 285 specimens during the nesting season at Tamaulipas, obtained data on the biology of behavior of the species, weight and measurements, character of the nests, time of incubation, and environmental factors. Transferred almost 30,000 for protection. One-hundred hatchlings taken to the biological lab to study growth, feeding habits, and parasites. This year first good job of control. Ten marked turtles recovered, and data listed.

CHAVEZ, HUMBERTO, MARTIN CONTRERAS G., and T. P. EDUARDO HERNANDEZ D. 1967. Aspectos biológicos y protección de la tortuga lora, *Lepidochelys kempi* (Garman), en la costa de Tamaulipas, Mexico. Inst. Nac. Invest. Biol. Pesqueras 17. 39 pp.

In 1965 a fishery biology station subordinate to the National Institute of Investigations—Fishery Biology was established in the port of Tampico, Tamaulipas. Part of its job was to study the ridley and formulate a plan for their protection. Data on measurements and weights of the young and adult females, nesting information from tagging studies, measurements of eggs, incubation period, factors of external environment, predators, and conservation of these turtles discussed. Provides the most complete information on Kemp's ridley to date.

CHAVEZ, HUMBERTO, MARTIN CONTRERAS G., and T. P. EDUARDO HERNANDEZ D. 1968. On the coast of Tamaulipas, Parts I and II. Int. Turt. Tort. Soc. J. 2(4): 20-29, 37 and 2(5): 19, 27-34.

Reprint in English of Chavez, Contreras, and Hernandez, 1967.

CHIN, LUCAS. 1969. Notes on orang-utans, bird ringing project and turtles. Sarawak Mus. J. 16(32/33): 249-252.

Egg production of the green turtle *Chelonia mydas* for 1967 and 1968.

CHOPARD, L. 1966. Les grandes migrations des tortues marines n'ont pas encore livré tous leurs secrets. Nature, Paris 3371: 94-96.

CLARK, H. WALTON, and JOHN B. SOUTHALL. 1920. Fresh water turtles: a source of meat supply. Rept. U.S. Comm. Fish Fish. Doc. 889. App. 7, p. 20, pl. 8.

Recipes and methods of handling. Encouragement to use this meat as a substitute for beef or fowl.

COGGER, HAROLD G. 1960. Snakes, lizards and chelonians. Australian Mus. Mag. 13(8): 250-253.
> Green, loggerhead, hawksbill, and leatherback turtles regularly sighted in waters of Broken Bay, Sydney Harbor, and Botany Bay.

COGGER, H. G., and D. A. LINDNER. 1969. Marine turtles in northern Australia. Amer. Zool. 15(2): 150-159.

COKER, R. E. 1906. Natural history of cultivation of the Diamondback terrapin, with notes on other forms of turtles. N. Carolina Geol. Survey Bull. 14.
> Distribution: from Buzzard's Bay, Mass., to Texas. Although thought to be of one species, Hay has shown differently. They breed in captivity, are carnivorous, and grow about an inch a year. In males the proximal part of the tail is thick after the second year's growth. Males, called bulls, are inferior in market value. *Chelonia* (1906): at writing they are seldom seen in Carolina, although they were plentiful in other years. *Thallasochelys colpochelys* (Kemp's turtle) commonly seen. *Dermochelys coriacea*, the leather turtle, only occasionally seen. One record weighed 800 pounds. *Thallasochelys caretta*, the loggerhead, lays eggs during the months of May to August. Data on eggs and nests: over a hundred eggs in a nest, sometimes 130, and eggs were found about a foot beneath the surface of the beach. North Carolina apparently too far north for *Eretmochelys imbricata*. Notes also on *Thallasochelys colpochelys kempii* (Garman).

COKER, R. E. 1910. The fisheries and guano industry in Peru. Bull. U.S. Bur. Fish. 28: 333-365.

COKER, R. E. 1920. The Diamond-back terrapin: past, present, and future. Sci. Mo. 11: 171-186.

COLLINS, J. W., and HUGH M. SMITH. 1891. A statistical report on the fisheries of the Gulf States. Bull. U.S. Fish Comm. 11: 93-184.
> Catch by counties.

COLLINS, R. LEE, and GARDNER LYNN. 1936. Fossil turtles from Maryland. Proc. Amer. Phil. Soc. 76(2): 151-173.
> The genus *Chelonia* is represented here in findings from the Cretaceous period to Pleistocene epoch.

CONANT, ROGER. 1958. A field guide to reptiles and amphibians. Houghton Mifflin Co., Boston. 366 pp.

CONTU, P. 1953. Ricerche sulla glioarchitettonica dei Rettili. Arch. Ital. Anat. Embriol. 58(3): 295-320.
> Neuroglia of brain and spinal cord of *Ophidia*, *Sauria*, and *Chelonia* studied. Neuroglia framework in central nervous system of reptilia considered intermediate between the structure in amphibians and birds. Optic lobes and cerebellum show signs of higher differentiation than in birds.

COOKER, R. E. 1905. Gadow's hypothesis of orthogenetic variation in *Chelonia*. Johns Hopkins Univ. Circ. 178.

COOKER, R. E. 1910. Diversity in the scutes of Chelonia. J. Morph. Phila. 21: 1-75, 14 pls. (original abstract in Science, n.s. 21(532): 384 (1905).

COPE, E. D. 1875. Check list of North American Batrachia and Reptilia; with a systematic list of the higher groups, and an essay on geographical distribution. Based on the specimens contained in the U.S. National Museum. Bull. U.S. Nat. Mus. pp. 1-104.

Calls *Caretta, Thallasochelys caouana*. Puts luth in different group. Original references provided.

COPE, E. D. 1887a. Catalogue of batrachians and reptiles of Central American and Mexico. Bull. U.S. Nat. Mus. 32: 1-98.

Lists *Chelonia imbricata and Chelonia aggassizi* only.

COPE, E. D. 1887b. List of the batrachians and reptiles of the Bahama Islands. Proc. U.S. Nat. Mus. 10(645): 436-439.

Lacertilia and Ophiuridae only two groups mentioned. The title too all-embracing inasmuch as sea turtles omitted.

COPE, E. D. 1890. Scientific results of exploration by the U.S. Fish Commission Steamer *Albatross*, No. 3, Report on the batrachians and reptiles collected in 1887. Proc. U.S. Nat. Mus. 12: 141-147.

Of no value in sea turtle work.

COPE, E. D. 1896. Ancestry of Testudinata. Amer. Nat. 30.

COPLEY, HUGH. 1956. Review of Kenya Fisheries, 1955. Government Printer, Nairobi. 45 pp.

Pictures of turtle fishing with remoras on pp. 23, 24.

CRAIG, ALAN K. 1966. Geography of fishing in British Honduras and adjacent coastal waters. Louisiana State Univ. Press, Coastal Studies Ser. No. 14: 143 pp.

Covers contemporary and colonial methods of turtling.

Cuba's fishing industry, 1958. 1959. U.S. Fish Wildlife Serv. Commer. Fish. MN-1.

Produced 59,997 pounds of turtle.

CUNNINGHAM, BERT, and A. P. HURWITZ. 1936. Water absorption by reptile eggs during incubation. Amer. Nat. 70(731): 590-595.

Repeated weighings and measurements of the incubating eggs of *Malaclemys centrata, Sceloporus undulatus,* and *Caretta caretta* show an increase in both weight and size. Desiccation indicates that the increased wight of *M. centrata* and *C. caretta* eggs can be attributed to water absorption. Similar studies not made on *S. undulatus* eggs, but it seems reasonable to suppose that the increase in weight is due to the same factor. Volume increase less than weight increase, which may account for part of the increased turgidity.

DANIEL, R. S., and K. V. SMITH. 1947. Migration of newly hatched loggerhead turtles toward the sea. Science 106(2756): 398-399.

Brighter illumination from the surf elicits a positive phototropic

response in newly hatched turtles. The mother always selects a
nest within sight of the surf.

DAVENPORT, G. A. 1896. The primitive streak and notochordal canal
in *Chelonia*. Radcliffe Coll. Monogr. 8.

DE BETTA. 1874. Rettili ed anfibi. Fauna d'Italia, part e quarta, pp.
14-15.
Chelonia mydas called *Chelonia albiventes;* mentioned as being
very rare in the Adriatic.

DECARY, RAYMOND. 1950. La faune malgache, son rôle dans les
croyances et usages indigènes. Payot, Paris. 236 pp.
Short section on marine turtles, including discussion of remora
fishing.

DELANEY, PATRICK ARTHUR. 1929. On specialized phagocytic
mesothelium in the Chelonia. Anat. Rec. 43(1): 65-97.
A discussion of the peculiar mesothelial cells covering the pleuro-
pericardial and peritoneal surfaces. Detailed histological study.

DEPARTMENT COMMERCE AND AGRICULTURE, PORTO RICO.
1944. Fishery Bull. Div. Fish Wildlife Conserv. Dept. Agr. Commerce
of Porto Rico, January.
A summary of recent laws and appropriations for study of the
fishery resources of Puerto Rico.

DERANIYAGALA, P. E. P. 1930*a*. The Testudinata of Ceylon. Ceylon
Jour. Sci. Section B. Zool. Geol. Spolia Zeylanica 16(1): 43-88.
Four common sea turtles listed as well as information regarding
food, reproduction, ovoposition, variation, and distribution. Extensive bibliography. Adolescent stage of *Dermochelys* has never
been seen. Excellent treatment of taxonomy.

DERANIYAGALA, P. E. P. 1930*b*. Testudinata evolution. Proc. Zool.
Soc. London Pt. 4: 1057-70, 3 pls.
A scholarly analysis of the ancestral history of Testudinata.

DERANIYAGALA, P. E. P. 1932*a*. Herpetological notes (from Ceylon). Ceylon J. Sci. Sec. B. Zool. Geol. Spolia Zeylanica 17(1):
44-55.
Caretta with nine pairs of costal scutes recorded. Fontanelles in
the carapace of *Eretmochelys imbricata* described. In the latter
species there is a change, after a certain age, from imbrication to
juxtaposition. In *Chelonia mydas* and other marine turtles the
mean between the lengths of the carapace and plastron of the
newly hatched young equals the egg diameter. Coprophagous
nature of pilot fish, *Naucrates ductor,* found seeking refuge near
the anus of *Dermochelys coriacae*. Five to nine costal scutes
known for loggerheads. This explained as atavism in cases of more
than five scutes. Variations in carapace of hawksbill turtles discussed. Data on diameter of sea turtle eggs given.

DERANIYAGALA, P. E. P. 1932*b*. Notes on the development of the
leathery turtle, *Dermatochelys coriacea*. Ceylon J. Sci. Sec. B. Zool.
Geol. Spolia Zeylanica 17:73-102.

Excellent embryological study. Plates and figures provided; data given for several embryos.

DERANIYAGALA, P. E. P. 1933. The loggerhead turtles (Carettidae) of Ceylon. Ceylon J. Sci. Sec. B. Zool. Geol. Spolia Zeylanica 18(1): 61-73.

Systematic account of two subspecies, *C. olivacea* and *C. gigas* (p. 66); the latter is "cosmopolitan in all tropical and temperate seas." Skulls and carapaces described and pictured. Excellent bibliography.

DERANIYAGALA, P. E. P. 1934a. Relationships among loggerhead turtles (Carettidae). Ceylon J. Sci. Sec. B. Zool. Geol. Spolia Zeylanica 18: 207-209.

DERANIYAGALA, P. E. P. 1934b. Some phylogenetic features of the leathery turtle, *Dermochelys coriacea*. Ceylon J. Sci. Sec. B. Zool. Geol. Spolia Zeylanica 18: 199-206, 8 pls.

DERANIYAGALA, P. E. P. 1936a. A further comparative study of *Caretta gigas*. Ceylon J. Sci. Sec. B. Zool. Geol. Spolia Zeylanica 19(3).

The author separates the Carettidae into three genera, which are separable into four distinct species. The resemblance between them is close. Descriptive key provided.

DERANIYAGALA, P. E. P. 1936b. Some post natal changes in the leathery turtle, *Dermochelys coriacea*. Ceylon J. Sci. Sec. B. Zool. Geol. Spolia Zeylanica 19: 225-239.

Infantile scales reached their limit of expansion when turtlet about 18 days old. Ecdysis of these infantile scales began about the 22nd day and ended about the 46th. Scale boundaries became more and more indistinct with age as the majority thinned out and disappeared.

Great detail in this report concerning skeletal features, color platelets, secondary characters, plastron, and extremities.

The oldest individual observed until the 662nd day following hatching. Data on growth rate indicate a growth of 545 mm in 662 days. Growth was in captivity, and the animal died because sewage was allowed to enter his tank.

DERANIYAGALA, P. E. P. 1936c. The nesting habit of the leathery turtle, *Dermatochelys coriacea*. Ceylon J. Sci. Sec. B. Zool. Geol. Spolia Zeylanica 19: 311-336.

1. Makes four false holes before digging the nest.
2. Emits strong fish odor while laying.
3. Large number of abnormal eggs.
4. Disguises nest site.
5. Lays during the full of the moon.
6. From 21 to 24 February 4:15 A.M. Finished in 20 minutes.
7. 125 eggs. Of these, 5 were one-half normal size, 9 were one-third normal size (2 of these with prominences), 7 were one-quarter size, and 4 were very small (last laid).
8. *Dermachelys* probably does not bellow.

9. Breeds year round. Two maximums, May and June, and October to December.

10. One turtle marked by shark bite appears every three months.

DERANIYAGALA, P. E. P. 1938a. The Mexican loggerhead turtle in Europe. Nature 142:540.

Mexican loggerhead, *Colpochelys kempii* Garman. This species very localized in the Gulf of Mexico. Finding it off the west coast of Ireland is evidence of transfer by currents. Two such specimens exist, 256 mm and 245 mm carapace. *Caretta caretta* also drifts into Ireland occasionally. The possibility of using sea turtles as indicators of ocean currents should not be overlooked. Mexican loggerhead differs from loggerhead in possessing four enlarged inframarginals instead of three on each side.

DERANIYAGALA, P. E. P. 1938b. The loggerhead turtles in the National Museum of Ireland, with special reference to those taken in Irish waters. Irish Natural. J. 7(3): 66-70.

DERANIYAGALA, P. E. P. 1939a. Terapod reptiles of Ceylon. Columbo Mus. Publ.

Excellent taxonomy, anatomy, embryology, biology, and bibliography.

DERANIYAGALA, P. E. P. 1939b. The distribution of the Mexican loggerhead turtle, *Colpochelys kempi* Garman. Bull. Inst. Oceanogr. Monaco 272: 1-4.

DERANIYAGALA, P. E. P. 1939c. The Mexican loggerhead in Europe. Nature 144: 156.

DERANIYAGALA, P. E. P. 1939d. Names of some Atlantic loggerhead turtles. Nature 144: 673.

DERANIYAGALA, P. E. P. 1943. Subspecies formation in loggerhead turtles (Carettidae). Spolia Zeylanica 23(2): 79-92.

Key to the two genera and the subspecies of the Carettidae and descriptions of the four known forms given. From studies of the zoogeography and paleontology, the author concludes that the original home of the family is the Indo-Pacific, from where they have spread into the Atlantic to form two subspecies of the coast of America. History of the taxonomic problem given with lists of synonyms and original authors, publications, and dates. Excellent bibliographical inclusions.

DERANIYAGALA, P. E. P. 1945. Some subspecific characters of the loggerhead *Caretta caretta*. Spolia Zeylanica 24(2): 95-98.

The author puts all loggerheads into one family, the Carettidae. The group previously thought of as a polymorphic genus. The family divided into monotypic genera, each species being dimorphic. The two genera are *Lepidochelys* and *Caretta*. Keys provided to the genera and subspecies, and the points of difference discussed with diagrams and extensive notes. Skeletal characters, including variations in neural and costal plates.

Key to the genera of Carettidae:

1. Dorsal color olive-green; on each side four enlarged inframar-

ginal scutes with a pore in each, neurals equilateral in a continuous series . . . . *Lepidochelys* Fitzinger, 1843.
2. Dorsal color brown red; three enlarged, poreless, inframarginal scutes on each side, neurals with elongate posterolateral sides and sometimes interrupted by costals. . . . .
Caretta Rafinesque, 1814.

Key to subspecies of *Caretta:*
1. Neural bones 7-12, frequently interrupted by the costals when less than 9; temperament fierce . . . . *Caretta c. gigas.*
2. Neural bones 7-8, very seldom interrupted by costals; temperament mild. . . . . *Caretta c. caretta.*
Caretta c. gigas inhabits the Indo-Pacific and probably the east Atlantic.
Caretta c. caretta inhabits the western Atlantic and is essentially American.

DERANIYAGALA, P. E. P. 1946. Marginal scutes in races of the brown red loggerhead, *Caretta caretta* Linné. Spolia Zeylanica 24(3): 195-196.
Indo-Pacific material and American material compared.
Caretta c. gigas—marginal scutes 14-11, usually 13 on each side.
Caretta c. caretta—marginal scutes 13-11, usually 12 on each side.
DERANIYAGALA, P. E. P. 1952. The loggerhead turtles (Carettinae) of Europe. Herpetologica 8(3): 57-58.
Existing nomenclature of the Carettinae should be demolished if law of priority enforced. Atlantic has two races of ridleys and two races of loggerheads: east Atlantic—*Caretta c. gigas, Lepidochelys o. olivacea,* and a small colony of *Lepidochelys olivacea kempi:* west Atlantic—*Caretta c. caretta* and *Lepidochelys olivacea kempi.*
DERANIYAGALA, P. E. P. 1953. A colored atlas of some vertebrates from Ceylon. Vol. 2: Tetrapod Reptilia. Ceylon Natl. Mus. Publ. 101 pp.
DERANIYAGALA, P. E. P. 1957. The breeding grounds of the luth and the ridley. Herpetologica 13(2): 110.
Most prolific breeding grounds of *Dermochelys coriacea* found in Ceylon and certain parts of the east coast of Malaya. Author suggests that both the ridley and the luth nest upon beaches neighboring Miami, Florida.
DERANIYAGALA, P. E. P. 1961. Some little known characters of the two subspecies of *Lepidochelys olivacea* (Eschscholtz). Spolia Zeylanica 29(2): 196-201.
Author contends that differences are subspecific rather than specific. Characters that differ are:

Character	*Lepidochelys o. olivacea*	*Lepidochelys olivacea kempi*
Carapace color (adult)	dull olive green	gray, probably olive green in old adult

Character	Lepidochelys o. olivacea	Lepidochelys olivacea kempi
No. of costa scutes	5 to 9, variable	5 pairs, rarely more
Enlarged inframarginals	4 on each side	4, sometimes 3, on each side
Color or carapace margin of hatchling	white	brownish gray anteriorly
Color of manus margin of hatchling	white	lt. brown posterior proximal part

Data are given on measurements, meristic characters, and osteology.

DERANIYAGALA, P. E. P. 1964. A comparison of the cephalic scalation of *Dermochelys coriacea* with that of the Cheloniidae (Reptilia, Testudinata). Senckenberg Biol. 45(3-5): 349-352.

Scalation of young from the Atlantic and from Ceylon shows that
they are one species. A few enlarged scutes in Cheloniidae replace
head scales in *Dermochelys*. Scales and certain anatomical characters indicate that the Cheloniidae are more specialized, contrary
to the perfectly adapted shape of *Dermochelys*.

DE ROOIJ, N. 1915. Reptiles of the Indo-Australian Archipelago. Vol.
1. Leiden Press.

DE SILVA, G. S. 1969. Statement on marine turtles in the state of
Sabah. *In* Marine turtles. IUCN Publ. New Ser., Suppl. Paper No. 20:
75-79.

Covers species status, exploitation, conservation, research objectives, and national requirements.

DE SOLA, C. R. 1931. Turtles of the northeastern states. Bull. N.Y.
Zool. Soc. 34(5).

DE SOLA, C. R., and F. ABRAMS. 1933. Testudinata from S.E.
Georgia. Copeia 1:12.

Chelonia mydas (Linne), Atlantic green turtle. Occasionally taken
in shrimp trawls off the Sea Islands (Sapelo, St. Simon's, Jekyl,
and Cumberland) and within St. Simon's Sound.

Eretmochelys imbricata (Linne), Atlantic hawksbill turtle. Rarely
seen on Georgia coast, although one specimen was taken in a
pound net off Savannah late in July, 1931.

Caretta caretta (Linne), Atlantic loggerhead turtle. Common off
the Sea Islands, where it breeds during June and July and into
early August, having mated in April and May. Hatching occurs in
November and December of the same year.

Caretta kempii Garman, (Kemp's bastard turtle). Often confused
with the preceding species. Erroneously thought to be the hybrid
offspring of the hawksbill and the loggerhead, although records
prove the species to be common. Regarding size, which is usually
overstated owing to the confusion of the species with a much
larger one, the loggerhead, it is well to cite the records made by

C. M. Breder, Jr., of the New York Aquarium and those made by us in Brunswick, proving the turtle to be a small species with adults rarely over 2 feet in length. The Dissection of 2-foot specimens revealed well-developed eggs and showed that, although the intestinal tract measures seven times the body length and would appear to be fitted for a vegetable diet, stomach contents indicated the spotted lady crab, *Platyonichus ocellatus,* to be the mainstay of the animal's regime. Turtles of this size weigh about 8 pounds and have the same habits and places of breeding as those given above for the loggerhead.

The following key can be used by naturalists in differentiating between confusing species which are alive or intact that heretofore have been separated on skull characters by dissection.

A. Limbs in form of flippers; five costal plates on each side.

   B1. Body golden brown above, immaculate yellow beneath; fore flippers with two claws each—Loggerhead turtle, *Caretta caretta.*

   B2. Body uniform dusky gray above, pale white beneath; fore flippers with three claws each—Kemp's bastard turtle, *Caretta kempii.*

Dermochelys coriacea (Linne), trunkback turtle. Seldom recorded from this coast although we saw one good-sized specimen off Cape Romain, South Carolina, on 5 August, aboard the *S.S. City of Savannah.*

DESPOTT, G. 1930. Cattura di due esemplare di *Chelone mydas* nei mari di Malta. (Capture of two *Chelone mydas* near Malta). Naturalista Siciliana 7(1/12): 73-75, 2 fig.

   States that *Thallasochelys caretta* is fairly common in the Mediterranean.

DETWILLER, SAMUEL R. *Vertebrate photoreceptors.* The Macmillan Co., New York.

   References to turtles scattered and not well indexed. Work highly technical. Excellent bibliography.

DIMOND, M. T. 1965. Hatching time of turtle eggs. Nature 208(5008): 401-402.

   Duration of incubation dependent on environmental conditions, especially temperature. Hatchling size positively correlated with egg size. Two loggerhead eggs required 54 and 55 days to hatch at 30°C.

DITMARS, R. L. 1910. Reptiles of the world. The Macmillan Co., New York.

   Less than a dozen species of sea turtles. Live in northern waters until cooler weather. Two widely separated families. *Dermochelys* are survivors of an extinct group. Others have evolved from modern types and show a close relationship to the *Testudinidae.* Slight differences between Pacific and Atlantic.

DITMARS, R. L. 1936. Reptiles of N. America. Doubleday Doran & Co., New York.

All sea turtles from *Reptiles of the World* are known for the United States.

DOBIE, JAMES L., LARRY H. OGREN, and J. F. FITZPATRICK, JR. 1961. Food notes and records of the Atlantic ridley turtle (*Lepidochelys kempi*) from Louisiana. Copeia 1961(1): 109-110.

Studied fourteen specimens captured between 1952 and 1958. Skeletal measurements and food contents included.

DOLLO, L. 1901. Sur l'Origine de la Tortue Luth, D. coriacea. Bull. Soc. Roy. Sci. Med. Nat. Bruxelles.

DOMANTAY, JOSE S. 1952-1953. The turtle fisheries of the Turtle Islands. Bull. Fish. Soc. Philippines 3-4: 3-27.

DOMM, S. B. 1971. The uninhabited cays of the Capricorn Group, Great Barrier Reef, Australia. Atoll Res. Bull.: 137-148.

All of the sand islands used extensively for nesting by *Chelonia mydas* and *Caretta caretta*.

DONOSO-BARROS, R. 1964a. Nota sobre *Lepidochelys kempi* en las costas de Cumana. Lagena 2: 20-21. (*L. kempi* is *L. olivacea* according to Bill Rainey, personal communication.)

DONOSO-BARROS, R. 1964b. Anotaciones sobre las tortugas marinas de Venezuela. Lagena 3: 26-31.

Do turtles sniff their way to Ascension? 1969. New Sci. 41(636): 355.

Migration of *Chelonia mydas* 1,400 miles from Brazil to Ascension Island may be by smelling a chemical trait of the island.

DUELLMAN, WILLIAM E. 1961. The amphibians and reptiles of Michoacán, Mexico. Univ. Kansas Publ., Mus. Nat. Hist. 15(1): 1-148.

DUERDEN, J. E. 1901. The marine resources of the British West Indies. West Indian Bull. 2.

In 1900, green turtles valued at £7,248 and hawksbill turtles valued at £1,693 exported from Jamaica. Rapid depletion points at need for cultivation. Value of tortoiseshell varies from 10 shillings to 20 shillings a pound. Evidence of marked turtles traveling from Jamaica to the Mosquito coast, a distance of four or five hundred miles. Duerden feels that methods of improving the transport of green turtles should be investigated thereby lowering the mortality. Grenada: turtle shell £400. St. Lucie: £100. Most of the sea turtles now come from the Mosquito coast of Central America. Some caught in the Cayman group. Green turtle shipped alive as far as England.

DUNLAP, CHARLES E. 1955. Notes on the visceral anatomy of the giant leatherback turtle (*Dermochelys coriacea* Linneaus). Bull. Tulane Med. Fac. 14(2): 55-69.

Autopsies of two females, 600 and 478 pounds: (1) muscular sphincter in pulmonary arteries appears capable of diverting blood flow from pulmonary to systemic circulation; (2) histologic evidence of continuing production of nephrons in kidney; (3) both were either sexually immature or at least had never laid eggs —intact hymenal membrane and no scars in ovaries; (4) interrenal body might be true ovary; (5) uric acid in urine was twice the concentration of urea; (6) one turtle had amoeba in intestinal tract that resembled *Endamoeba histolytica*.

DUNN, EMMETT REID. 1944. Los géneros de anfibios y reptiles de Colombia. Caldasia 10: 497-529.

Summary by orders, families, and genera, with keys to all categories. Genera discussed and listed, together with an account of distribution. Species of Colombia for each genus described.

EARLL, EDWARD. 1887. Eastern Florida and its fisheries. The fisheries and fishery industries of the United States. U.S. Comm. Fish Fish. Sect. 2, Part 14.

Statistics.

EHRENFELD, DAVID W. 1968. The role of vision in the sea-finding orientation of the green turtle (*Chelonia mydas*): 2. Orientation mechanism and range of spectral sensitivity. Animal Behavior 16(2,3): 281-287.

EHRENFELD, DAVID W., and ARCHIE CARR. 1967. The role of vision in the sea-finding orientation of the green turtle (*Chelonia mydas*). Animal Behavior 15(1): 25-36.

Experiments performed on adult females captured just after laying and on 525 hatchlings. Adults fitted with spectacles with filters of different colors. Blindfolded the turtles were unable to find the sea; red, blue, and 0.4 neutral density filters significantly decreased orientation scores. Sea finding by the young in an arena was highly successful.

EHRENFELD, DAVID W., and A. L. KOCH. 1967. Visual accommodation in the green turtle. Science 155(3764): 827-828.

Turtle eye is emmetropic in water but extremely myopic in air, which precludes migrating turtles using stars for navigation.

ELLIS, RICHARD A. 1964. Intercellular channels in the salt-secreting glands of marine turtles. Science 144(3624): 1340-1342.

Tissue from the salt glands of two loggerheads and four green turtles used for electron microscopy and cytochemical tests. Histological features of both species similar; secretory lobules consist of myriads of closely packed, branched tubules radiating outward from a central duct or canal. At peripheral ends are small terminal cells with little cytoplasm. Long pleomorphic microvilli project from the walls of adjacent principal secretory cells, and scant, irregular ones project from the apical surface of the cells into the lumen of the tubule. A mucopolysaccharide fills the intercellular channels and may act as an ion trap to facilitate concentration of electrolytes. High concentration of mitochondria and intercellular system of agranular membranes similar to the cells of salt gland of marine birds, chloride cells of fishes, and others, which add evidence that these organelles participate directly in secretion of electrolytes. Architecture of secreting cells in turtles differs from that in birds.

ELLIS, RICHARD A., and JOHN H. ABEL. 1964. Electron microscopy

and cytochemistry of the salt gland of sea turtles (*Caretta caretta*
and *Chelonia mydas*). Anat. Rec. 148(2): 278-279. (Abstract only)
Covered in Ellis (1964).

EVERMANN, B. W. 1900. Investigations of the aquatic resources and
fisheries of Puerto Rico. Bull. U.S. Fish Comm. 20.
Turtles mentioned only incidently as being fished with gill nets in
some localities. Mentioned by Schmidt. Hawksbill and green
mostly at east end. Scarcity due to lack of sandy bottom.

EVERMANN, B. W. 1901. Fisheries of the Middle Atlantic States.
Rept. U.S. Comm. Fish Fish. 28:433-543.
Raw data on production by pounds and value. Since there is some
doubt as to what is meant by "turtles" in this article, the figures
and statistics contained therein should be qualified.

EVERMANN, B. W., and B. A. BEAN. 1896. Indian River and its
fisheries. Rept. U.S. Comm. Fish Fish. 22: 227-248.
Statistics and production.

FABER. 1883. Fisheries of Adriatic and Fish thereof. Pt. 2, p. 178.
Reptilia: *Chelonia mydas*, called *albiventes*, is probably a young
mydas. Only two specimens had been found in Adriatic.

FAHY, WILLIAM E. 1954. Loggerhead turtles, *Caretta caretta caretta*,
from North Carolina. Copeia 1954(2): 157-158.
Male captured on 10 March 1953 weighing 400 pounds, 41 inch
carapace. Seven females captured on 20 March 1953. Measurements included.

FAULKNER, J. M., and CARL A. L. BINGER. 1927. Oxygen poisoning in cold blooded animals. J. Exp. Med. 46(5): 865-871.
Turtles are immune to oxygen poisoning at ordinary temperatures. However, when 37.5°C is used, the immunity is lost. They
react like mammals, losing appetite, breathing rapidly, dying.
Autopsy shows hemorrhagic extravasations in the lungs.

FERREIRA, M. M., 1968. Sobre a alimentacao de aruana, *Chelonia
mydas* Linnaeus, au longo da costa do estado de Ceara. Acq. Estac.
Biol. Mar. Univ. Fed. Ceara 8(1): 83-86.
Feeding habits of the green turtle along the coast of Ceara.

FIEDLER, R. H. 1928*a*. Trade in fresh and frozen fishery products and
related marketing considerations in Jacksonville, Fla. U.S. Bur. Fish.
Doc. 1036.
Insignificance of the present turtle industry clearly shown. Industry ranks 34th in importance in a list of 48 fisheries products
marketed in Jacksonville. Types of containers listed. Hotels and
restaurants almost the only demand for this product.

FIEDLER, R. H. 1928*b*. Trade in fresh and frozen fishery products and
related marketing considerations in Atlanta, Ga. U.S. Bur. Fish. Doc.
1039.
Florida listed as the principle source of supply. Product received
as meat in 50-pound boxes, primarily for hotels and restaurants.

FIEDLER, R. H. 1938. Fishery industries of the U.S. (1936). U.S. Bur.
Fish. Admin. Rept. 27.

Fisheries products were tabulated for the following years:

1880—Entire U.S.	1932—Entire U.S.
1908—Entire U.S.	1934—Gulf and S. Atlantic states.
1931—Entire U.S.	

Statistics of South Atlantic and Gulf states were contained in the following issues:

1880	1890	1901	1920	1930	1933
1887	1891	1904	1925	1931	1934
1888	1897	1908	1929	1932	1935

FIEDLER, R. H. 1940. Fishery industries of the U.S. (1938). U.S. Bur. Fish. Admin. Rept. 37.

The catch for Florida listed and the value given.

FIEDLER, R. H. 1941. Fishery industries of the U.S. (1939). U.S. Bur. Fish. Admin. Rept. 41.

Florida turtle fishery discussed and the catch value listed.

FIEDLER, R. H., M. J. LOBELL, and C. R. LUCAS. 1943a. The fisheries and fishery resources of the Caribbean area. A report of the Caribbean fishery mission. Mimeographed. U.S. Dept. of the Interior, Washington, D.C.

Gives brief accounts of methods and general oceanographic background of the entire area.

FIEDLER, R. H., M. J. LOBELL, and C. R. LUCAS. 1943b. The fisheries and fishery resources of Nicaragua. A report of the Caribbean fishery mission. Mimeographed. U.S. Dept. of the Interior, Washington, D.C.

Exported up to $8,000 in 1941.

FIEDLER, R. H., M. J. LOBELL, and C. R. LUCAS. 1943c. The fisheries and fishery resources of Costa Rica. A report of the Caribbean fishery mission. Mimeographed. U.S. Dept. of the Interior, Washington, D.C.

Exported 163,000 kilograms valued at $8,600 and shell valued at $2,197 in 1939.

FIEDLER, R. H., M. J. LOBELL, and C. R. LUCAS. 1943d. The fisheries and fishery resources of British Honduras. A report of the Caribbean fishery mission. Mimeographed. U.S. Dept. of the Interior, Washington, D.C.

Very little information.

FIEDLER, R. H., J. R. MANNING, and F. F. JOHNSON. 1932. Fishery industries of the U.S. for 1932. Rept. U.S. Comm. Fish Fish. App. 3.

California, Louisiana, and Florida listed. Total pounds of catches, values, and methods of procuring discussed.

FIEDLER, R. H., J. R. MANNING, and F. F. JOHNSON. 1934. Fishery industries of the U.S. for 1933. Rept. U.S. Comm. Fish Fish. App. 1.

Production of turtle by pounds and values tabulated according to states of the Gulf coast and southeastern group. Florida produced 31,068 pounds of green turtle valued at $1,896 and 14,690 pounds of soft-shelled turtle valued at $233. Louisiana produced 27,820 pounds of loggerheads valued at $556.

FISCHER, KLAUS. 1964. Spontanes Richtungsfinden nach dem Sonnenstand bei *Chelonia mydas* L. (Suppenschildkröte). Naturwissenschaften 51(8): 203.

Young in tank oriented in SW-NE direction when sea was SSE. Similar results when sea was on all sides except west. When conditioned to a diurnal cycle six hours out of phase of normal, turtle oriented about 90° from the previous directions, indicating determination of compass direction by use of sun and internal clock. Experiments with *Caretta caretta* did not yield similar results.

FISCHER, P. H. 1966. Instincts et tropismes chez les tortues marines du Queensland. Cah. Pacif. 9: 7-9.

FISHERIES. 1894. Bull. Pan Amer. Union 1:67. Washington, D.C.

FISHERY RESOURCES OF THE U.S. 1945. A letter of Secretary of the Interior reporting to Senate of the 79th Congress. Doc. 51.

FISHERY STATISTICS OF THE U.S. 1968. 1971. Stat. Dig. 62. Nat. Mar. Fish. Ser., Washington: 528 pp.

FISHERY STATISTICS of the U.S. 1969. 1972. Stat. Dig. 63. Nat. Mar. Fish. Ser., Washington: 474 pp.

FITZINGER. 8143. Systema Reptilium.

Early taxonomic treatment.

FLORES, C. 1966. Nuevos registros de *Lepidochely kempi* (Garman) en la costa oriental de Venezuela. Lagena 12: 11-14. (*L. kempi* is actually *L. olivacea* according to William Rainey in personal communication.)

FLORIDA STATE BOARD OF CONSERVATION. 1940. Fourth Biennial Report. Tallahassee, Florida.

Statistics given for counties reporting. Four counties reported in 1939 and 1940.

FLORIDA STATE BOARD OF CONSERVATION. 1942. Fifth Biennial Report. Tallahassee, Florida.

Nine counties reported in 1941. Seven counties reported in 1942.

FLORIDA STATE BOARD OF CONSERVATION. 1944. Sixth Biennial Report. Tallahassee, Florida.

Seven counties reported in 1944. Eight counties reported in 1943.

FLORIDA STATE BOARD OF CONSERVATION. 1946. Seventh Biennial Report. Tallahassee, Florida.

Statistics provided on all counties that reported: thirteen counties in 1945 and nine in 1946.

FLOWER, STANLEY S. 1925. Contributions to our knowledge of the duration of life in vertebrate animals. No. 3. Reptiles. Proc. Zool. Soc. London 95, pp. 911-981.

Chelonia mydas—6 years in the New York Aquarium.

Chelonia virgata—(Pacific green turtle) 15 years in the New York Aquarium.

Chelonia imbricata—(hawksbill) probably 32 years old. Same turtle that was in New York Aquarium for 3 years and 9 months.

Thallasochelys caretta— (loggerhead) was in the New York Aquarium 14 years and freed. Another specimen was 12 years in the Monaco Aquarium.

FLOWER, STANLEY S. 1937. Further notes on the duration of life in animals. No. 3. Reptiles. Proc. Zool. Soc. London 107: 1-39.

Growth of *mydas* and *virgata* about equal, hatching at 2.5 inches, reaching 8 inches when 1 year old. Female mature at 35 inches and a 44 inch specimen is about 10 years old.

Three green turtles each about 1 pound and 5 inches in length received by the society's aquarium grew to over 50 pounds each in nine years. One that was 448 pounds grew little. Several lived over 12 years in London. Green turtles do poorly in Berlin, but the other two common species do well. Hawksbills: 10 to 15 years in London and Berlin. Loggerhead: 20 grams when hatched, 48 by 35mm. One reared in captivity in Key West, 4.5 years: 37 kilos (81.5 pounds), 0.63 meters (2 feet, 1 inch) by (1 foot, 11 inches).

FORBES, RICHARD B., and DOROTHY McKEY-FENDOR. 1968. A green turtle for Oregon coast. Can. J. Zool. 46(5): 1079.

FORREST, H. E. 1931. Hawksbill turtle on the Welsh coast. Northwestern Naturalist 6(1): 26-27.

On *Chelonia imbricata*, new to the fauna of North Wales.

FOWLER, HENRY W. 1906. Some cold-blooded vertebrates of the Florida Keys. Proc. Acad. Nat. Sci., Philadelphia, Pennsylvania.

A brief synopsis of a trip taken through the Keys with notations of species of turtles seen and mentioned by local inhabitants. Sea turtles mentioned.

FRAIR, WAYNE. 1969. Aging of serum proteins and serology of marine turtles. Serol. Mus. Bull. 42: 1-3.

FRANCESCON, A. 1930. Sulla Natura del Ganglio del Tronco del Vago nei Cheloni. (Character of the ganglion of the trunk of the vagus in Chelonians). Arch. Ital. Anat. Embriol. 28(1): 59-74.

FREIBERG, MARCOS A. 1967. Tortugas de la Argentina. Cienc. Invest. 23(8): 351-363.

Chelonia mydas, Dermochelys coriacea, and *Caretta caretta caretta* mentioned. Descriptions with notes on behavior and distribution for these and other Argentine turtles.

FRY, D. B. 1913. On the status of *Chelonia depressa* Garman. Rec. Austral. Mus. 10: 159-185.

FUGLER, C. M., and R. G. WEBB. 1957. Some noteworthy reptiles and amphibians from the states of Oaxaca and Veracruz. Herpetologica 13(2): 103-108.

Reports three juvenile *Lepidochelys olivacea kempi* purchased at Alvarado, Veracruz, and said to have come from immediate vicinity. Another from Nautla, Veracruz. Average carapace length of the four: 43 mm.

FUJINOKI, Y., and SH. TONEGAUNA. 1957. A leatherback turtle taken off No, Echigo Provence. Saishu to Shiiku 19: 302. (In Japanese)

FUJIWARA, M. 1966. The early development of the marine turtle with special reference to the formation of germ layers in Amniota. Bull. Tokyo Gakugei Univ. 18, Ser. IV (1): 47-60. (In Japanese)

GADOW, H. 1899. Orthogenetic variation in shells of Chelonia. Zool. Results (Willey) 3, p. 207.
Variations in number and arrangement of scutes in the loggerhead.

GADOW, H. 1905. Orthogenetic variations. Science 22: 637-640.

GADOW, H. 1909. Cambridge Natural History 8: 312-329. The Macmillan Co., New York.
General description, anatomy, and classification of sea turtles.
1. *Dermatochelys coriacea*
Leathery turtle, Luth. "Overaton" by Agassiz. Wide range but rare, most common in W. Atlantic from Florida to Brazil, and Indian Ocean.
2. *Chelonia mydas*
Believed to be poisonous at some seasons.
3. *Chelonia imbricata*
Carnivorous. Method of heating carapace in order to loosen shields is described.
4. *Thallasochelys caretta*

GAGE, S. H., and S. P. GAGE. 1886. Aquatic respiration in soft shelled turtles: a contribution to the physiology of respiration in vertebrates. Amer. Nat. 20: 233-236.
1. Soft shelled—under water from 2 to 10 hours.
2. Fill and empty mouth 16 times a minute.
3. Mucous membrane "villified," increasing surface.
4. Water tests on tank water of turtles showed considerable gaseous exchange.

GALLAGHER, R. W., and MALCOLM HOLLINGER. 1973. Sea turtles nesting on Hutchinson Island, Florida, 1972. In press.

GARMAN, SAMUEL. 1880. On certain species of Chelonicidae. Bull. Mus. Comp. Zool. 6(6): 123-124.
Thalassochelys Kempii

C. Agassizii	Northwest Pacific
C. virgata	Northwest Pacific
C. depressa	Northwest Pacific

Also, *C. depressa*, which was probably the previous two, in Teneriffe, Rio de Janeiro, Cape of Good Hope, and Indian Ocean. *C. Agassizii* is also known as *C. virgata*, 1814 and 1857 of tropical Pacific.

GARMAN, SAMUEL. 1884. Contributions to the natural history of the Bermudas. Reptiles. Bull. U.S. Nat. Mus. 25: pp. i-xxiii, 1-353.

Five hundred eggs in one female. Forty turtles caught in one day by two boats. All sea turtles mentioned except Kemp's. Early reports, from 1543 on, relating to abundance. By 1620 decline had started. An act was passed against killing turtles 18 inches in diameter or under. One writer met turtles in mid-ocean. Maximum size: 1,200 pound leatherback, 850 pound green (worth 4 to 10 cents per pound alive or 12 to 18 cents per pound dressed), 450 pound loggerhead, 160 pound hawksbill. One shark had a ten pound green turtle in its stomach. Complete list of synonyms.

GAYMER, R. 1968. Amphibians and reptiles of the Seychelles. Brit. J. Herp. 4: 24-28.

GHAI, S. P. 1931. Abstracts of papers. Proc. Indian Sci. Congr. 18: Sec. 4: 219-221.

A systematic study of the cestode parasites of reptiles, as well as of birds and mammals.

GIRAL, FRANCISCO. 1955. Grasas de tortugas mexicanas. Ciencia 15(4,5): 65-69.

Previous work on three sea turtles (ridley, loggerhead, and green) and one Mexican river turtle summarized. Fats in the oils encompass almost all fatty acids known in reptiles and amphibians. Great variability of proportions.

GOETTE, A. 1899. Ueber die Entwicklung des Knocherner Rückenschildes (Carapax) der Schildkröten. Zeitschr. Wiss. Zool. 66: 407-434.

GOIN, COLEMAN J. 1968. Comments upon the origin of the herpetofauna of Florida. Quart. J. Fla. Acad. Sci. 21(1): 61-70.

Chelonia, Eretmochelys, Caretta, Lepidochelys, and *Dermochelys* listed as Tropicopolitan, one of five groups given based on geographic affinities.

GOODRIAN, J. 1946. Rapport ten behoeve van het welraatsplan Nederlandische Antillen, p. 30.

"It has attracted our attention that in various places along the coast turtles are depositing their eggs, but that the possibilities which are thereby created, are being nipped in the bud by the fact that these eggs are used for food by the population. Systematical breeding of turtles deserves serious consideration with regard to both the meat and the shell. In a period of three years the turtle already has grown sufficiently (approximately 55 lbs.). For breeding purposes certain parts of a bay, as for instance the Lac on Bonaire, should be fenced in and closed off with wirenetting. Personnel would be required to guard against thieves.

For further protection it would be advisable to prohibit buying and selling of turtle eggs and turtles, as well as having them in one's possession with a view to sell them. An exception could be made by the issuance of permits.

Over forty years ago Dr. Boeke reported about this cultivation that experiments in this direction 'will ultimately undoubtedly be necessary to lead to the required results' " (p. 129).

GOODRICH, E. S. 1916. On the classification of the Reptilia. Proc. Roy. Soc. London Sec. B. 89: 261-276.

Evolutionary dissertation on hearts. Chelonian structures discussed. Different groups of reptiles differ in heart structures.

GOODRICH, E. S. 1919. Note on the reptilian heart. J. Anat. 53: 298-304.

Discussion elaborating more fully on the differences of hearts and associated structures in the principal reptilian groups.

GRANDA, A. M., and K. W. HADEN. 1970. Retinal oil globule counts and distributions in two species of turtles: *Pseudemys scripta elegans* (Wied) and *Chelonia mydas mydas* (Linnaeus). Vision Res. 10: 79-84.

Globules usually conjugated with cone structures; in both species cones predominate and rods are few. *Pseudemys:* inferior temporal area that participates in binocular vision dense in globules. Superior temporal field not so differentiated. Globules provide filter for harsh glare, permitting acute vision for turtle, which locates in the water attending to stimuli from above. *Chelonia:* distribution of globules showed no definite pattern. Authors conclude that since in normal sea habitat differential glare and acuity in the binocular field play small roles, this lack of areal differentiation not surprising.

GRANT, CHAPMAN. 1956. Aberrant lamination in two hawksbill turtles. Herpetologica 12(4): 302.

Two hatchlings taken near Banes, Oriente, Cuba. Specimen 1: first and second neurals fused, scute passes from marginal to marginal (fusion of fourth and fifth neurals and fourth costals), succeeding scute extends to right marginal. Specimen 2: seven neurals, one of which extends to marginals, 11 left marginals.

GRAPER, LUDWIG. 1932. Die das Zungenbein und Zunge Bewegenden Muskeln der Schildkröten. I und II. Jenaische Zeitschr. Naturwiss. 66(1): 169-198.

The physiological, anatomical, and neurological adaptations of the turtle that enable it to "breathe" through its tongue discussed.

GRAY, J. E. 1855. Catalogue of the shield reptiles in the British Museum. London.

Also a series of papers on the Testudinata in the Proc. Zool. Soc. London. 1861 to 1873.

GRAY, J. E. 1869. Notes on the families and genera of tortoises, and on characters of their skulls. Proc. Zool. Soc. London 12.

Turtle are classified and described, including the family Cheloniidae: *Caretta, Chelonia mydas.* Family Sphargididae, *Dermatochelys.*

GREAVES, J. B. 1933. Nesting of *Caretta olivacea.* J. Bombay Nat. Hist. Soc. 37: 494.

GREEN, R. H. 1971. Sea turtles round Tasmania: The first record of the green turtle *Chelonia mydas* (Linne, 1758) and the hawksbill turtle *Eretmochelys imbricata bissa* (Ruppell, 1835) from Tasmanian waters. Rec. Queen Victoria Mus. 38: 1-4.

Large green caught on hand line April 1959 at Burnie, Northwest Tasmania. Small hawksbill found dead December 1969 on beach on King Island, Bass Straight.

GREGORY, E. R. 1900. Observations on the development of the excretory system of turtles. Zool. Jahrb. 13(4): 1-34.

Aromochelys. Platypeltis spinnifer. Detailed discussion plus incidental observations on developing embryos.

GUPTA, S. P. 1961. On some trematodes from the intestines of the marine turtle, *Chelone mydas,* from the Caribbean Sea. Canadian J. Zool. 39(3): 293-298.

Trematodes found in a turtle from Trinidad: *Cricocephalus albus, Pleurogonius mehrai*—fam. Proncephalidae; *Nectargium travassosi, Deuterobaris chelonei*—fam. Angiodictyidae; *Schizamphistomordes chelonei*—fam. Paramphastomidae.

HADZISELIMOVIC, H., and M. ANDELIC. 1967. Contribution to the knowledge of the ear in the sea turtle. Acta Anat. 66(3): 460-477.

Two sea turtle heads (species not stated) used for descriptive anatomy of the ear. Pictures, drawings, and text give detailed information on structure, with the conclusion that sea turtles possess, from the viewpoint of topological correlation, a highly developed otic region.

HAINES, R. W. 1935. Some muscular changes in the tail and thigh of reptiles and mammals. J. Morph. 58(2): 355-385.

Detailed comparative study with drawings and plates. Bibliography.

HALSTEAD, BRUCE W. 1956. Animal phyla known to contain poisonous marine animals. *In* Venoms. Papers presented at the First International Conference on Venoms 27-30 December 1954 at the annual meeting of the American Association for the Advancement of Science, Berkley, Calif., AAAS Pub. No. 44.

Eretmochelys imbricata and *Dermochelys coriacea* listed as poisonous. Symptoms given; treatment and chemistry or toxicology unknown.

HAMERTON, A. E. 1935. Report on the deaths occurring in the Society's gardens during the year 1934. Proc. Zool. Soc. London 2: 443-474.

Records the causes of death of 222 mammals, 613 birds, and 233 reptiles and amphibians with records of parasitic subspecies found.

HARDY, SIR ALLISTER. 1959. The open sea: its natural history, Pt. II: fish and fisheries. Houghton Mifflin Co., Boston. 322 pp.

Four species recorded for Britain; *Dermochelys coriacea, Eretmochelys imbricata, Caretta caretta,* and *Lepidochelys kempii. Chelonia mydas* reported occasionally but never confirmed. Suggested that ridleys and loggerheads in these waters are strays from the Gulf of Mexico and adjacent waters.

HARDY, JERRY D., JR. 1962. Comments on the Atlantic ridley turtle, *Lepidochelys olivacea kempi*, in the Chesapeake Bay. Chesapeake Sci. 3(3): 217-220.

Five specimens studied; meristic data and case histories given.

HARLAN, RICHARD. 1827. Genera of North American Reptilia, and a synopsis of the species. J. Acad. Nat. Sci., Phila. 5: 317-372, 6: 7-38.

Order Chelonia: sea tortoises

1. *Chelonia mydas*
2. *Chelonia caretta*
3. *Chelonia Caouana*
4. *Coruido coriacea* Luth.

HARPER, ROLAND M. 1927. Natural resources of southern Florida. Fla. State Geol. Survey 18th Ann. Rept.

Sea turtles mentioned and some statistics given. Latter are lumped together with sponges, crayfish, etc., so do not hold much meaning for turtles alone.

HARRISSON, TOM. 1950. The Sarawak turtle island's "Semah." Royal Asiatic Soc. J. Malayan Branch 23(3): 105-126.

Brief review of history of egg taking (*Chelonia mydas*) on three Malayan islands. Observations and discussions of "Semah"— ceremonies concerned with "opening the river mouth" at the close of the monsoon season. Appendix of turtle island egg yields, 1948-49.

HARRISSON, TOM. 1951. The edible turtle (*Chelonia mydas*) in Borneo, 1. Breeding season. Sarawak Mus. J. 5(3): 592-596.

Adults never killed for food; eggs collected, sold for 5.5 cents each (Straits currency). Turtles breed in every month of the year, with a peak from May through September.

HARRISSON, TOM. 1952. Breeding of the edible turtle. Nature 169(4292): 198.

Breeding occurs all months of the year on three islands off the Sarawak coast, with a summer peak. Incubation period: 50 to 65 days from 90 clutches in August; average 52 days.

HARRISSON, TOM. 1954. The edible turtle (*Chelonia mydas*) in Borneo, 2. Copulation. Sarawak Mus. J. 6(4): 126-128.

Copulation occurs mostly during nonmonsoon months. Act usually difficult to perform; males remain mounted for over an hour at times. Suggested that copulation occurs after laying (highest frequency between 5 A.M. and 4 P.M.) and that one act supplies sperm for more than one laying.

HARRISSON, TOM. 1955. The edible turtle (*Chelonia mydas*) in Borneo, 3. Young turtles (in captivity). Sarawak Mus. J. 6(6): 633-640.

Hatchling turtles come out at night; 50% hatching success or less is frequent. Turtles were fed up to three years on fish and/or prawns without any vegetable matter. Young turtles feed by at least three stimuli: (1) scent; (2) sight; (3) texture and taste. Comments on weight and growth and the need for basic studies on this valuable resource included.

HARRISSON, TOM. 1956a. The edible turtle (*Chelonia mydas*) in Borneo, 4. Growing turtles and growing problems. Sarawak Mus. J. 7(7): 233-239.
   Comments on learning, behavior, and mortality and its causes. Largest turtle raised weighed 18 pounds 4 ounces after 3.5 years. Great deal of variability in growth, some of which reflected different rearing conditions. Artificial incubation discussed.

HARRISSON, TOM. 1956b. The edible turtle (*Chelonia mydas*) in Borneo, 5. Tagging turtles (and why). Sarawak Mus. J. 7(8): 504-515.
   Problems associated with tagging discussed as well as historical information on the status of turtles in Sarawak. Four thousand tagged from 1953 to 1955. Results so far indicate that the turtles lay two to four times a season every three years.

HARRISSON, TOM. 1956c. Tagging green turtles. Nature 178: 1479.
   Marking started in 1951. Cow ear tags selected by 1953 with the tag on the front flipper. Fourteen returns in 1956 of tags put on in 1953 indicate a three-year laying cycle.
   System met with success.

HARRISSON, TOM. 1958. Notes on the green turtle (*Chelonia mydas*). 6. Semah ceremonies, 1949-58. Sarawak Mus. J. 8: 482-486.

HARRISSON, TOM. 1959. Notes on the green turtle (*Chelonia mydas*). 7. Long-term tagging returns, 1952-8. Sarawak Mus. J. 8: 772-774.

HARRISSON, TOM. 1960. Notes on the green turtle (*Chelonia mydas*). 8. First tag returns outside Sarawak, 1959. Sarawak Mus. J. 9: 277-278.

HARRISSON, TOM. 1961. Notes on the green turtle (*Chelonia mydas*). 9. Some new hatching observations. Sarawak Mus. J. N.S. 10: 293-299.

HARRISSON, TOM. 1962a. Notes on the green turtle (*Chelonia mydas*). 10. Some emergence variations. Sarawak Mus. J. N.S. 10: 610-613.

HARRISSON, TOM. 1962b. Notes on the green turtle (*Chelonia mydas*). 11. West Borneo numbers, the downward trend. Sarawak Mus. J. N.S. 10: 614-623.

HARRISSON, TOM. 1962c. Notes on the green turtle (*Chelonia mydas*). 12. Monthly laying cycles. Sarawak Mus. J. N.S. 10: 624-630.

HARRISSON, TOM. 1963. Notes on marine turtles. 13. Growth rate of the hawksbill. Sarawak Mus. J. N.S. 11: 303-304.

HARRISSON, TOM. 1964a. Notes on marine turtles. 15. Sabah's turtle islands. Sarawak Mus. J. 11(23, 24): 624-627.

HARRISSON, TOM. 1964b. Stirbt die Suppenschildkroete aus? Umschau 64(11): 340-343.

HARRISSON, TOM. 1965. Notes on marine turtles. 16. Some loggerhead (and hawksbill) comparisons with the green turtle. Sarawak Mus. J. N.S. 12: 419-422.

HARRISSON, TOM. 1966. Marine turtles in South-east Asia and the Western Pacific. Pacific Science Congress, 11th Proc. (Abstract only)

HARRISSON, TOM. 1969a. The marine turtle situation in Sarawak. *In* Marine turtles. IUCN Publ. New Ser. Suppl. Paper No. 20: 71-74.
　　Covers general status, exploitation, conservation, research, and national requirements.
HARRISSON, TOM. 1969b. The turtle tragedy. Oryx 10(2): 112-115.
HASSE, C. 1871. Das Gehororgan der Schildkroten. Hasse's Anatomische Studien, Heft 2, p. 225.
　　Anatomical discussion of ear organs.
HAY, O. P. 1898. On Prostega, the systematic position of *Dermochelys* and the morphogeny of the Chelonian carapace and plastron. Amer. Nat. 32: 929-950.
HAY, O. P. 1901. The composition of the shell of turtles. Biological Academy of Science, New York.
HAY, O. P. 1908a. The fossil turtles of North America. Carnegie Inst. Wash. Pub. 75.
　　Excellent work. Cheloniidae back to the Upper Cretaceous, discussion of present forms and their relation to ancestors.
HAY, O. P. 1908b. On three existing species of sea turtles, one of them (*Caretta remivaga*) new. Proc. U.S. Nat. Mus. 34 (1605): 183.
　　The bastard turtle, *Colpochelys kempii* Garman, discussed anatomically and taxonomically. It is fairly common along the coasts of the southeastern states. Garman first recognized it as being separate from *Caretta caretta* (1880). Superficially the animal closely resembles the loggerhead, but in osteology it is distinct. *Caretta remivaga* n. sp. based on skull U.S. Nat. Mus. Cat. No. 9973, collected by Prof. F. Suminchrast in Ventosa Bay, Mexico, 1870 (west coast of Mexico). *Lepidochelys olivacea* mentioned.
HAY, O. P. 1922. On the phylogeny of the shell of the Testudinata and the relationships of *Dermochelys*. J. Morph., Phila. 36: 421-441.
HAY, O. P. 1928. Further consideration of the shell of Chelys and of the constitution of the armor of turtles in general. Proc. U.S. Nat. Mus. 73(3): 1-12.
　　This is a highly controversial article dealing with the evolutionary development (hypothetical) of the bony plates of turtles and the relation of the shell to other bones of the body.
HAYCROFT, J. B. 1891. The development of the carapace of the Chelonia. Trans. Roy. Soc. Edin. 36(2): 335-342.
HEFFINGTON, VIRGINIA. 1970. Hatching a new steak. Tropic 4(33): 28, 30.
　　Brief account of turtle culture project on Grand Cayman Island. Schroeder projects 3,500 green turtles in 1.5 years at market size (150 pounds), and 7,000 for the second harvest. Eggs come from the wild, and 1% of the yearlings released to preserve the population. Turtles raised in round plastic tanks and later moved to concrete tanks.
HELDT, H. 1933. La tortue Luth *Sphargis coriacea*. Contribution à l'étude anatomique et biologique. Ann. Sta. Oceanog. de Salammbo 8: 40, fig. 18.

HENDRICKSON, JOHN R. 1958. The green sea turtle, *Chelonia mydas* (Linn.), in Malaya and Sarawak. Proc. Zool. Soc. London 130(4): 455-535.

Studies of South China Sea area (eastern coast of Malaya—four nesting beaches, and Sarawak—two nesting beaches). Descriptions of nesting, mating, development of young; discussion of hatchery methods, predators, parasitism, and conservation. Comments on the fishery for eggs. Excellent work, recommended for those interested in green turtles.

HENDRICKSON, JOHN R. 1969. Report on Hawaiian marine turtle populations. *In* Marine turtles. IUCN New Publ. Ser., Suppl. Paper No. 20: 89-95.

Covers present status, exploitation, conservation, research, and requirements.

HENDRICKSON, JOHN R., and ERIC R. ALFRED. 1961. Nesting population of sea turtles on the east coast of Malaya. Bull. Raffles Mus. 26: 190-196.

Estimated that two million turtles eggs constituting over 50 tons of high-grade protein food are consumed each year in Malaya. Exclusive rights to collect turtle eggs on specified areas of beach granted by government licenses yearly on a competitive bid basis. Four species nest on Malayan east coast: *Dermochelys coriacea, Chelonia mydas, Lepidochelys olivacea,* and *Eretmochelys imbricata.* Figures on egg production and egg prices. Authors suggest the conservation of a small number of the nests.

HENDRICKSON, JOHN R., and E. BALASINGAM. 1966. Nesting beach preferences of Malayan sea turtles. Bull. Natl. Mus. Singapore 33(10): 69-76.

Lack of homogeneity of breeding turtles along beaches of eastern coast of Malaya appears to be due to the selectivity of different species. Hawksbills nest infrequently; ridleys show no tendency to congregate in particular areas for nesting; greens and leatherbacks nest in large numbers, usually on different sites. Green turtle prefers fine sand, shallow slopes from high beach platforms to the sea, shallower water near shore. Leatherbacks prefer coarse sand, steeper slopes, and deeper water. Possible function of these factors in beach preference discussed.

HENDRICKSON, JOHN R., and J. S. WINTERFLOOD. 1961. Hatching leathery turtle eggs. Bull. Raffles Mus. 26: 187-189.

Dermochelys eggs considered a delicacy by Malayans and harvested heavily. Transplanted 102 eggs to a hatchery site; 72 hatchings emerged 58 to 59 days after laying. Attempts to keep young in captivity failed; all were dead after four months. The 70% hatch, however, warrants further hatchery attempts as a conservation measure.

HERMANN, H., and L. MERKLEN. 1926. Des effets physiologiques de la reduction du champ de l'hématose chez les chéloniens par ligature d'une bronche. Bull. Soc. Nancy 2(6): 685-690.

The effects of ligating one broncus discussed. Article is a continuation of a work previously done on the same subject.

HERNANDEZ, JESUS VASQUEZ. 1966. Marcado de tortugas marinas frente al Puerto de Mazatlán, Sinaloa. Bol. Prog. Nac. Marcado Tortugas Mar. 1(5): 3 pp. (mimeo).

June is not the month of greatest abundance; turtles mostly captured in May, therefore marking will be done in this month. June to September the Pacific ridley is most abundant; corresponds to the period of reproduction. List of 24 marked turtles included.

HERRICK, C. JUDSON. 1922. Neurological Foundations of Animal Behavior. Pp. 209-210. Henry Holt & Co.

Brief history of the evolution of the fore brain in reptiles.

HESSE, RICHARD, W. C. ALEE, and K. P. SCHMIDT. 1937. Ecological Animal Geography. John Wiley & Sons, Inc., New York.

Brief·notes only on the occurrence of sea turtles.

HEWITT, J. 1933. New reptiles and a frog. Occas. Papers Rhodesian Mus. No. 2, p. 45.

HIGGINS, ELMER, and RUSSELL LORD. 1926. Preliminary report on the marine fisheries of Texas. U.S. Bur. Fish. Doc. 1009.

Reference included primarily because it contains no notice of turtles, which would indicate the low status of turtle fishing as compared with previous years.

HILDEBRAND, HENRY H. 1963. Hallazgo del área de anidación de la tortuga marina "lora" Lepidochelys kempi (Garman), en la costa occidental del Golfo de México. Ciencia 22(4): 105-112.

HILDEBRAND, SAMUEL F. 1929. Review of experiments on artificial culture of Diamond-back Terrapin. Bull. U.S. Bur. Fish. 45:25-70.

HILDEBRAND, SAMUEL F. 1932. Growth of Diamond-back Terrapins, size attained, sex ratio and longevity. Zoologica 9(15): 551-563.

HILDEBRAND, SAMUEL F. 1938. Twinning in turtles. J. Heredity 29(7): 243-253.

Literature tells of only 21 cojoined. Six described in this article. Ordinary twins difficult to distinguish. Two pairs from unhatched eggs, one from egg at hatching. Two monsters in 100,000 turtles, 25 years. Sea turtle in 1751 with "twin" head. Silver Springs, Florida: three freaks in 27 terrapin eggs; one twisted jaw, one double headed, and two fused plastron to plastron. Chilling or low oxygen can instigate. Excellent bibliography.

HILDEBRAND, SAMUEL F., and CHARLES HATSEL. 1927. On the growth and care and behavior of loggerhead turtles in captivity. Proc. Nat. Acad. Sci. 13(6): 374-377.

Nest containing 135 eggs of Caretta caretta found on Bogue Banks, Beaufort, North Carolina, presumably on the morning it was made. Eggs transferred and reburied in sandy beaches near the U.S. Fisheries Laboratory. Eggs rotted when placed where the nest was covered by water several times during high tide.

HILLABY, JOHN. 1963. The fate of sea turtles. New Sci. 20(371): 776-777.
Popular article on taxonomy, status, and fate of sea turtles.
HILLABY, JOHN. 1968. The fate of the sea turtles. Sea Frontiers 11(1): 4-13.
Informational article for the layman on general biology, conservation, and commercial exploitation of marine turtles.
HINDS, V. T. 1964-65. The green sea turtle in South Arabia. Port of Aden Annual: 54-57.
HIRTH, HAROLD F. 1962. Cloacal temperatures of the green and hawksbill sea turtles. Copeia 1962(3): 647-648.
Temperatures taken on seven green turtles before laying and seven after laying, and on two hawksbills after laying. Turtles show no significant difference in temperature before and after laying in the green, but turtle temperatures slightly higher than water temperature. Limited data suggest that the body temperature of sea turtles differs very little from that of their natural environment.
HIRTH, HAROLD F. 1969. Marine turtles in the Seychelles and Aldabra. *In* Marine turtles. IUCN New Publ. Ser. Suppl. Paper No. 20: 54-55.
Nesting areas, exploitation, conservation, and national requirements discussed.
HIRTH, HAROLD F., and ARCHIE CARR. 1970. The green turtle in the Gulf of Aden and the Seychelles Islands. Verhandelingen der Koninklijke Nederlandse Akademia van Wetenschappen, AFD. Natuurkunde TweedeReeks 58(5). 44 pp.
Deals with aspects of the life history of green turtles and contains some information on hawksbills as well. Some of the most important green turtle rookeries are located on the coast of South Yemen. In the Seychelles, nesting populations correlated with the degree of exploitation. Measurements on eggs, hatchlings, and adults included; beaches described. Nesting behavior, feeding habits, long-distance travel, taxonomic problems, exploitation, and natural mortality discussed.
HOGE, A. R. 1950. Notas erpetológicas, 7. Fauna erpetológica da Ilha da Quermado Grande. Mem. Inst. Butantan 22: 151-172.
Chelonia mydas and *Caretta caretta* two of the species described.
HOLBROOK, J. E. 1840. North American Herpetology. 4 vols. J. Dobson, Philadelphia.
HOLMES, W. N. 1965. Endocrine controls in water and electrolyte metabolism: some aspects of osmoregulation in reptiles and birds. Arch. Anat. Microscop. Morphol. Exp. 54(1): 491-514.
Summary and discussion of the effects of the adrenocortical steroids on the renal and extrarenal excretory mechanisms.
HOLMES, W. N., and R. L. McBEAN. 1964. Some aspects of electrolyte excretion in the green turtle *Chelonia mydas mydas*. J. Exp. Biol. 41(1): 81-90.

Experiments conducted on juveniles to measure: (1) plasma and urine electrolyte composition and salt gland weights of juveniles maintained in salt water and in freshwater; (2) the excretion rates of sodium and potassium by fed and unfed turtles; (3) the excretion rates of sodium and potassium by saline-loaded juveniles; (4) the electrolyte composition of urine from two species of adult marine turtles—*Chelonia mydas mydas* and *Lepidochelys olivacea.* Results indicated: (1) salt gland, located in the orbit of the eye, is primary route of sodium and potassium excretion; the kidney appears to be incapable of maintaining a positive water balance in the face of electrolyte loads presented by seawater and food; (2) excretion of electrolytes by the salt gland appears to be at least partly dependent upon a fully functional adrenal cortex.

HONEGGER, R. E. 1967. The green turtle (*Chelonia mydas japonica*) Thunberg in the Seychelles Islands. British J. Herp. 4: 8-11.

HOOKER, D. 1908a. Preliminary observation on the behavior of some newly hatched loggerhead turtles (*Thallasochelys caretta*). Carnegie Inst. Wash. Yearbook 6: 111-112.

HOOKER, D. 1908b. The breeding habits of the loggerhead turtle and some early instincts of the young. Science 27: 490-491.

Breeds April to June. Multiple nests: 100 eggs, 50-day incubation. Brief discussion of behavior.

HOOKER, D. 1909. Report on the instincts and habits of newly hatched loggerhead turtles. Carnegie Inst. Wash. Yearbook 7: 124.

Same as Papers Tortugas Lab., Carnegie Inst. Wash. 3: 69-76. 1911.

HOOKER, D. 1911. Certain reactions to color in the young loggerhead turtle. Papers Tortugas Lab., Carnegie Inst. Wash. 3: 69-76.

Sun not important.

1. Photophobic opaque and transparent red, orange, green.

2. Photophillic - blue.

HOOPER, S. N., and R. G. ACKMAN. 1970. Trans-6-hexadeconoic acid in the Atlantic leatherback *Dermochelys coriacea coriacea* L. and other marine turtles. Lipids 5(3): 288-292.

Depot fat from *Dermochelys* contained about 3% of this fat. Depot fat from the loggerhead and the ridley contained this acid, in a lower proportion in the ridley. Structural details of acid elucidated.

HORNELL, J. 1905. Marine biological reports. Pearl fishery of Lake Tamblegam, Vol. I, part 2(2): 47.

HORNELL, J. 1927. The turtle fisheries of the Seychelles Islands. H. M. Stationery Office.

HORNELL, JAMES. 1950. Fishing in many waters. Cambridge Univ. Press, London. 210 pp.

Description of spears used for turtles at Wake Island and Manokwari and of iron-headed harpoons used along Geelvink Bay and in the Schouten Islands. Discussion on the use of the remora for capturing greens and hawksbills.

HOUCK, WARREN J., and JAMES J. JOSEPH. 1958. A northern record for the Pacific ridley, *Lepidochelys olivacea.* Copeia 1958(3): 219-220.

> In October 1957 a ridley found on the beach near Table Bluff, California, with a carapace length of 24.1 cm. This record is northward extension of the range by about 800 miles.

HUGHES, GEORGE. 1969*a*. Marine turtle hatchlings of Tongaland. African Wildlife 23(1): 5-19.

> Ten loggerhead nests and two leatherback nests transplanted to a hatchery site during 1967-1968 season. Forty percent hatching success in loggerhead nests after 72 days incubation. Tongaland hatchlings almost invariably emerge at night. Hatching and movement to sea discussed. Hatchlings swept south by the Agulhas Current; found on beaches between Durban and Cape Town. Plastic tags on the inframarginal bridge have been used on 631 loggerhead hatchlings.

HUGHES, GEORGE. 1969*b*. Report to the survival service commission on marine turtles in Southern Africa. *In* Marine turtles. IUCN New Publ. Ser., Suppl. Paper No. 20: 56-66.

> Brief discussion of turtle status in Angola, southwest Africa, Mozambique, Malagasy, and Cape Province. Natal only area in South Africa where research and legal restrictions established for a number of years. Nesting sites and abundance, exploitation, conservation, research, and national requirements covered.

HUGHES, GEORGE R. 1970*a*. Marine turtles: an introduction to the sea turtles of South East Africa. S. Afr. J. Sci. 66(8): 239-246.

HUGHES, GEORGE R. 1970*b*. Further studies on marine turtles in Tongaland: III. Lammergeyer 12: 7-25.

> Tagging of *Caretta caretta* hatchlings discussed. Method of estimating nests and substantiation of lack of definite reproductive cycle in loggerheads presented. Movements of hatchlings of *Caretta caretta* and *Dermochelys coriacea* discussed. Hatchlings influenced by Agulhas Current, and large numbers exist in mixed-waters zone, Cape of Good Hope, where temperature changes from 22°C to 10°C. Inability to survive this shock may account for relatively small population.

HUGHES, GEORGE R. 1970*c*. Further studies on marine turtles in Tongaland: IV. Lammergeyer 12: 26-36.

> New methods discussed. Growth of tagged *Dermochelys coriacea* after three years is negligible. Termination of digging stimulus found to be same as Hendrickson 1958.

HUGHES, GEORGE R. 1971. Further studies on marine turtles in Tongaland: V. Lammergeyer 13: 7-24.

> New method of tagging *Caretta caretta* hatchlings in field: implanting 3-mm length of stainless steel wire is suitable for limited number of years. Estimated number of females is 466. Hatching program success described. Hatchling and juvenile movements discussed. Leatherback data suggest two-year nesting cycle.

HUGHES, GEORGE, A. J. BASS, and M. T. MENTIS. 1967. Further studies on marine turtles in Tongaland, I. Lammergeyer 7: 7-54.
Studies from 1963 to 1966 conducted on the coast of Tongaland in northeastern Natal. Data include weights and measurements; nesting season, aspects of life history, etc., discussed for logger-heads and leatherbacks. Short notes included on hawksbills, greens, and ridleys (no local breeding known).

HUGHES, GEORGE, A. J. BASS, and M. T. MENTIS. 1968. New African record for ridley turtles (*Lepidochelys olivacea*). Copeia 1968(2): 423.
Olive ridley captured off coast of Natal.

HUGHES, GEORGE, and M. T. MENTIS. 1967. Further studies on marine turtles in Tongaland, II. Lammergeyer 7: 55-72.
Report of 1966-67 survey of leatherback and loggerhead nesting. New tag used. Nesting interval of loggerheads of 14 to 15 days, with a possible two-year cycle. Measurements included on nesting females, hatching success, and hatchlings.

HUNT, TIMOTHY J. 1957. Notes on diseases and mortality in Testudines. Herpetologica 13(1): 19-24.
A blood parasite, *Trypanosoma testudinis* has been recorded in *Testudo exculenta* (probably a synonym for *Chelonia mydas mydas*).

HYMAN, L. H. 1932. A laboratory manual for comparative vertebrate anatomy. Univ. of Chicago Press, Chicago, Ill.
Useful dissection handbook.

INGLE, ROBERT M. 1972. Florida's sea turtle industry in relation to restrictions imposed in 1971. *In* Annual summary. Marine Florida Commercial Marine Landings. Pp. 55-62.
Survey of turtle production in Florida in 1970, just prior to restrictive action.

INGLIS, WILLIAM G. 1957. A revision of the nematode genera *Kathtania* and *Tonaudia*. Ann. Mag. Nat. Hist. 10(119): 785-800.
Tonaudia tonaudia reported from *Caretta caretta* in Egypt.

JACOBS, W. 1939. Die Lunge der Seeschildkröte *Caretta caretta* als Schwebeorgan. Zeitschr. vergleich. Physiol. 27(1): 1-28.
A study of compensations in breathing and swimming with weights placed at different locations. Air that a turtle breathes can be manipulated to increase bouyancy of a given part and to change the center of gravity of the animal.

JARVIS, NORMAN D. 1932. The fisheries of Puerto Rico. U.S. Bur. Fish. Invest. Rept. 13.
The fact that sea turtles are not mentioned reflects the insignificance of the industry of this island.

JOHLIN, J. M. and FERRIN B. MORELAND. 1933. Studies of the blood picture of the turtle after complete anoxia. J. Biol. Chem. 103(1): 107-114.
Chemical discussion of the blood changes in turtles that have been placed in pure N_2 for as long as 28 hours.

JONES, S., and A. B. FERNANDO. 1968. The present status of the turtle fishery in the Gulf of Mannar and Palk Bay. Symp. Living Resources Seas Around India, Indian Counc. Agr. Res. 1968.

KAPPERS, C. U., G. CARL HUBER, and E. C. CROSBY. 1936. The comparative anatomy of the nervous system of vertebrates, including man. The Macmillan Co., New York.

Incidental references to the sea turtle groups appear regularly. Excellent bibliography. Highly technical and greatly detailed work of over 1,800 pages.

KAUFMANN, REINHARD. 1966. Das Vorkommen von Meeresschild-kröten in Kolumbien und ihre Nutzung als Nahrungsquelle. Natur. Mus. 96(2): 44-49.

Discusses the species of sea turtles found in Colombia (*Dermochelys coriacea, Eretmochelys imbricata, Chelonia mydas*, and *Caretta caretta*—all but the last now being rare) and their utilization as a food source.

KAUFMANN, REINHARD. 1967. Wachstumsraten in Gefangenschaft gehaltener Meeresschildkröten. Mitt. Inst. Colombo-Aleman Invest. Cient. 1: 65-72.

Growth data for 26 loggerheads (up to seven months old), 25 hawksbills (up to five months), and 4 green turtles (up to five months).

KAUFMANN, REINHARD. 1968. Zur Brutbiologie der Meeresschild-kröte *Caretta caretta caretta* L. Mitt. Inst. Colombo-Aleman Invest. Cient. 2: 45-56.

Loggerhead spawns from mid-April to mid-August on beaches east of Santa Marta, Colombia. Description of beaches, population size and its reduction due to turtle trapping, nest building, and nesting behavior. Recommendations given for conservation.

KAUFMANN, REINHARD. 1971. Die Lederschildkroete *Dermochelys coriacea* L. in Kolumbien. Mitt. Inst. Colombo-Aleman Invest. Cient. 5: 87-94.

First report of leatherback nesting on Caribbean coast of Colombia. On beach east of Santa Marta in 1970, seven females, four other nests, and seven emergences observed. Natural history notes compared with loggerhead.

KEATING, BERN. 1961. Comeback of the giant turtle. Saturday Evening Post 10 June 1961: 37-38, 67-68.

Dermochelys.

KLOSS, C. B. 1907. Notes on the capture of a rare leathery turtle, *Dermochelys coriacea*, in Johore waters. J. Strts. Br. Roy Asiat. Soc. Pp. 63-65.

KLUGER, JOSEF. 1931. Methusaleme der Tierwelt. Studien über die optimale Lebensdauer. Josef Kluger: Wünschelburg-Schles.

Discussion of various ages supposedly attained by various animals. Summary concludes that the reptiles, especially turtles, have a great life expectancy. Examples cited.

KNOEPFFLER, L. P. 1962. Une curieuse anomalie de la carapace chez *Caretta caretta caretta* (Linneaus 1758). Vie et milieu 13(2): 327-331.

Carapace length of 42 cm and weight of 15 kilograms. Plate 4 separated from 3 by third costals, and 5 separated from 4 by fourth and fifth costals, which join at median; the fifth vertebral plate has a secondary plate on the left, and the carapace is "hunched." No color or texture modifications of plates. Plastron has four inframarginals.

KOCH, A. L., ARCHIE CARR, and D. W. EHRENFELD. 1969. The problem of open-sea navigation: the migration of the green turtle to Ascension Island. J. Theor. Biol. 22(1): 163-179.

Mechanisms for migration of *Chelonia* 1,400 miles between Brazil and Ascension Island. Visual acuity in green turtles is poor, and therefore they cannot use stars for guidance. Detection of a chemical substance gradient as part of orientation basis evaluated, along with its possible evolution.

KOENIG, D. 1934. Der vordere Augenabschnitt der Schildkröten und die Funktion seiner Muskulatur. Jenaische Zeitschr. Naturwiss. 69(2): 223-284.

A study of turtle eye muscles after the eye has been destroyed.

KRABBE, K. H. 1935. Recherches embryologiques sur les Organes pariétaux chez certain Reptiles. K. Danske Videnskab. Skelek. Biol. Meddelel 12(3): 1-111.

KURATA, Y. 1958. Notes on sea turtles. Ushio, Tokyo 19: 9-10. (In Japanese)

LABATE, MARIO. 1964. Catture di *Dermochelys coriacea* (L.) nelle acque della costa pugliese. Atti. Soc. Peloritana Sic. Fis. Mat. Natur. 10(2): 165-169.

Three captures reported along the coast of Puglio, Italy in July.

LAMPE, E. 1901. Katalog der Reptilien-Sammlung (Schildkröten) des naturhistorischen Museums Wiesbaden. Jahrbücher Nassauischen Vereinsnaturkunde, Johrg. 54: 177-222.

LARSELL, O. 1932. The cerebellum of reptiles: chelonians and alligators. J. Comp. Neurol., Wistar Inst. Phila. 56(2): 299-345.

Embryonic, postembryonic, and adult stages examined in toto and in serial sections. *Chelonia mydas* was one of those studied.

LARSELL, O. 1933. Morphological studies on the cerebellum. 2. In chelonians and alligators. J. Comp. Neurol., Wistar Inst. Phila. 56(2): 127, 3 pls., 103 figs.

LATREILLE, 1801. Hist. Nat. Rept. 1: 22.

Early taxonomic treatment.

LAYCOCK, GEORGE. 1969. America's endangered wildlife. W. W. Norton & Co., Inc., New York. 226 pp.

Chapter on the green turtle.

LAYNE, JAMES N. 1952. Behavior of captive loggerhead turtles, *Caretta caretta caretta* (Linneaus). Copeia 1952(2): 115.

Three turtles (approximately 15 inches carapace length) observed for 2.5 months. Behavior docile; turtles divided their time about equally between swimming and resting.

LEARED, ARTHUR. 1862. Description of new parasite found in the heart of the edible turtle. Quart. J. Micr. Soc. London, n.s. 2: 168-170.

A description of *Distomum constrictum.*

LEARY, TERRANCE R. 1957. A schooling of leatherback turtles, *Dermochelys coriacea coriacea,* on the Texas coast. Copeia 1957(3): 232.

Observed an estimated 100 leatherback turtles along a 30 mile line, approximately 75 yards from the beach, extending north from Port Arkansas, Texas. Associated with the turtles were *Stomolophus meleagris.*

LE BUFF, CHARLES R., JR., 1969. The marine turtles of Sanibel and Captiva islands, Florida. Sanibel-Captiva Conserv. Found. Spec. Publ. No. 1.

LE BUFF, CHARLES R., JR., and RICHARD W. BEATLY. 1971. Some aspects of nesting of the loggerhead turtle, *Caretta caretta caretta* (Linne), on the Gulf coast of Florida. Herpetologica 27(2): 153-156.

First discussion of biology of loggerhead turtles nesting on southwest Florida coast. Behavior similar to Atlantic coast individuals, but small differences occur.

LIEBMAN, P. A., and A. M. GRANDA. 1971. Microspectrophotometric measurements of visual pigments in two species of turtle, *Pseudemys scripta* and *Chelonia mydas.* Vision Res. 11(2): 105-114.

In *Chelonia mydas* P502 was found in rods and P440, P502, and P562 in cones. Findings rule out theory that turtles see with single-detector visual pigment coupled with a number of differently colored discriminator filters. Findings are similar to distribution of visual pigments among freshwater and saltwater fish.

LIMPUS, COLLIN J. 1971. The flatback turtle, *Chelonia depressa* Garman in southeast Queensland, Australia. Herpetologica 27(4): 431-445.

Nesting from October to January; mating at beginning of season; maximum four clutches, two-week intervals, 50 large eggs average; 53-day incubation period; 80 to 90% hatching success. Foxes, dingos, monitor lizards are significant predators.

LINDBLAD, J. 1969. Journey to red birds. Collins, London. 176 pp.

Includes popular account of work on leatherback turtles by Naturalists Club Patrol in Trinidad.

LINDNER, M. J. 1948. The fisheries and fishery resources of Mexico. U.S. Fish Wildlife Ser. No. 212.

Although sea turtles not specifically mentioned, the fishery resources of Mexico discussed in general terms. Luxury items are apparently the only well-exploited fishery (this would presumably include sea turtles).

LINER, ERNEST A. 1954. The herpetology of Lafayette, Terrebonne and the Vermilion parishes, Louisiana. Proc. Louisiana Acad. Sci. 17: 65-85.

> List of species includes *Lepidochelys olivacea kempi*—11 specimens caught in trawls while shrimping in the Gulf of Mexico off Terrebonne coast. Stomach contents: crab shells, *Callinectes* spp., and an occasional barnacle. Eight specimens were immature females; weights given.

LINNE. 1758. Syst. Nat. Ed. 10, Vol. I.

> Early taxonomy.

LINNE. 1766. Syst. Nat. Ed. 12, Vol. I.

> Early taxonomy.

LINTON, EDWIN. 1910. Helminth fauna of the Dry Tortugas, 11: Trematodes. Carnegie Inst. Wash. Pub. 133, Papers Tortugas Lab. 4: 11-98.

> Five species listed from loggerhead turtle. No other sea turtle mentioned.

Lista de tortugas marinas marcadas por la estación de biología pesquera de el Sauzal, B.C. 1966*b*. Bol. Prog. Nac. Marcado Tortugas Mar. 1 (2): 4 pp. (mimeo)

> Marked 20 turtles in Gulf of Baja, California; have not found nesting area. Arrived when turtles were scarce or fishermen had captured them. Turtles marked were 18 *Chelonia mydas agassizii*, 1 *Caretta caretta gigas*, and 1 *Chelonia mydas carrinegra*.

LOENNBERG, ELNAR. 1894. Note on reptiles and batrachians collected in Florida in 1892 and 1893. Proc. U.S. Nat. Mus. 17: 317-339. Pub. 1003.

> Green turtle, hawksbill, and loggerhead mentioned and discussed.

LONG. 1774. History of Jamaica.

> In the eighteenth century the garrisons in Jamaica derived their most important supply of fresh meat from turtles found in abundance around the Cayman Islands.

LOOSS, A. 1899. Weitere Beiträge zur Kenntnis der Trematoden Fauna Aegyptens, zugleich Versuch einer natürlichen Gliederung des Genus Distomum Retzius. Zool. Jahrb., Jena, Abt. f. Syst. 12: 521-784, figs. 1-90.

> Mentioned by Price (1934). Contains references to sea turtle parasites.

LOOSS, A. 1902. Trematoden aus Seeschildkröten. Zool. Jahrb. Syst. 16(30): 411-894.

LOVERIDGE, ARTHUR. 1941. Report on the Smithsonian-Firestone Expedition's collection of reptiles and amphibians from Liberia. Proc. U.S. Nat. Mus. 91: 113-140.

LOVERIDGE, ARTHUR. 1945. Reptiles of the Pacific world (with a foreword by Fairfield Osborn). The Macmillan Co., New York.

> Very complete descriptions of the animals, habits, with keys and bibliography as well as practical methods of catching, etc. Excellent habit, growth, and natural history accounts.

LOVERIDGE, ARTHUR. 1946. New Guinean reptiles and amphibians in the Museum of Comparative Zoology and United States National Museum. Bull. Mus. Comp. Zool. 101(2).

Three usual species plus *Lepidochelys olivacea* (Eschscholtz), plus excellent references and bibliography. Excellent spot locations in Far East.

LOVERIDGE, ARTHUR, and E. WILLIAMS. 1957. Revision of the African tortoises and turtles of the suborder Cryptodira. Bull. Mus. Comp. Zool. 115(6): 163-557.

Key given to marine turtles breeding in Africa: *Dermochelys coriacea, Eretmochelys imbricata, Caretta caretta,* and *Lepidochelys olivacea.* Synonyms listed, descriptions given; range, habitat, size, and weight, breeding season, and enemies discussed.

LOWE, CHARLES H., JR., and KENNETH S. NORRIS. 1955. Measurements and weight of a Pacific leatherback turtle, *Dermochelys coriacea schlegeli,* captured off San Diego, Calif. Copeia 1955(3): 256.

Female, 768 pounds, captured 26 June 1953 near Coronados Islands southwest of San Diego. Other measurements included.

LUBOSCH, W. 1933. Untersuchungen über die Visceralmuskulatur der Sauropsiden. (Untersuchungen über die Kaumuskel der Wirbeltiere 3). Jahrb. Morph. u. Mikrosk. Anat. Abt. 1, Gegenbaurs Morph. Jahrb. 72(4): 584-666.

The origins, insertions, innervations, and homologies of the visceral musculature of various reptiles, including the green sea turtle.

LUCAS, F. A. 1922. Historic tortoise and other aged animals. Nat. Hist. 22: 301-305.

An article in the popular vein telling, among other things, of a tortoise that lived about 150 to 200 years, most of the time in captivity. No species given.

LUCKE, B., and H. SCHLUMBERGER. 1942. Common neoplasms in fish, amphibians and reptiles. J. Tech. Methods Bull. Int. Assoc. Med. Mus. 22: 4-17.

Among other animals listed, the green turtle mentioned as having multiple papillomas of the skin and eye.

LUDICKE, M. 1936. Ueber die Atmung von *Emys orbicularis* L. Zool. Jahrb. Abt. Allg. Zool. u. Physiol. 56(1): 82-106.

The accessory mechanism for obtaining oxygen in turtles discussed fairly thoroughly here. Such items as the increased capillary bed in the tongue, pharynx, and surface described quantitatively. An interesting article on the adaptations of water-living reptiles to oxygen procurement and respiration.

LUDICKE, M. 1940. Die Blutmengen in der Lunge und in der Niere der Schlangen. Zool. Jahrb. Abt. Allg. Zool. u. Physiol. Tiere 59(4): 463-504.

Highly detailed comparative study. *Caretta caretta* mentioned specifically.

LUHMAN, MARION. 1935. Two new trematodes from the loggerhead turtle (*Caretta caretta*). J. Parasitology 21(4): 274-276.

A list of trematodes reported from *C. caretta* in America. New distribution record for *Styphlodora solitaria* and *Pleurogonius trigonocephalus*. *Hapalotrema synorchis* (p. 274) from the heart, and *Pyelosomum lingicaecum* (p. 276) from the intestine of loggerhead from Tortugas, Florida described. Twenty-one species known previously in loggerhead.

LUMSDEN, T. 1923. Observations on the respiration centers. J. Physiol. 57: 354-367.

Tortoises, turtles, alligators, and crocodiles show apneustic characteristics in the mechanisms of their breathing. Breathing in these reptiles much resembles that of a cat whose pneumotaxic center has been removed and in which continuous ventilation prevents the rapid onset of asphyxial conditions.

LUMSDEN, T. 1924. Chelonian respiration (tortoise). J. Physiol. 58: 259-266.

Lumsden states that tortoises resist attempts to chloroform them by refusing to breathe for two to three hours at a stretch. Mechanics of breathing discussed. Parts of the central nervous system concerned with breathing discussed, and roles of various nervous components examined.

LUTHER, G. 1959. On an abnormal egg of the turtle, *Lepidochelys olivacea olivacea* (Eschscholtz) with observations on hatching of the eggs. J. Mar. Biol. Assoc. India 1(2): 261.

Egg dumbbell shaped, 72 mm long. Hatching percentage of a clutch of eggs in two artificial nests was small. Costal scutes of three hatchlings: 6-7, 7-8, 7-7.

LYLES, CHARLES H. 1965. Fishery statistics of the U.S. 1963. U.S. Fish Wildlife Ser., Stat. Dig. No. 57. 522 pp.

LYLES, CHARLES H. 1966. Fishery statistics of the U.S. 1964. U.S. Fish Wildlife Ser., Stat. Dig. No. 58. 541 pp.

LYLES, CHARLES H. 1967. Fishery statistics of the U.S. 1965. U.S. Fish Wildlife Ser., Stat. Dig. No. 59. 756 pp.

LYLES, CHARLES H. 1968. Fishery statistics of the U.S. 1966. U.S. Fish Wildlife Ser., Stat. Dig. No. 60. 679 pp.

LYLES, CHARLES H. 1969. Fishery statistics of the U.S. 1967. U.S. Fish Wildlife Ser., Stat. Dig. No. 61. 490 pp.

McALLISTER, H. J., A. J. BASS, and H. J. van SCHOOR. 1965. Marine turtles on the coast of Tongaland, Natal. I. Lammergeyer 3(2): 12-40.

Description of habitat (location: 27°44' south latitude to 26°50! south latitude), tagging technique, nesting behavior, nesting cycle, and distribution of *Caretta* and *Dermochelys*. Discusses hatchlings and their seaward movement and parasites and predators. Recommendations for conservation included.

MacCALLUM, W. G., and G. A. MacCALLUM. 1918. On the anatomy

of *Ozobranchus branchiatus* (Menzies). Bull. Amer. Mus. Nat. Hist. 38: 395-408.

The leech found by Nigrelli (1943) parasitic upon papillomas of *Chelonia mydas.*

McCANN, CHARLES. 1966a. Key to the marine turtles and snakes occurring in New Zealand. Tuatara 14(2): 73-81.

Records mostly from dead or dying turtles stranded possibly as a result of sudden changes in temperature. Most common on northern shores. Four species listed: *Chelonia mydas, Caretta imbricata, Caretta caretta,* and *Dermochelys coriacea.*

McCANN, CHARLES. 1966b. The marine turtles and snakes occurring in New Zealand. Rec. Dominion Mus. 5: 201-215.

Similar to McCann (1966a). Loggerhead, *Caretta,* listed as having *Lepidochelys* as synonymy.

McCANN, CHARLES. 1969. First southern hemisphere record of the platylepadine barnacle *Stomatolepas elegens* (Costa) and notes on the host *Dermochelys coriacea* (Linne). N.Z.J. Mar. Freshwater Res. 3(1): 152-158.

Host animal was a young leatherback.

McCARTHY, FREDERICK D. 1955. Aboriginal turtle hunters. Australian Mus. Mag. 11: 283-288.

Aborigines hunt turtles today at Palm Island and along northern coast from eastern Cape York to northwestern Australia. Ancient and modern methods of turtling discussed, including turning, harpooning (sometimes with the aid of a remora), and capture by hand. Green, leatherback, and hawksbill are caught. Methods of preparing discussed.

MacCASKIE, I. B., and C. R. FORRESTER. 1962. Pacific leatherback turtles (*Dermochelys*) off the coast of British Columbia. Copeia 1962(3): 646.

Sighting in Sedgwick Bay most northerly to date (water temperature of 58°F). Earlier reports of sightings mentioned.

McEWEN, R. W. 1938. Vertebrate embryology. Henry Holt & Co., New York.

McFARLANE, ROBERT W. 1963. Disorientation of loggerhead hatchlings by artificial road lighting. Copeia 1963(1): 153.

Hatchling loggerheads apparently attracted by road and city lighting, causing movement toward and subsequent death from traffic. Suggested that this destruction occurs frequently on populated shores and may represent a real threat to turtle survival.

McGINNIS, S. M. 1968. Respiration rate and body temperature of the Pacific green turtle *Chelonia mydas agassizii.* Amer. Zool. 8: 766. (Abstract only)

Animal is eurythermal, temperatures were recorded by observation and radio telemetry; the respiration rate is directly proportional to the degree of activity and the body temperature.

McNEILL, FRANK. 1955. Saving the green turtle of the Great Barrier Reef. Australian Mus. Mag. 11: 78-82.

Summary of events leading to law prohibiting the harvesting of green turtles or their eggs in Queensland waters, pending investigation of the turtles' biological status.

MAKINO, SAJIRO. 1952. The chromosomes of the sea turtle, *Chelonia japonica*, with evidence of female heterogamety. Annot. Zool. Japonenses 25(1, 2): 250-257.
Male has diploid number of 56, female has 55. Difference due to sex chromosome.

MANTER, H. W. 1932. Continued studies on trematodes of Tortugas. Carnegie Inst. Wash. Yearbook 31: 287-288.

Marcado de tortugas marinas en el Caribe Mexicano. 1966. Bol. Prog. Nac. Marcado Tortugas Mar. 1(3): 2 pp. (mimeo)
Successful culturing of eggs taken from womb of *Chelonia mydas*. Program was initiated in 1963 and is closely related to the marking program. Ordinance issued to protect eggs of captured female turtles and aid in their cultivation, but an influx of turtle meat from Caribbean countries lowered prices in U.S. and resulting decrease in fishing hindered efforts for cultivation. Data on 10 loggerheads and 1 green turtle marked on Isla Mujeres and Cozumel included.

Marcado de tortugas en el Pacífica Mexicana. 1966. Bol. Prog. Nac. Marcado Tortugas Mar. 1(4): 8 pp. (mimeo)

Marcado de tortugas marinas en las costas de Baja California. 1967. Bol. Prog. Nac. Marcado Tortugas Mar. 1(9): 2 pp. (mimeo)
Lists data on 48 *Lepidochelys olivacea* marked.

MARCELIN, P. 1926. Two marine turtles. Bull. Soc. d'Etude Sci. Nat. Nimes 44: 151-152.
Two recent captures of *Thalassochelys corticata* off the coast of Gard. France: Mediterranean coast.

Marine turtles. *In* Symposium on investigations and resources of the Caribbean Sea and adjacent regions. 1968. Sect. IV: 3 pp.
Sea turtles in the Caribbean threatened to some degree with extinction and represent a neglected and mostly unmanaged source of protein. Five-point plan by Carr on research and restoration of worked stocks of sea turtles: (1) range reconnaissance; (2) exploitation surveys; (3) migration and population studies; (4) international regulation and protection; (5) pilot culture projects.

MARQUEZ, RENE. 1966. La cría artificial de la tortuga blanca (*Chelonia mydas mydas* Linneaus) en Tortuguero, Costa Rica. Inst. Nac. Invest. Biol.-Pesq., Div. Vert. Marin, Mexico: 29 pp.

MARQUEZ, RENE. 1969. Additional records of the Pacific loggerhead turtle, *Caretta caretta gigas*, from the North Mexican Pacific Coast. J. Herpet. 3(12): 108-110.
Reports occurrences of loggerheads (two) in the Gulf of California, in the waters off California (one), and off Baja California (four). Counts and measurements given.

MARQUEZ, RENE, and MARTIN CONTRERAS. 1967. Marcado de Tortuga lora (*Lepidochelys kempi*) en la costa de Tamaulipas, 1967.

Bol. Prog. Nac. Marcado Tortugas Mar. II(1): 8 pp. (mimeo)
During second season of marking in Tamaulipas 271 females marked during the nesting season, 3 May to 18 July 1967. Five important *arribadas*, with the most numerous and prolonged one on the 7th, 8th, and 9th of June. Three turtles found renesting 20 to 24 days later and 1 found 42 days later. Some marked in 1966 noticed. List of marks and accompanying information given.

MARTIN, H. N., and W. A. MOALE. 1895. A handbook of vertebrate dissection. Part 1. How to dissect a Chelonian. The Macmillan Co., New York.

MARTIN, W. E., and J. W. BAMBERGER. 1952. New blood flukes (Trematoda: *Spirorchidae*) from the marine turtle, *Chelonia mydas* (L.). J. Parasitol. 38(2): 105-110.
Haemoxelelon stunkardi and *H. chelonenecon* described. They were found in the mesenteric veins.

MARTINEZ, J. L. 1948. The Cuban fishing industry. U.S. Fish Wildlife Serv., Fish. Leaflet 308.

MARTINEZ T., AGAPITO. 1967. Marcación de tortugas marinas en la costa occidental de la península de Baja California. Bol. Prog. Nac. Marc. Tortugas Mar. 1(7). (mimeo)
Loggerheads scarce from October to March; arrive in April to September. Ridleys most abundant in October to March. Marked 46 ridleys and 1 loggerhead; data on marks given.

MAST, S. O. 1911. Behavior of the loggerhead turtle in depositing its eggs. Papers Tortugas Lab., Carnegie Inst. Wash. 3: 63-67.
Observations of one instance. Laying supposedly 150 eggs first time; less second time; about 80 third time. Out of water 52 minutes.

MASTERS, CHARLES O. 1970. Sea turtles. Ward's Bull. 10(70): 1,5.
Brief popular article on general biology.

MATTHEY, R. 1932. Nouvelle contribution à l'étude des chromosomes chez les sauriens. Bull. Soc. Vaudoise Sci. Nat. 57(231): 587-588.
Existing data prompt the author to conclude that in all but two groups of the Reptilia the chromosome number is 48. This, it is assumed, applies to sea turtles.

MATTOX, NORMAN T. 1936. Annular rings in the long bones of turtles and their correlation with size. Trans. Ill. State Acad. Sci. 28: 225-226.
Chrysemys marginata: Although each ring does not correlate to a definite length of time, in general, the more rings, the older the animal.

MAWSON, N. 1921. Breeding habits of the green turtle *Chelonia mydas*. J. Bombay Nat. Hist. Soc. 27: 956-957.

MAYER, A. G. 1909. Annual Report from the Director of the Department of Marine Biology. Carnegie Inst. Wash. Yearbook 7: 121.
Loggerhead young attracted to blue. Turn from sea if behind yellow, green, or red glass. Tend to crawl downhill. Low intensity of light positive tropism.

MEHRA, H. R. 1932. Nouveaux Monostromes de la Famille des Prono-cephalidae des Tortes d'eau douce de l'Inde. Ann. Parasit. 10: 225-247.

MELLEN, I. 1925. Marine turtles sleep on Hawaiian sands. Zool. Soc. Bull. N.Y. 28. 6: 160.

Basking habit of *Chelonia mydas.*

MERTENS, R., and H. WERMUTH. 1955. Die rezenten Schildkröten, Krokodile und Brückenechsen. Eine Kritische Liste der heute leben-den Arten und Rassen. Zool. Jahrb., Syst. (8315): 323-440.

MERTENS, R., and H. WERMUTH. 1960. Die Amphibien und Rep-tilien Europas. Verlag Waldemar Kramer, Frankfurt am Main. 264 pp.

MINATO, AKIRA, and SUSMO OTOMO. 1969. Studies on the constit-uents of turtle oil: V. Sterol composition of turtle oil. Yakugaku Zasshi 89(8): 1056-1060. (In Japanese)

MITSUKURI, K. 1886. On the formation of the germinal layers in Chelonia. Quart. J. Micr. Sci. 27: 17-48.

MITSUKURI, K. 1892. Further studies on the formation of the germi-nal layers in Chelonia. J. Coll. Sci. Imp. Univ. Japan 5(1): 35-52.

MITSUKURI, K. 1893. On the process of gastrulation in Chelonia. J. Coll. Sci. Imp. Univ. Japan 6(4): 227-277.

MITSUKURI, K. 1904. The cultivation of marine and fresh water ani-mals in Japan. Bull. U.S. Bur. Fish. 24: 259-289.

Snapping turtle, or soft-shell tortoise ("suppon"), *Trionyx japon-icus,* culture methods are described. Some of the techniques may be applicable to sea turtle farming.

MJOBERG, ERIC. 1930. Forest life and adventures in the Malay Ar-chipelago. Translated from the Swedish by Anna Barwell. Georg Allen and Unwein, London.

Egg-laying habits of the green turtle are mentioned.

MONROE, RALPH M. 1897. The green turtle and possibilities of its protection and consequent increase on the Florida coast. Bull. U.S. Fish Comm. 17: 273-275.

Eggs. May to August with 130 to 180 per hatch. Incubation 10 to 12 weeks. Two to three percent survive first week. No apparent decline. Young should be protected.

MONTICELLI, F. S. 1896. Di un ematozoo della *Thallassochelys caret-ta* Linn. Internat. Monatschr. f. Anat. u. Physiol. Leipzig 13: 141-172.

Deals with *Hapalotrema mistroides.*

MONTALBANO, WILLIAM. 1973. The first great turtle roundup. Tropic 7(11): 20-24, 33.

MONTOYA, A. E. 1966. Programa nacional de marcado de tortugas marinas. Inst. Nac. Invest. Biol-Pesq., Mexico: 1-39.

MONTOYA, A. E. 1969. Programas de investigación y conservación de las tortugas marinas en México. *In* Marine turtles. IUCN New Publ. Ser., Suppl. Paper No. 20: 34-53.

List of principle nesting sites, species, and nesting times. Conservation efforts discussed: limited licensing, closed seasons (Gulf of Mexico—1 May to 31 August), national education program. Research, national and international requisites commented on. Maps and charts included.

MONTOYA, A. E., and EMMANUEL VARGAS M. 1968. Marcado de tortuga lora [*Lepidochelys kempi* (Garman)] en la costa de Tamaulipas. Bol. Prog. Nac. Marcado Tortugas Mar. II(2): 10 pp. (mimeo)

From 29 April to 22 June marked 323 nesting ridleys on a 17 kilometer stretch of beach from Barra de Tordo to Barra San Vicente. Nine turtles found returning a _cond time to nest and are listed. Intervals between nesting ranged from 1 to 46 days. Nine turtles marked in two previous seasons (6,3) were also sighted.

MOORHOUSE, F. W. 1933. Notes on the green turtle (*Chelonia mydas*). Repts. Great Barrier Reef Comm. 4(1): 1-22.

At Heron Island, near the southern extremity of the Great Barrier Reef of Queensland, 50 adult female green turtles that came to the island to lay during the breeding season November to February of 1929 to 1930 were marked by attaching a numbered label to one or the other of the pygal plates. These animals returned several times at (approximately) fortnightly intervals. Maximum times: seven. Average number of eggs: 120. Incubation period: 9.5 to 10.5 weeks. Percent of hatch per nest varied from 0 to 86. Young turtles that are very carnivorous when young can be kept successfully in aquaria. Loggerhead incubation period is similar to green turtle. This treatise contains much factual information and should be considered required reading for anyone interested in sea turtles. Life histories, growth, behavior, notes on production in various parts of the world, and other important aspects are well presented.

MOREJOHN, G. V. 1969. Occurrence of a Pacific ridley and a young fur seal in Monterey Bay. Calif. Fish Game 55(3): 239-242.

Observed and photographed *Lepidochelys olivacea* 8 November 1967.

MORTENSEN, T. 1907. Om. Fiskeriene par vore vestindiske Oer. Atlanten 43: 139-142. Copenhagen.

This article is referred to in Schmidt's turtle marking paper. Mentions that turtle fishery is on decline. He also brings out the fact that measures should be taken to inject life into the industry.

MOULTON, J. M. 1963. The recapture of a marked leatherback turtle in Casco Bay, Maine. Copeia 1963(2): 434-435.

Sightings of leatherbacks in Casco Bay in August 1962 occurred several times within two weeks. One was harpooned, released, and later recaptured.

MOWBRAY, LOUIS S., and DAVID K. CALDWELL. 1958. First record of the ridley turtle from Bermuda, with notes on other sea turtles and the turtle fishery in the islands. Copeia 1958(2): 147-148.

A 15 pound ridley captured near Warwick, Bermuda in 1949. The same turtle weighed 40 pounds eight years later. Fewer than 100 turtles taken by fishermen each year. Most are green, some are hawksbills. Loggerheads seen frequently and leatherbacks seen occasionally, although neither are fished for. Majority of greens taken weigh 40 to 60 pounds, but some 125 to 140 pounds. Authors suggest that greens comprise an itinerant population of juveniles carried to Bermuda by the Gulf Stream.

MROSOVSKY, NICHOLAS. 1967. How turtles find the sea. Science J. 3(11): 52-57.

Popular review of orientation research by Mrosovsky and Carr (1967), Ehrenfeld and Carr (1967), Carr and Ogren (1960), and others.

MROSOVSKY, NICHOLAS. 1968. Nocturnal emergence of hatchling sea turtles: control by thermal inhibition of activity. Nature 220(5174): 1338-1339.

Tests with temperature-adapted green turtle hatchlings and temperature measurements show that photic activity is inhibited above 28.5°C and that this inhibition would usually hold the turtles in the nest until darkness at Bigi Santi Beach, Surinam, and in other parts of the world.

MROSOVSKY, NICHOLAS. 1970. The influence of the sun's position and elevated cues on the orientation of hatchling sea turtles. Anim. Behav. 18(4): 648-651.

Chelonia mydas and *Eretmochelys imbricata* hatchlings reacted to sun position by deviation from shortest route to water. Tests included cutting off cues from close to horizon and reestablishing artificial cues. Results suggest almost any visual stimulus has some effect on the relatively uncomplicated tropotactic reaction.

MROSOVSKY, NICHOLAS, and ARCHIE CARR. 1967. Preference for light of short wavelengths in hatchling green turtles, *Chelonia mydas,* tested on their natural nesting beaches. Behavior 28(314): 217-231.

Hatchlings showed preference for blue and green stimuli over red when given a choice. Showed a preference for light of greater intensity. Blue and green stimuli more effective than red in distracting turtles on their way to the sea. Results discussed in relation to visual mechanisms in turtles.

MROSOVSKY, NICHOLAS, and P. C. H. PRITCHARD. 1971. Body temperatures of *Dermochelys coriacea* and other sea turtles. Copeia 1971(4): 624-631.

Temperatures of female leatherbacks, greens, and loggerheads determined by taking temperature of eggs at laying, at three different sites in Guianas in 1968 and 1970. Temperatures of leatherbacks, greens, and ridleys were each significantly higher than the sea and each species significantly higher than preceding ones. Authors conclude leatherbacks normally average 3.0°C above ambient; the difference in temperature between species may be related to rates of occurrence in northern waters.

MROSOVSKY, NICHOLAS, and SARA J. SHETTLEWORTH. 1968. Wavelength preferences and brightness cues in the water finding behaviour of sea turtles. Behaviour 32(4): 211-257.

    1. Hatchlings preferred blue or yellow over red, but this preference could be reversed by red light of sufficiently high intensity.

    2. Weather conditions or large visual obstructions affected orientation.

    3. Reaction to photic stimuli became weak in animals taken from environments above about 24°C.

MULVILLE, DAN. 1960. Trade winds and turtles. Putnam & Company Ltd., London. 248 pp.

    Travels of 40-foot sailing vessel from Canary Islands to Antigua and then around Caribbean. Trip to Aves Island for rescue, salvage, and turtling included.

MURPHY, R. C. 1914. *Thallassochelys caretta* in the South Atlantic. Copeia No. 2.

    During November, 1912, the writer observed numbers of loggerhead turtles in the South Atlantic Ocean between the latitudes of 32°54' S and 37° S, and the longitudes of 42°15' W and 46° 29' W. The area included within these limits lies 400 to 500 miles east of the coast of Uruguay. The specific dates and notes are as follows:

    "Nov. 3. Two loggerheads, with carapaces fully a meter in length noted separately.

    Nov. 4. Three seen, of which one was harpooned and captured. Its carapace was grown over with algae and its stomach contained Chondrophoridae (Velella). A Cape Verde sailor who was suffering from rheumatism drank a cup of the blood of the turtle as medicine.

    Nov. 8. Rough weather. Many loggerheads seen throughout the day. One was observed swimming or floundering on its back, raising one pectoral flipper above the surface of the water as it paddled.

    Nov. 9. One seen. This loggerhead lay idly at the surface until it was grazed by the ship. Beneath its plastron was a veritable cloud of small fishes which kept their position when the turtle darted away."

MURPHY, WILLIAM S., et al. 1934. Studies on barbiturates. IV. Effect of barbiturates in experimental nephrosis. J. Pharmacol. Exp. Therap. 52(1): 70-77.

    The effect of barbiturates, with or without accompanying drugs, is reported. Animals used included mammals, turtles, fowls, etc.

MUSGRAVE, A., and G. P. WHITLEY. 1926. From sea to soup. An account of the turtles of Northwest Islet. Austr. Mus. Mag. 2(10): 331-336, 11 figs.

    Detailed account of egg-laying habits of *Chelonia mydas*. Egg laying November to January. According to this article, turtles of all three species apparently are present.

NEILL, WILFRED T. 1957. Objections to wholesale revision of type localities. Copeia 1957(2): 140-141.
Objections include some for marine turtles.

NEILL, WILFRED T. 1958. The occurrence of amphibians and reptiles in saltwater areas, and a bibliography. Bull. Mar. Sci. Gulf. Car. 8(1): 1-97.
Good review, marine turtles included.

NEWMAN, N. H. 1905. The significance of scute and plate "abnormalities" in Chelonia. (A contribution to the evolutionary history of the Chelonian carapace and plastron). Biol. Bull. 10: 68-114.

NICK, L. 1912. Das Kopfskelett von *Dermochelys coriacea* L. Zool. Jahrb. Abt. f. Anat. 33: 1-238.

NIGRELLI, R. F. 1940. Observations on trematodes of the marine turtle, *Chelonia mydas*. Anat. Rec. 78(4) Suppl. 178.

NIGRELLI, R. F. 1941. Parasites of the green turtle, *Chelonia mydas* L., with special reference to the rediscovery of trematodes described by Loos from this host species. J. Parasitology, 26(6) Suppl.
An abstract.

NIGRELLI, R. F. 1942. Leeches (*Ozobranchus branchiatus*) on fibro-epithelial tumors of marine turtles (*Chelonia mydas*). Anat. Rec. 84(4): 539-540.
Leeches found attached to papillomata and fibromata of green turtle. Etiology of tumors unknown. Worms might act as vectors for viral or other parasitic forms capable of inducing neoplasms. Leeches secrete hirudin, which might be a factor.

NIGRELLI, R. F., and G. M. SMITH. 1943. The occurrence of leeches, *Ozobranchus branchiatus* Menzies, on fibro-epithelial tumors of marine turtles, *Chelonia Mydas* L. Zoologica (New York) 28(2): 107-108.
The role of hirudin secreted by the leeches is discussed in connection with the growth of fibro-epithelial tumors of the turtles. It is not known if the leeches instigate the tumors directly or indirectly by being vectors of an organism capable of stimulating the neoplasms. In fact, the leeches may just be opportunists laying their eggs in already well-developed papillomas. Good bibliography.

NILSSON-CANTELL, C. A. 1930. Diagnosis of some new Cirripedes from the Netherlands Indies collected by the expedition of His Royal Highness the Prince Leopold of Belgium in 1929. Bull. Mus. Roy. Hist. Nat. Belgique 6(4): 1-2.
Stomatolepas transversa, a barnacle (n. sp.) was found on five *Chelonia mydas* in the Aroe Archepelago (Dutch Indies).

NILSSON-CANTELL, C. A. 1932. The barnacles *Stephanolepas* and *Chelonibia* from the turtle *Eretmochelys*. Ceylon J. Sci. (B) 16: 257-263.
Stephanolepas bores into *Eretmochelys*.

NISHIMURA, S. 1960. Visits by unusual aquatic animals to the sea coasts of Niigata prefecture, Japan Sea, in the winter of 1959-60. Saisho to Shiiku 22: 213-216.

NISHIMURA, S. 1964a. Considerations on the migrations of the leatherback turtle, *Dermochelys coriacea* (L.) in the Japanese and adjacent waters. Publ. Seto Mar. Biol. Lab. 12(2): 177-189.

Considerable number of records of occurrences in Japanese waters may be due to offshore habits of turtle. Fifty-six occurrences listed by month and geographical area. Distribution cannot be explained by seasonal variation of water temperature. Suggested that the Kuroshio and the Tsushima Strait currents transport these animals into the Japanese waters. Two hypotheses of migrations discussed pertaining to offshore stream of warm current and drift currents generated by monsoon winds.

NISHIMURA, S. 1964b. Records of occurrence of the leatherback turtle in adjacent waters to Japan. Seiri Seita 12: 286-290. (In Japanese)

Seventy-two records listed covering the period from the early seventeenth century to March 1963. Turtles captured along Japan seacoast of Honshu almost exclusively during the cold stormy winter season in contrast to warm season occurrence of the animals on the coasts of Hokkaido and Pacific Honshu.

NISHIMURA, S. 1967a. Records of the hawksbill turtle, *Eretmochelys imbricata* (Linne), in the Japan Sea. Pub. Seto Mar. Biol. Lab. 15(4): 297-302.

Hawksbill is an occasional visitor to Japanese waters; 39 records listed with date, locality, size, source, and remarks. Most are young or immature individuals less than 45 cm carapace length. In the warm season (June to October) records are concentrated in the westernmost district of Honshu or the west coast of Hokkaido. In the cold season (November to March) records are from districts between the two extremities.

NISHIMURA, S. 1967b. The loggerhead turtles in Japan and neighboring waters (*Testudinata: Cheloniidae*). Publ. Seto Mar. Biol. Lab. 15(1): 19-35.

Turtles thought to be one species, *Caretta caretta gigas,* until 1963 when some turtles were ascertained to be *Lepidochelys olivacea.* Discussion of breeding locations and distribution of *Caretta* in Japan, with counts and measurements given on 78 specimens. Worldwide distribution of *Caretta* is an example of antitropical distribution; *Lepidochelys* common in tropical and subtropical waters and distribution fades toward temperate regions.

NISHIMURA, S., and K. HARA. 1967. The status of sea turtles of the genera *Caretta* and *Lepidochelys* in Japanese waters (*Testudinata: Cheloniidae*). Acta. Herpet. Japan 2: 21-35. (In Japanese)

NOBLE, GLEN A., and ELMER R. NOBLE. 1940. A brief anatomy of the turtle. Stanford University Press, Stanford, California.

Although intended primarily as a laboratory guide, this little book is very complete and instructive. There are many excellent drawings and a good bibliography. There also appears a summary of the embryology of the turtle that was originally put down by Agassiz (1857).

NOPCSA, F. 1923a. Reversible and irreversible evolution in Reptiles. Proc. Zool. Soc. London, Part 2.

NOPCSA, F. 1923b. Die Familien der Reptilien. Berlin.

NOPCSA, F. 1928. Genera of Reptiles. Palaeobiologica.

NOPCSA, F. Heredity and evolution. Proc. Zool. Soc. London: 633-665.

NYE, WILLARD, JR. 1886. Fish and fishing at Abaco Island. U.S. Fish Comm. Bull. 6: 125-126.

O'DONOGHUE, C. H. 1918. The heart of the leathery turtle. J. Anat. 52.

OLIVEIRA, JEJEUNE P. H. 1951. De nota previa sobre a fauna e flora marinha bentonica da Ilha de Trinidade. Mem. Inst. Oswaldo Cruz 49: 443-456.

    Notes presence of many loggerheads on dry shore.

OLIVER, JAMES A. 1946. An aggregation of Pacific sea turtles. Copeia 2: 103.

    A large number of *Lepidochelys olivacea* were encountered 50 miles off the west coast of Mexico in November 1945. Description of the aggregation and the methods used to collect specimens.

OLIVER, JAMES A., and CHARLES E. SHAW. 1953. The amphibians and reptiles of the Hawaiian Islands. Zoologica 38(4): 65-95.

    Marine turtles listed: *Chelonia japonica, Eretmochelys imbricata squamata,* and *Dermochelys coriacea shlegeli.* Western Pacific green most common, hawksbill next; it is of little commercial importance since the decline of the tortoiseshell industry. The leatherback is not common.

OWEN, R. 1849. On the development and homologies of the carapace and the plastron of the Chelonian reptiles. Phil. Trans. Roy. Soc. London 139: 151-171.

PARKER, G. H. 1901. Correlated abnormalities in the scutes and bony plates of the carapace of the sculptured tortoises. Amer. Nat. 35: 17-24.

PARKER, G. H. 1922. The crawling of young loggerhead turtles toward the sea. J. Exp. Zool. 36: 323-331.

    Three factors operate: geotropism, retinal images, and color. Turtles react to all three in getting into the sea. Work done at Miami, Florida.

PARKER, G. H. 1925. The time of submergence necessary to drown alligators and turtles. Occas. Papers, Boston Soc. Nat. Hist. 5: 157-159.

    Forty to sixty minutes for loggerheads. Recorded elsewhere—10 hours for turtles. Very active Kemp's died in 1.5 hours. Highly vascular anal and oral regions of turtles helps them to maintain life by exchange of gases with surrounding water.

PARKER, G. H. 1926. The growth of turtles. Proc. Nat. Acad. Sci. 12(7): 422-424.

    Although turtles grow more rapidly than thought previously, their growth varies a great deal. *Caretta* at hatching weighed 20 grams.

At 4.75 months: 800 grams. At three years: 19 kilograms. Time to reach maximum growth of 500 pounds is not known.

PARKER, G. H. 1928. The direction of the ciliary currents in the oviducts of vertebrates. Amer. J. Physiol. 87(1): 93-96.

There are two systems of cilia in the oviduct of the painted turtles *Chrysemys*. One beats away from the ovaries and the other beats toward them. The latter, it is assumed, is for the purpose of helping the sperm up the duct.

PARKER, G. H. 1929. The growth of the loggerhead turtle. Amer. Nat. 63(687): 367-373.

Loggerhead: 20 grams on hatching. Carapace: 4.8 cm. Individual at Key West, then 4.5 years, weighed 37 kilograms, or a little over 25% of the average adult weight. Carapace on this one: 63 cm by 50 cm. Rate of growth several times that of other turtles kept under almost similar conditions. Even lower rates indicate more rapid growth of turtles than was previously supposed.

PARKER, W. K. 1880. Report on the development of the green turtle. Report of the scientific results of the voyage of H. M. S. Challenger during 1873-1876, Vol. I. The Macmillan Co., New York.

PARRISH, FRED K. 1958. Miscellaneous observations on the behavior of captive sea turtles. Bull. Mar. Sci. Gulf Carib. 8(4): 348-355.

Behavior of 27 green, loggerhead, hawksbill, and ridley turtles observed for 4.5 months at Marineland, Florida. Temperament, feeding behavior, diet, scratching, respiration, territoriality, resting, and sleeping discussed.

PARSCHIN, A. N. 1929. Bedingte Reflexe bei Schildkröten. (Conditioned reflexes of the turtle.) Pfluger's Arch. Ges. Physiol. 222(3): 328-333.

In view of experiments performed here, Parschin believes that turtles have color vision, but he offers no proof.

PARSONS, JAMES J. 1962. The green turtle and man. Univ. of Florida Press, Gainesville.

Impressive monograph of the green turtle and its relation to man.

PARSONS, THOMAS S. 1958. The choanal papillae of the Cheloniidae. Breviora Mus. Comp. Zool. 85: 1-5.

Gross anatomy and histological structure of choanal papillae described. Papillae appear to prevent the contents of the mouth from entering the nasal cavities.

PARSONS, THOMAS S. 1968. Variation in the choanal structure of recent turtles. Can J. Zool. 46(6): 1235-1263.

Choanal regions of all living genera and almost all living forms described. Unlike other families, Cheloniidae and Dermocheliidae do not have ridges and flaps along the lateral margins of choanae. Dermochelyids have no species structures along the lateral choanal margins; Cheloniids have papillae. Possible taxonomic and phylogenetic implications of findings discussed.

PATHAK, S. P., and L. M. DEY. 1956. The fatty acid composition of Indian turtle fat. Biochem. J. 62(3): 448-451.

A sample of body fat from hawksbill from Bay of Bengal showed significant differences in the proportions of saturated and unsaturated acids compared to amphibian animal fats; high content of unsaturated acids is typical of marine animal fats.

PAX, FERDINAND, and WALTHER ARNDT. 1930. Die Rohstoffe des Tierreichs. 2. Gebrüder Bornträger, Berlin.

The raw materials of the animal kingdom are discussed. Oil from sea turtles and tortoiseshell mentioned.

PEARSE, A. S. 1923. The abundance and migration of turtles. Ecology 4: 24-28.

Land and freshwater species. Tagging experiments. Not of value to present objectives.

PEARSE, A. S. 1949. Observations on flatworms and nemerteans collected at Beaufort, N.C. Proc. U.S. Natl. Mus. 100(3255): 25-38.

Bicornuata, Gorgoderidae, type *B. caretta,* new species, described from *Caretta caretta.*

PEARSE, A. S., S. LEPKOVSKY, and LAURA HINTZE. 1925. The growth and chemical composition of three species of turtles fed on rations of pure foods. J. Morph. Physiol. 41: 191-216.

An excellent study. The experiments indicate that in regard to the value of foods as a basis for nutrition and growth there is no essential difference between poikilothermal and homoiothermal animals.

PENYAPOL, COMMDR. AMPORN. 1958. A preliminary study of the sea turtles in the Gulf of Thailand. Siam Soc. Nat. Hist. Bull. 17: 23-36.

Study of green and hawksbill turtles at KoKram and Kokru 1956-57. Contains breeding, embryological development, and food value. Breeding season year round, as in Sarawak, with certain peak times.

PETERS, JAMES A. 1954. The amphibians and reptiles of the coast and coastal sierra of Michoacán, Mexico. Occ. Pap. Mus. Zool. 554: 1-37.

Chelonia mydas is only sea turtle listed; observed nesting in Maruata in August of 1950 and July of 1951.

PETERS, JAMES A. 1957. The eggs (turtle) and I. The Biologist 39: 21-24.

Popular account of green turtle nesting in Bay of Maruata, August 1950: 127 eggs laid, 1 5/8 to 1 3/4 inches in diameter.

PETERS, JAMES A. 1960. Notes on the faunistics of southwestern and coastal Michoacán, with lists of reptilia and amphibia collected in 1950 and 1951. *In* Donald D. Brand et al., Coalcoman and Motines del Oro. Publ. for Institute of Latin Amer. Stud., Univ. Texas. The Hague: Martinus Nijhoff: 319-335.

Discussion of biotic position of region, history of zoological exploration, and analysis of fauna and its relationships. *Chelonia mydas* only sea turtle mentioned.

PETERS, W. C. H. 1838. Observationes ad anatomiam Cheloniarum. Berolini. (pls.).

PHISALIX. 1934. Action du venin d'abeilles sur les reptiles et leur

résistance à ce venin. Bull. Mus. Nat. Hist. Paris 6(2): 166-170.
Reptiles and especially turtles were seemingly more immune to bee stings than mammals and birds tested. Sting more virulent than injections of ground glands containing venom.

PINNER, ERNA. 1967. Orientierungs-und Navigationsprobleme der Karibischen Suppenschildkröte. Naturwiss. Rundsch. 20(12): 530-531.
Orientation and navigation problems of the green turtle in the Caribbean.

POGLAYEN-NEUWALL, IVO. 1953a. Untersuchen der Kiefermuskulatur und deren Innervation bei Schildkröten. Acta. Zool. (Stockholm) 34(33, 4): 241-249.
Pterygoid muscles lacking, studies of trigeminus muscles confirm results of earlier investigators. Presence of inframandibular muscle demonstrated. Diagram of branching of trigeminus nerve of *Chelonia*.

POGLAYEN-NEUWALL, IVO. 1953b. Die Besonderheiten der Kiefermuskulatur von *Dermochelys coriacea*. Anat. Anz. 100(1, 4): 22-31.
Trigeminus musculature and nerve distribution essentially like that of the Cheloniidae. No remnant of embryonic $C_1 d$ muscle in adult, contrary to previous observations.

POPE, C. H. 1935. the reptiles of China. Nat. Hist. Cent. Asia, Amer, Mus. Nat. Hist. 10:lii, 604 pp., map, 27 pls., 78 figs.

POPE, C. H. 1939. Turtles of the U.S. and Canada. Alfred A. Knopf, New York.
All turtles discussed and described, and many photographs. Extensive bibliography. Habits and habitats are treated. Popular in style, but accurate and comprehensive.

POWER, E. A. 1958. Fishery statistics of the U.S. 1956. U.S. Fish Wildlife Serv., Stat. Dig. No. 43. 476 pp.

POWER, E. A. 1959. Fishery statistics of the U.S. 1957. U.S. Fish Wildlife Serv., Stat. Dig. No. 44. 429 pp.

POWER, E. A. 1960. Fishery statistics of the U.S. 1958. U.S. Fish Wildlife Serv., Stat. Dig. No. 49. 424 pp.

POWER, E. A. 1961. Fishery statistics of the U.S. 1959. U.S. Fish Wildlife Serv., Stat. Dig. No. 51. 457 pp.

POWER, E. A. 1962. Fishery statistics of the U.S. 1960. U.S. Fish Wildlife Serv., Stat. Dig. No. 53. 529 pp.

POWER, E. A. 1963. Fishery statistics of the U.S. 1961. U.S. Fish Wildlife Serv., Stat. Dig. No. 54. 460 pp.

POWER, E. A., and C. H. LYLES. 1964. Fishery statistics of the U.S. 1962. U.S. Fish Wildlife Serv., Stat. Dig. No. 56. 466 pp.

PRATT, H. S. 1914. Trematodes of the loggerhead turtle of the Gulf of Mexico. Arch. Parasit. 16: 411-427.

PRICE, EMMETT W. 1934. New genera and species of blood flukes from a marine turtle, with a key to the genera of the family Spirorchidae. J. Wash. Acad. Sci. 24(3): 132-141.
This article is especially good for work on sea turtles since the

animal used was *Chelonia mydas*. Included is a dissertation on the classification of sea turtle flukes, especially the family Spirorchidae.

PRICE, EMMETT W. 1939. A new genus and two new species of digenetic trematodes from a marine turtle. Proc. Helminthol. Soc. Wash. 6(1): 24-25.

> *Rhytidodoides intestinalis* and *R. similis*. Both are from *Chelonia mydas*.

PRITCHARD, P. C. H. 1964. Turtles of British Guiana. J. Brit. Guiana Mus. 39: 19-45.

PRITCHARD, P. C. H. 1966a. Sea turtles of Shell Beach, British Guiana. Copeia 1966(1): 123-125.

> Nesting by sea turtles occurs on a number of beaches, Shell Beach in northwest British Guiana (now Guyana) is the site of the author's report. Shells, bones, and skulls found for olive ridley, hawksbill, green, and leatherback, but no nesting observed. Estimated that largest number of nesting turtles are ridleys. Measurements and counts on 14 ridley shells and four hatchlings. Three ridley egg clutches of 186, 159, and 156 eggs. One green turtle observed to nest.

PRITCHARD, P. C. H. 1966b. Occurrence of mesoplastra in a Cryptodiran turtle, *Lepidochelys olivacea*. Nature 210(5036): 652.

> Plastron found on Shell Beach, British Guiana. *Lepidochelys* is most primitive Cheloniidae, mesoplastra may be true homology with the mesoplastra of primitive turtles; however, author suggests that more likely the specimen merely shows a casual division of embryonic ossification centers.

PRITCHARD, P. C. H. 1967. To find the ridley. Int. Turt. Tort. Soc. J. 1(4): 30-35, 48.

PRITCHARD, P. C. H. 1969a. Summary of world sea turtle survival situation. IUCN Bull. 2(11): 90-91.

> Summary of Working Meeting of Marine Turtle Specialists held at Morges, Switzerland, 10-13 March 1969, sponsored by IUCN. Five of the seven species are probably declining. Exceptions are two well-protected and localized species, *Lepidochelys kempii* and *Chelonia depressa*. Includes national situations and requirements and international conservation and research requirements.

PRITCHARD, P. C. H. 1969b. Report on sea turtle survival situation in the Guianas. *In* Marine turtles. IUCN New Publ. Ser. Suppl. Paper No. 20: 17-18.

> Shell Beach, Guyana is heavily harvested; it is especially important hawksbill nesting site. In French Guiana the situation is not as serious; Silebach Beach contains possibly the largest breeding population of leatherbacks in the hemisphere.

PRITCHARD, P. C. H. 1969c. The survival status of ridley sea turtles in American waters. Biol. Conserv. 2(1): 13-17.

PRITCHARD, P. C. H. 1969d. Sea turtles of the Guianas. Bull. Fla. St. Mus., Biol. Sci. 13(2): 85-140.

Summarizes investigations of turtle nesting beaches in Guyana, Surinam, and French Guiana. Data given on nesting by *Chelonia mydas*, *Eretmochelys imbricata*, *Dermochelys coriacea*, and *Lepidochelys olivacea*, including size, weight, incubation times, and nesting periodicity. Survival and conservation of sea turtles in South America are discussed.

PRITCHARD, P. C. H. 1971. The leatherback or leathery turtle *Dermochelys coriacea*. IUCN Monograph No. 1, Morges, Switzerland: 39 pp.

Authorative, succinct monograph on the leatherback turtle. Compiles published and unpublished data on all aspects of leatherback biology. Recommended.

PRITCHARD, P. C. H., and W. G. GREENHOOD. 1968. The sun and the turtle. Int. Turt. Tort. Soc. J. 2: 20-25, 34.

PROCTER, J. B. 1922. A study of the remarkable tortoise, *Testudo loveridgii* Blgr., and the morphogeny of the chelonian carapace. Proc. Zool. Soc. London 34(3): 483-526.

The author concludes after a detailed embryological study that fenestration in this and other species is caused by arrested development and not, as previously supposed, by absorption with age. Proctor feels that the neurals and costals are of dermal origin and gives evidence supporting this view. An excellent bibliography is provided.

PUFAHL, H. 1915. Methods of working up horn, tortoise shell and other wastes. (German) Kunstoffe 5: 174-175, 197-201.

Pufahl provided a very good summary of methods and procedures to be followed by anyone interested in the manufacturing aspect of tortoiseshell.

RADOVICH, JOHN. 1961. Relationships of some marine organisms of the northeast Pacific to water temperatures, particularly during 1957 through 1959. Calif. Fish Game, Fish Bull. 112: 1-62.

Green turtle caught off southern California. Sightings of turtles (presumably greens) off central California and as far north as Nootka Sound, British Columbia. Leatherbacks also seen and captured. Frequency of turtle sightings and captures may be related to the warm water temperature.

RAGOTZKIE, ROBERT A. 1959. Mortality of loggerhead turtle eggs from excessive rainfall. Ecology 40(2): 303-305.

Sapelo Island, Georgia, 1955-57: only 2 of 17 marked nests produced hatchlings. Heavy September rains flooded nests and killed late-developing embryos. Nesting season from mid-May to mid-July. Author concludes that eggs laid after 1 July have poor chance of survival owing to heavy September rains.

RATHKE, H. 1846a. Sur le développement des Chéloniens. Ann. Sci. Nat. Paris Zool. Ser. 3, tome 5, pp. 161-170.

RATHKE, H. 1846b. Ueber die Luftröhre, die Speiseröhre und den Magen der *Spargis coriacea*. Archiv f. Anat. u Physiol.

RATHKE, H. 1848. Ueber die Entwickelung der Schildröten. Braunschweig, pp. 1-268 (10 pls.).

RAVEN, H. C. 1946. Predators eating turtle eggs in the East Indies. Copeia 1: 48.

The eggs of the sea turtle (*Chelonia mydas*) are eaten by both mammals (*Sus barbatus*) and reptiles (*Varanus* sp.) on the coast and offshore islands of eastern Dutch Borneo.

RAY, CARLTON, and W. COATES. 1958. Record and measurements of a leatherback turtle from the Gulf of Maine. Copeia 1958(3): 220-221.

Leatherback tangled in a lobster pot line on 10 August 1957 a few yards offshore of island of Vinalhaven; 635 pounds and 209 cm carapace length (other measurements included). Turtle kept at the New York Aquarium for two days; death caused by rough handling, which resulted in severe hemorrhaging of both lungs. Flesh from the pectoral region was frozen and eaten on 18 October 1957. Reported to taste like sirloin, "but with a touch of the gaminess of venison."

REED, CLYDE F. 1957. Contributions to the herpetofauna of Virginia, 2: The reptiles and amphibians of Northern Neck. J. Wash. Acad. Sci. 47(1): 21-23.

Sea Turtles listed are the loggerhead, ridley, and leatherback. A leatherback, largest sea turtle ever collected in the Chesapeake Bay, illustrated.

REED, CLYDE F. 1958. Contributions to the herpetofauna of Maryland and Delmarva, No. 17: Southeastern herptiles with northern limits on coastal Maryland, Delmarva, and New Jersey. J. Wash. Acad. Sci. 48(1): 28-32.

Four species of sea turtles listed as incidental to the area: *Caretta caretta caretta, Chelonia mydas, Dermochelys coriacea,* and *Lepidochelys (olivacea) kempii.*

REINHARDT, J., and C. F. LUTKEN. 1862. Bidrag til det vest indiske Origes og naunligen til de dansk-vestindiske Oers Herpetologie. Videnskabelige Meddelelser fra den naturhistoriske Forening i København for Aaret 1862, pp. 284-290.

No positive proof that loggerheads breed in Danish West Indies. A remarkable capture of leatherneck turtles off Bajo Reef, near Nootka Sound, west coast of Vancouver Island, B.C., 1931, 1932. Rept. Prov. Mus. Nat. Hist. (Victoria, B.C.).

Two specimens of *Dermochelys schlegelii* taken in 1931 constitute the northernmost record for the species on the Pacific coast of America.

REMLINGER, P., and J. BAILY. 1931. Sur la longue persistance (302 jours) du virus rabique dans l'encéphale de la tortue. Compt. Rend. Soc. Biol. 108(30): 446-468.

Two strains of rabies virus injected intracererally into tortoises (*Testudo mauritanica*). When taken out and injected into animals after varied intervals, the virus was still capable of producing the disease. However, the turtles did not seem to suffer ill effects. Authors maintain that the long persistence of the virus is due to the existence of nonpathogenic phase in the life cycle of the rabies organism.

Report on Kenya Fisheries 1957. 1958. Government Printer, Nairobi. 16 pp.

Regulations to be imposed in 1958: no taking of laying turtles; reporting of catch (size, sex, number). Number of turtles caught in 1957 unknown.

Report on Kenya Fisheries 1958. 1959. Government Printer, Nairobi. 18 pp.

Turtle fishermen must have licenses. Twenty-three skippers licensed on the basis of previous fishing using remoras. 11 dealers licensed.

Report on Kenya Fisheries 1959. 1960. Government Printer, Nairobi. 25 pp.

Exported 225,000 pounds of green turtles (33,000 shilling value) from Lamu District.

Report on Kenya Fisheries 1960. 1961. Government Printer, Nairobi. 27 pp.

Exported 11,420 pounds (1,520 shilling value) of green turtles from Lamu District.

Only 166 turtles were caught (138 exported) compared with 416 of previous year.

Report on Kenya Fisheries 1961. 1962. Government Printer, Nairobi. 24 pp.

Exported 176 turtles, 220 green turtles taken, 8 licensed skippers, and 9 dealers. Capture prohibited on beaches or in sea within 500 yards of high water mark. Turtles taken from area of Bapun Islands are caught with sucker fish.

Report on Kenya Fisheries 1962. 1963. Government Printer, Nairobi. 31 pp.

Estimated 128 turtles exported to Europe in 1962; about 100 fishermen. It is suspected that a large number of turtles are caught and killed illegally and eaten by the local population. Additional short comments on fishing methods and marketing.

Report on Kenya Fisheries 1963. 1964. Government Printer, Nairobi. 33 pp.

8 licenses, 128 turtles (32,000 pounds) caught. Exported to Europe 25,853 pounds frozen turtle and 2,934 pounds of turtle oil.

Report on Kenya Fisheries 1964. 1966. Government Printer, Nairobi. 30 pp.

Forty-six turtles caught. Fishery is economically of small importance. No export.

Report on Kenya Fisheries 1965. 1967. Government Printer, Nairobi. 43 pp.

Sixty-three turtles taken. No export of green turtles, which have become increasingly rare and hard to catch.

RICHARD, C., and NGUYEN-THI-LAU. 1961. Les oeufs de tortue de mer (*Chelonia mydas*) aliment traditionnel vietnamien. Composition chimique et valeur alimentaire. Rev. Elevage et Méd. Vét. Pays Trop. 14(3): 329-35.

Average weight of green turtle egg: 30.8 g. Composition: 8.75 g (28.4%) white, 20.75 g (67.3%) yolk, and 1.33 g (4.3%) shell. White: 97.3% water. Yolk: 16.75% protein, 13.18% total lipids, 0.2% total phosphorus, 0.08% lipoid phosphorus, 2.08% lecithin, and 0.33% cholesterol. Average egg has 39 calories.

RICHARDS, HORACE G. 1930. Notes on the barnacles from Cape May County N.J. Proc. Nat. Acad. Sci. Phila. 82: 143-144.

Platylepas hexastylos (Fabr.) from the skull of *Chelonia mydas*. *Chelonibia testudinaria* (L.) on the shell of a large turtle, probably *Caretta caretta*.

RIDGWAY, SAM H., J. PALIN, J. H. ANDERSON, E. G. WEVER, and J. G. McCORMICK. 1969. Hearing in the giant sea turtle, *Chelonia mydas*. Proc. Nat. Acad. Sci. 64(3): 884-890.

Aerial and mechanical stimulation of the ear in three green turtles showed cochlear potentials with a maximum sensitivity between 300 and 400 Hz. Authors conclude the useful span is about 60 to 1,000 Hz and is therefore a low-frequency receptor. Anatomical considerations and correlations with freshwater turtles included.

RISLEY, PAUL. 1936. Centrioles in germ cells of turtles, including observation on the "manchette" in spermatogenesis. Zeitschr. Wiss. Zool. Abt. A 148(1): 133-158.

Cytological discussion of spermatogenesis in turtles as well as observations on oogenesis.

RODBARD, SIMON. 1948. Body temperature, blood pressure, and hypothalamus. Science, n.s. 108 (2807): 413-415.

Correlation found between blood pressure and body temperature within normal range of variance. Various tests indicate a brain center that reacts to temperature to regulate blood pressure. Turtles, rabbits, and chickens have the lowest blood pressures.

ROTHLEY, H. 1930. Ueber den feineren Bau der Luftröhre und Lunge der Reptilien. Zeitschr. Wiss. Biol. Abr. A. Zeitschr. Morph. Oekol. Tiere. 20(1): 1-62.

Comprehensive anatomical account of adaptations of reptiles, including *Caretta*, to breathing in their various environments.

ROUTA, ROBERT A. 1967. Sea turtle survey of Hutchinson Island, Fla. Quart. J. Fla. Acad. Sci. 30(4): 287-294.

Bulk of nesting population is loggerhead, although a few green turtles nest also. Turtles begin nesting in May and continue through August, with a peak in the last week in June. Estimates of nests: 5,265 nests (658,125 eggs); destroyed: 412 nests (51,500 eggs). No correlation between nesting activity and moon phase.

ROZE, J. A. 1955. Las tortugas marinas de Venezuela. Rev. Pecuaria (Caracas) No. 240: 9-11.

Key given to four species found in Venezuelan waters.

Chelonia mydas: 15 to 20 kilograms, 40 kilograms maximum; mating season on Aves Island from 15 July to 15 October, in the West Indies from May to October; 75 to 200 eggs.

Eretmochelys imbricata: omnivorous; no migration; mating season May to August.

Caretta caretta: rare.

Dermochelys coriacea: occasional.

RUCKER, HERBERT. 1929. Studies in Chelonian osteology. Annals N. Y. Acad. Sci. 31: 31-120.

Detailed discussion of turtle osteology.

SACHSSE, WALTER. 1970. Eine Aufzuchtmethode fuer junge Seeschildkroeten mit einigen zusaetzlichen Beobachtungen. Salamandra 6(3/4): 88-93.

Two loggerheads reared to one year of age in plastic aquaria 15-50 liters in suspension of unicellular algae (0.2-2.5% volume) of predominantly *Nannochloris* spp. Requires only monthly change of water and sunlight. Differences in growth rate ended by separation. Feeding ceased at temperatures below 17°C or specific gravity above 1.037.

SAENZ, A. 1931. Sur le bacille paratuberculeux de la torteux. Ann. Inst. Pasteur (Paris) 47(1): 4-28.

Friedmann's paratubercle tortoise bacillus injected into various animals to discover is any immunity was carried over for the tuberculosis of that species. No gross immunity observed.

Saving marine turtles. 1969. S. Afr. J. Sci. 65(11): 320.

SCATTERGOOD, L. W. and C. PACKARD. 1960. Records of marine turtles in Maine. Maine Field Natur. 16(3): 46-50.

SCHEER, BRADLEY T. 1948. Comparative physiology. John Wiley & Sons, New York.

Scattered throughout are isolated facts of turtle physiology that could apply throughout the Chelonian groups. In each case a reference provided. Book constitutes a good bibliographical start for workers interested in sea turtle physiology. In one table the fatty acid composition of depot fat of *Chelonia mydas* is listed (p. 428). Isolated facts comparing reptilian systems with those of fish, amphibians, birds, and mammals.

SCHMID, FELIX. 1933. Zerlegungsbefunde bei Reptilien und Amphibien. Sitzungsber. Bes. Naturforsch. Freunde. Berlin (8-10): 462-477.

Records of the parasites of 37 species of Ophidia, 17 Lacertilia, 1 Testudinata, and 3 Amphibia that died in the Zoology Gardens in Berlin.

SCHMIDT, C. 1962. Conservation of sea turtles. Interzoo Yrbk. 4(2): 70-71.

SCHMIDT, JOHN. 1916. Marking experiments with turtles in the Danish West Indies. Meddelelser Kommissionen Hovundersogelser, serie: Fiskeri 5(1): 1-26.

Natural history, catch records, and migration data. A very comprehensive treatise; considered one of the most valuable works for anyone interested in sea turtles. All aspects of sea turtle biology examined.

SCHMIDT, KARL P. 1922. The amphibians and reptiles of lower California and the neighboring islands. Bull. Amer. Mus. Nat. Hist., pp. 507-707, pls. 47-57.
No sea turtles mentioned.

SCHMIDT, KARL P. 1946. Turtles collected by the Smithsonian Biological Survey of the Panama Canal Zone. Smithsonian Misc. Coll. 106(8): 1-9.
An annotated list of 10 species of turtles, with discussion of the status of the sea turtles to be expected. The Panamanian specimen of Chelydra referred to is without postfemoral tubercles in the male.

SCHMIDT, KARL P. 1953. A check list of North American amphibians and reptiles. 6th ed. Amer. Soc. Icthy. Herpet. 280 pp.

SCHMIDT, STEPHEN, and P. ROSS WITHAM. 1961. In defense of the turtle. Sea Frontiers 7(4): 211-219.
House of Refuge Museum near Stuart, Fla. has launched a conservation plan for sea turtles. Eggs transplanted to protective grounds of the Museum. Project began in 1956, and by 1961 green, loggerheads, and hawksbills had been hatched and raised. Trunkback hatchlings will only eat ripe tomatoes, presumably because they are attracted to the color. Have obtained some green turtle eggs from Costa Rica and from local nestings and are trying to restock these turtles in the Indian River area. Factors affecting the decline include prolonged cold spell, hurricanes, predators, development of nesting beaches, and exploitation.

SCHMIDTGEN, OTTO. 1907. Die Cloake und ihre Organe bei den Schildkröten. Zool. Jahrb. Abr. f. Anat. 24: 357-414.
Anatomy of the urogenital organs.

SCHMIDT-NIELSEN, KNUT, and RAGNAR FANGE. 1958. Salt glands in marine reptiles. Nature 182(4638): 783-785.
Salt gland in marine turtles located in the orbit of each eye. Suggested that the shedding of tears by laying turtles functions primarily as an osmoregulatory device, these tears being excretions of the salt gland. Salt concentration of the secretion well above that of sea water.

SCHOEPFF, J. D. 1792-1801a. Historia testudinum iconibus illustrata. J. J. Palm, Erlangen. 136 pp.

SCHOEPFF, J. D. 1792-1801b. Naturgeschichte der Schildkröten mit Abbildungen erläutert von ihm selbst übersetzt. J. J. Palm, Erlangen. 160 pp.

SCHROEDER, ROBERT E. 1966. Buffalo of the sea. Sea Frontiers 176-183.
Use should be made of vast pasturage of marine grasses on shallows from Florida to Brazil. This grass should be harvested and used as food for turtle farming. High reproductive rate makes hatchery management feasible for restoration of stocks. Author

suggests that with restoration it should be possible to operate turtle ranches similar to cattle ranches.

SCHROEDER, WILLIAM C. 1924. Fisheries of Key West and the clam industries of southern Florida. U. S. Bur. Fish. Doc. 962.

SCHULZ, J. P. 1969. National situation report re marine turtles in Surinam. *In* Marine turtles. IUCN New Publ. Ser. Suppl. Paper No. 20: 19-33.

Includes comments on nesting areas, species involved, relative abundance, exploitation, conservation, research, and future programs. Graphs on nest number and other factors.

SCHULZ, J. P. 1971. Nesting beaches of sea turtles in West French Guiana. Proc. K. Med. Akad, Wet. Ser. C Biol. Med. Sci. 74(4): 398-404.

Four (possibly five) species of sea turtles nest on beach between Organabo Creek and Marowijne River in west French Guiana. *Dermochelys coriacea* nests there in large numbers; may be the most important nesting area for them.

SCHUMACHER, G. H. 1953-54. Beiträge zur Keifermuskulatur der Schildkröten I. Mitteilung. Wissenschaftliche Zeitschrift der Universität Greifswald Math.-Nat. 3(6,7): 457-518.

SCHUMACHER, G. H. 1954-55a. Beiträge zur Keifermuskulatur der Schildkröten II. Mitteilung. Wissenschaftliche Zeitschrift der Universität Greifswald Math. Nat. 4(5): 501-518.

SCHUMACHER, G. H. 1954-55b. Beiträge zur Keifermuskulatur der Schildkröten III. Mitteilung. Wissenschaftliche Zeitschrift der Universität Greifswald Math.-Nat. 4(6, 7).

SCHUMACHER, G. H. 1956. Morphologische Studie zum Gleitmechanismus des M. adductor mandibularis extremus bei Schildkröten. Anatomischer Anzeiger 103(1, 4): 1-12.

Comparative and descriptive anatomy of *Chelonia, Caretta, Dermochelys,* and some freshwater turtles.

SCHWARTZ, ALBERT. 1954. A record of the Atlantic leatherback turtle (*Dermochelys coriacea*) in South Carolina. Herpetologica 10(1): 7.

Female taken 7 October 1952 at 33°N, 79°30'W. Weight 680 pounds, immature. Additional measurements and comments given on coloration.

SCHWARTZ, FRANK J. 1960. The barnacle, *Platylepas hexastylos,* encrusting a green turtle, *Chelonia mydas mydas,* from Chinoteague Bay, Maryland. Chesapeake Sci. 1(2): 116-117.

First record of green in Chinoteague Bay, 31 inch carapace length and 73 pounds. Hundreds of the barnacles attached to the carapace, plastron, dorsal portions of head and neck, and dorsum of all flippers.

SCHWARTZ, FRANK J. 1961. Maryland turtles. Md. Dept. Res. Ed., Educ. Ser. No. 50. 44 pp.

Includes general comments on green, loggerhead, leatherback, hawksbill, and Atlantic ridley sea turtles.

SCHWEIGGER. 1812. Königsberg. Arch. Naturw. Math. 1(3).
  Taxonomy.
SCOTT, E. O. G., and B. C. MOLLISON. 1956. The Indo-Pacific red
  brown loggerhead turtle, *Caretta caretta gigas* (Deraniyagala), and
  the leathery turtle, *Dermochelys coriacea* (Linne) in Tasmanian
  waters. Pap. Proc. Roy. Soc. Tasmania 90: 59-63.
SCOTT, P. B. C. 1957. The carotid arch in *Chelonia*, with special reference to the carotid sinus. Thesis, Univ. of Aberdeen.
SCUDDER, SAMUEL H. 1882. Nomenclator zoologicus. An alphabeti-
  cal list of all generic names that have been employed by naturalists
  for recent and fossil animals from the earliest times to the close of
  the year 1879. In two parts. 1. Supplemental list. 2. Universal index.
  Bull. U. S. Nat. Mus. pp. i-xxi, 1-376, 1-340.
      Chelone—1828, *Chelonia*—1838, *Caretta, Eretmochelys, Thalas-
      sochelys (imbricata)*—no dates.
SEALE, A. 1917. Sea products of Mindanao and Sulu. III. Sponges,
  tortoise shell, corals and trepang. Philippine J. Sci. 12(D): 191-212.
      1914: 2,296 kilos-34,947 pesos. Description of three principle sea
      turtles. Canning and soup of green turtle in Spain. Loggerhead
      eats fish; hawksbill, crabs, and mollusks, no fish. Green turtle eats
      some fish and weeds. Moros of Siasi and S. Ubian capture and
      keep young turtles. Mentions a turtle farm on Ascension Island.
      8,000 kilos and 100,000 pesos yearly in Philippines; most went to
      Japan.
SEARS, J. H. 1886. *Dermatochelys coriacea*, trunk back or leathery
  turtle. Bull. Essex Inst. 18: 87-94.
      Quotes from other records of the trunkback in New England
      waters.
Sea turtle research. 1970. S. Afr. Mar. Biol. Res. Bull No. 8: 21-25.
      Brief summary of research programs at Tongaland, Africa, with
      some correlation of other research programs around the world.
SEDGWICK, ADAM. 1905. A student's textbook of zoology. 2:
  402-415. The Macmillan Co., New York.
      Notes on classification and distribution of the sea turtles.
SETTE, OSCAR E. 1924. Fishery industries of the U.S. U.S. Bur. Fish.
  Doc. 997.
      Included in the statistics offered for the southeastern states are
      tabulations for turtle production. These figures are given by coun-
      ties of states mentioned and by apparatus.
SETTE, OSCAR E. 1925. Fishery industries of the U.S. U.S. Bur. Fish.
  Doc. 1010.
      The fisheries of the Gulf coast described, and data on turtle
      catches included. Values on catches are also given. Apparatus
      listed, and the number of turtles taken with each type of gear
      specified.
SHAH, R. V. 1962. A comparative study of the respiratory muscles in
  Chelonia. Breviora, Mus. Comp. Zool. No. 161: 1-16.
      The M. strictum pulmonale encloses the lung in the Cyclanor-

binae, is absent in the Trionychinae, Cheloniidae, Dermocheliidae, and Testudininae, and partly covers the lungs in all other
turtles. The Mm. diaphragmaticus and transversus abdominis,
which act in expiration, vary greatly within the order; much less
variation in the Mm. serratus magnus and obliquus abdominus,
which act in inspiration.

SHAH, R. V., and V. B. PATEL. 1964. Myology of the chelonian
pectoral appendage. J. Anim. Morphol. Physiol. 11(1): 58-84.
Comparative study of amphibious (*Lissemys punctata*), terrestrial
reptilian (*Testudo elegans*), and marine (*Eretmochelys imbricata*)
pectoral appendages. Muscles involved in the adduction and
abduction of the upper arm are best developed in the marine
form; these features essential for swimming. Skeletal elements of
the wrist and manus in extreme supination in the marine form,
intermediate in amphibious, and opposite in terrestrial. In these
regions the flexor muscles, in comparison to the extensor
muscles, better developed in *Eretmochelys*.

SHANNON, FREDRICK A. 1956. The reptiles and amphibians of
Korea. Herpetologica 12(1): 22-49.
Lists *Dermochelys coriacea schlegeli* and *Chelonia mydas japon-
ica*.

SHAW, RALPH J., and FRANCIS MARSH BALDWIN. 1935. The
mechanics of respiration in turtles. Copeia 1: 12-15.
Kymograph records and subsequent analysis summarized to give
rhythmic picture of turtle respiration. Full inspiration followed
by expiration in stages.

SIEGLBAUER, F. 1908. Muskeln und Nerven der Schildkrötenextremität. Anat. Anz., Jena 32. Erg. 11: 283-288.

SIEGLBAUER, F. 1909. Zur Anatomie der Schildkrötenextremität.
Archiv für Anatomie und Entwickelungsgeschichte. Pp. 183-280.
A highly detailed anatomical study complete with excellent plates
in color. An extensive bibliography provided.

SIMHA, SHYAM SUNDER, and DEVIKA RANI. 1969. Studies on the
family Rhytidodidae Odhner, 1926, with a description of a new
species, *Rhytidodes indicus*, from the intestine of *Eretmochelys
squamosa*, from Rameswaram, India. Riv. Parassitol. 30(2): 95-100.

SIMKISS, K. 1962. Sources of calcium for the ossification of the embryos of the giant leathery turtle. Comp. Biochem. Physiol. 7(1-2):
71-79.
No alteration of bone structure in adults that can be associated
with a storage of calcium prior to egg laying. Ossification of
skeleton of embryos occurs mainly in later half of incubation;
about 75% of calcium obtained from outside the egg contents.
Hatchlings contain a large quantity of magnesium, which may
indicate absorption of salts from the sea.

SIMONEAUX, N. E. 1934. The commercial fisheries of Louisiana. Bull.
Dept. Cons. La. 25: 135-136.

SMITH, F. G. W. 1950. Recommendations for the protection and rational exploitation of the sea turtles. Proc. Gulf. Car. Fish. Inst. 1: 114-116.

Industry should rigidly prohibit taking eggs or catching turtles on the beaches at any time of the year or should limit adult catches. Size limit of 75 pounds for the green and 25 pounds for hawksbill recommended. Should set up experimental turtle farm and hatchery for compilation of information. Effort should be made to collect statistics regarding growth, size, age, maturity, and fishing pressure. Regulations should be uniform throughout the Caribbean, where possible, for ease of enforcement. Should educate fishermen and encourage domestic consumption rather than export.

SMITH, F. G. W. 1954. Taxonomy and distribution of sea turtles. Fish. Bull. 89: 513-515.

Essentially the same as information in Ingle and Smith, 1949, the original edition of this book.

SMITH, G. M., and C. W. COATES. 1938. Fibro-epithelial growths of the skin in large marine turtles, *Chelonia mydas*. Zoologica 23: 93-98.

Fibro-epitheliomas occur in captive animals as well as in those in the wild state. No parasites found in four animals bearing these tumors. Microscopic structure of tumors described. Other tumors listed for *Chelonia mydas*.

SMITH, G. M., and C. W. COATES. 1939. The occurrence of trematode ova, *Hapalotrema constrictum* (Leared) in fibro-epithelial tumors of the marine turtle *Chelonia mydas* (Linnaeus). Zoologica 24: 279-382.

The fact that ova of a trematode were found in tumors of the eyelid and cornea of some sea turtles is regarded as a coincidence. No etiology exists, the authors state.

SMITH, G. M., C. W. COATES, and R. F. NIGRELLI. 1941. A papillomatous disease of the gall bladder associated with infection by flukes, occurring in the marine turtle *Chelonia mydas* (Linnaeus). Zoologica 26: 14-16.

Rhytidodoides similis (Price), 1939, has been found contiguous with 100 gall bladder neoplasms of benign nature in *Chelonia mydas*. Excellent discussion. The fluke previously described as *Haplotrema constrictum*, (1938, 1939), occurring with epithelial papillomata was later found to be *Leared leared*. Presumption is strong that the fluke is the causative agent for the tumors. *Haplotrema mistroides* mentioned as a parasite of *Caretta caretta*.

SMITH, HOBART M. 1961. Function of the choanal rakers of the green sea turtle. Herpetologica 17(3): 214.

Parallel in gross structure and function to gill rakers of fish. Author suggests that the choanal rakers prevent contents of the mouth from entering the nasal cavity, probably associated with the behavior of consistently pressing the tongue against the roof of the mouth in manipulating food and in preparing to swallow it.

SMITH, HOBART M., and EDWARD H. TAYLOR. 1950a. An annotated checklist and key to the reptiles of Mexico exclusive of the snakes. Bull. U.S. Natl. Mus. 199: 1-253.

SMITH, HOBART M., and EDWARD H. TAYLOR. 1950b. Type localities of Mexican reptiles and amphibians. Univ. Kansas Sci. Bull. 33(2): 313-380.

SMITH, HOMER W. 1929. The inorganic composition of the body fluids of the *Chelonia*. J. Biol. Chem. 82(3): 651-661.
> The perivisceral and pericardial fluids of the *Chelonia* are alkaline secretions in which the bicarbonate content may be three to four times as great as in the plasma. Chloride is diminished in the plasma so that the total bases of the two fluids is approximately the same. Emphasis placed upon the secretory properties of the pericardial and peritoneal membranes.

SMITH, HUGH M. 1894. Notes on a reconnaissance of the fisheries of the Pacific coast of the United States in 1894. Bull. U.S. Fish Comm. 14: 286.
> *Chelonia virgata* (green) reaches San Francisco markets from southern California coast and lower California.

SMITH, K. V., and R. S. DANIEL. 1946. Observations of behavioural development in the loggerhead turtle. (*Caretta caretta*). Sci. 104(2964): 154-156.
> Describes behavioral development within the egg.

SMITH, M. A. 1931. Fauna of British India, Reptilia and Amphibia. Vol. I.

SMITH, PHILIP W., and JAMES C. LIST. 1950. Notes on Mississippi amphibians and reptiles. Amer. Midland Nat. 53(1): 115-125.
> One specimen of *Lepidochelys kempii* (carapace length 69 mm) was found off Chandeleur Island, Chandeleur Sound, Louisiana. Five costal plates and four inframarginals. Stomach contained parts of crabs, *Callinectes* and *Hepatus*, plus numerous parts of gastropods. A skull and a juvenile are also mentioned as belonging to this species.

SMITH, W. G. 1968. A neonate Atlantic loggerhead turtle, *Caretta caretta caretta*, captured at sea. Copeia 1968(4): 880-881.
> Turtle, 64.3 mm carapace length, taken by net in the Gulf Stream, along with sargassum weed and juvenile fish characteristic of a sargassum community. Estimated to be about 11 weeks old.

SOMADIKARTA, S., and H. ANGGORDI. 1962. Sea turtle eggs as food. Commun. Veterinariae 6: 73.

SQUIRES, H. J. 1954. Records of marine turtles in the Newfoundland area. Copeia 1954(1): 68.
> August 1946: leatherback approximately 6 feet and 1,000 pounds. January 1953: loggerhead 99 cm long, caught in 100 fathoms. Sightings of a possible ridley and small loggerheads.

STARKS, E. C., and L. D. HOWARD. 1928. The dissection of the turtle. Stanford Laboratory Guides, Biology Series, Stanford University Press, Stanford, California.

STEARNS, SILAS. 1886. Some of the fisheries of Western Florida. Bull. U.S. Fish Comm. 6:465-467.

STEARNS, SILAS. 1887. The fisheries of the Gulf of Mexico. *In* The fisheries and fishery industries of the U.S. Sect. 2, Pt. 15, pp. 533-587. U.S. Comm. Fish Fish.

    Statistics.

STEBBINS, ROBERT C. 1954. Amphibians and reptiles of western North America. McGraw-Hill Book Co., Inc. New York. 528 pp.

STEINBECK, JOHN, and EDWARD F. RICKETTS. 1941. Sea of Cortez. The Viking Press, New York.

    An account of harpooning a hawksbill turtle off southern California. Notes included on stomach contents.

STEJNEGER, LEONHARD. 1894. On some collections of reptiles and batrachians from East Africa and the adjacent islands, recently received from Dr. W. L. Abbott and Mr. William Astor Chanler, with descriptions of new species. Proc. U.S. Nat. Mus. 16: 711-741.

    Although this area is thickly populated with sea turtles, none mentioned in this report.

STEJNEGER, LEONHARD. 1902. The herpetology of Puerto Rico. Rept. U.S. Nat. Mus. for year ending 30 June 1902, pp. 549-724.

    Of no value in the present connection.

STEJNEGER, LEONHARD. 1907. Herpetology of Japan and adjacent territory. Bull. U.S. Nat. Mus. 58: i-xx, 1-577, 409 figs., 35 pls.

    Discussion of *Caretta olivacea*, *Chelonia japonica*, and *Eretmochelys squamosa*. Complete taxonomic bibliography.

STEJNEGER, LEONHARD. 1910. The batrachians and reptiles of Formosa. Proc. U.S. Nat. Mus. 38, Art. 1731.

    Only *Caretta*, here listed as *olivacea*, mentioned. It is noted that the animal has not been captured, although it is known in surrounding waters.

STEJNEGER, LEONHARD. 1913. Results of the Yale Peruvian Expedition of 1911. Batrachians and reptiles. Proc. U.S. Nat. Mus. No. 1922.

    No sea turtles included.

STEJNEGER, LEONHARD, and THOMAS BALFOUR. 1943. A check list of North American amphibians and reptiles, 5th ed. Bull. Mus. Comp. Zool. 93: xix plus 260.

    Chelonia agassizii Bocourt, 1868, west coast of lower California to Guatemala. *Chelonia mydas* Linne, 1758, Ascension Island, etc. *Eretmochelys imbricata* Linne, 1776, American seas. *Eretmochelys squamata*, 1857, Agassiz, Indian, and Pacific oceans. Pacific Ocean-lower California. *Caretta caretta* Linne, 1758, about American islands. *Lepidochelys kempii* Garman, 1880. Ridley, bastard turtle (*Thalassochelys kempii*), northern part of Gulf of Mexico to Cape Hatteras, Azores, and Ireland. *Lepidochelys olivacea* (Eschscholtz), 1858, tropical Pacific and Indian oceans, west coast of Mexico to California coast. *Dermochelys coriacea* Linne, 1776, Mediterranean, Atlantic coast of the United

States. *Dermochelys schlegelli* Garman, 1884, tropical Pacific and Indian oceans, California coast.

STEPHEN, A. C. 1953. Scottish turtle records previous to 1953. The Scottish Natur. 65: 108-114.

STEVENSON, CHARLES H. 1889-91. Report on coast fisheries of Texas. Bull. U.S. Fish Comm. 17: 373-420.

STEVENSON, CHARLES H. 1898. The preservation of fishery products for food. Bull. U.S. Fish Comm. 18: 347-539.

STIEDA, L. 1875. Ueber den Bau des centralen Nervensystems der Schildkröte. Zeitschrift für Wissensch. Zoologie. Siebold, Kolliker und Ehlers, 25: 361-406.

STOSSICH. 1878. Bolletino della Società Adriatica di Scienze Naturali.
Mentions a *Chelonia mydas* preserved in museum of Fiume, collected at Adrea.

STRAUCH, ALEXANDER. 1890. Bemerkungen über die Schildkrötensammlung im zoologischen Museum der Kaiserlichen Akademie der Wissenschaften zu St. Petersburg. Mémoires, Acad. Sci. St. Petersburg, 74 serie, 38(2): 1-127.

STROMSTEN, FRANK A. 1911. A contribution to the anatomy and development of the posterior lymph hearts of turtles. Papers Tortugas Lab., Carnegie Inst. Wash. 3:77-87.
Histological study.

SUMNER, F. B., R. C. OSBURN, and L. J. COLE. 1911. A biological survey of the waters of Woods Hole and vicinity. Bull. U.S. Bur. Fish. 31: 169.

SWEAT, DONALD E. 1968. Capture of a tagged ridley turtle. Quart. J. Fla. Acad. Sci. 41(1): 47-48.
In seven months the turtle traveled 955 miles and increased from 4 cm to 69 cm carapace length. Captured near Dry Tortugas and released about 90 miles north of Tampico, Mexico.

SWINGLE, WAYNE E., ARTHUR E. DAMMANN, and JOHN A. YNTEMA. 1969. Survey of the commercial fishery of the Virgin Islands of the United States. Proc. Gulf. Carib. Fish. Inst. 22: 110-121.
Has small amount about the turtle fishery.

SZALAI, T. 1930. Bionomische und methodologische-systematische Untersuchungen an rezenten und fossile Testudinaten. Paleobiologica 3: 347-364.
Taxonomic and morphological study of recent and fossil turtles.

TAYLOR, DAN. 1962. Sea turtles provide clues to understanding animal orientation. Duquesne Sci. Counselor 25(4): 102-105.

TAYLOR, E. H. 1921. Turtles of the Philippine Islands. Philippine J. Sci. 16: 111-145.

TEMMINCK. 1836. Fauna Japonica (Reptilia).

TERCAFS, R. R., E. SCHOFFENIELS, and G. GOUSSEF. 1963. Blood composition of a sea-turtle *Caretta caretta* L., reared in freshwater. Arch Int. Physio. Biochem. 71(4): 614-615.
Plasma osmotic pressure lower than that of turtles living in seawater. Chloremia is very low.

THOMPSON, E. F. 1945. The fisheries of Jamaica. Development and Welfare Bull. No. 18, Bridgetown, Barbados.

Catch between 300 and 600 turtles per year, mostly hawksbill. Shell less than 12 shillings per pound. Total annual value $10,000. Fast disappearing. Offers plan for cultivation.

THOMPSON, E. F. 1946. The fisheries of British Honduras. Development and Welfare Bull. No. 21, Bridgetown, Barbados.

One paragraph only. Small industry, poor potentiality. Shell exported.

THOMPSON, E. F. 1947. The fisheries of Cayman Islands. Development and Welfare Bull. No. 22, Bridgetown, Barbados.

Green turtles mostly taken from Nicaragua and Honduras. Adults in Cayman Islands very rare. Cost of operating boats analyzed shows very poor livelihood. Hawksbill on the wane. Special trap net for hawksbill described.

THOMPSON, J. STUART. 1932. The anatomy of the tortoise. Sci. Proc. Roy. Dublin Soc. 20 (paper 28): 359-461.

This seems to be usual discourse except for a detailed discussion of the best methods and techniques for making dissections.

THORSON, THOMAS G. 1963. Body fluid partitioning in fresh-water, marine, and terrestrial chelonians. Amer. Zool. 3(4): 529. (Abstract only)

Body fluid partitioning measured in *Chelydra s. serpentina*, *Gopherus polyphemus*, *Chelonia m. mydas*, *Chelonia m. agassizi*, *Lepidochelys kempi*, *L. olivacea*, and *Caretta c. caretta*. Marine turtles had somewhat less water than freshwater turtle, *C. s. serpentina*. Proportionately more of the body water of the marine turtles was in the circulating or mediating fluid compartments and less was present as protoplasmic or intracellular water.

TINKLEPAUGH, O. L. 1932. Maze learning of a turtle. J. Comp. Psych. 13: 201-206.

A wood turtle, *Clemmys insculpta* (Le Conte), male, about 6 inches long was the subject. This turtle learned a comparatively difficult maze with a nest as the goal. Food was used later. In both cases the animal compared favorably with a rat. No bibliography.

TOMINAGA, NAOTOMO. 1955. Composition of egg shell of *Caretta olivacea*. Kagaku (Science) 25: 140-141.

Percentage composition given and amino acids listed. No great difference between composition of proteins from that of hen eggs. High organic substance content may account for elasticity of eggshell.

TOMITA, MASAJI. 1929. Chemical embryology of reptiles. J. Bio. Chem. Tokyo 10(2): 351-356.

Sea turtle *Thalassochelys corticata (Chelonia caouana)*. General data on the laying and hatching of the eggs and their chemical analysis.

TOWNSEND, CHARLES H. 1890. Reptiles from Clarion and Socorro

Islands and the Gulf of California with description of a new species. Scientific results of explorations by the U.S. Fish Commission Steamer *Albatross*. Proc. U.S. Nat. Mus. Publ. No. 800 15: 143-144.

Of no value in the present connection.

TOWNSEND, CHARLES H. 1897. Fisheries of the Gulf States. Rept. U.S. Comm. Fish Fish. 25: 105-170.

Statistics.

TOWNSEND, CHARLES H. 1906. Growth of confined hawksbill turtles. Bull. N. Y. Zool. Soc. 22: 291.

Two hawksbills from Key West: one 60 pounds with a 26 inch carapace, and one 50 pounds with a 24 inch carapace. Seven or eight years old, and raised in captivity in small saltwater pond. Seaweed, garden plants, clams, etc.

TRESSLER, DONALD K. 1923. Marine products of commerce. Reinhold Publishing Corp., New York. 762 pp.

Statistics, bibliography. Statistics for all the actively producing states in this country and incidental facts relative to the South American distribution are offered. Extensive discussion.

TRESSLER, DONALD K., and JAMES McW. LEMON. 1951. Marine products of commerce: their acquisition, handling, biological aspects and the science and technology of their preparation and preservation. New York, Book Division, Reinhold. 782 pp.

Green only true marine turtle that is commonly eaten; chief fishery of U.S. is Key West. More caught in West Indies and off eastern Nicaragua and Costa Rican coasts; gill nets used, season from March to September. Costa Rican fishery mostly turns turtle or ties a log to flippers of nesting turtles. Hawksbill chief source of tortoiseshell. Comments on methods of preparation and on leatherback, loggerhead, and ridley.

TRUE, F. W. 1884. The fisheries and fishery industries of the United States, Sec. 1, Pt. 2. The useful aquatic reptiles and batrachians. U.S. Comm. Fish Fish. 1893.

Life histories, ecological notes, and distribution outlined in this review.

TRUE, F. W. 1887. The fisheries and fishery industries of the United States, Sec. 5, Vol. 2, Pt. 19, pp. 493-504. Fisheries and Methods. U.S. Comm. Fish Fish.

Turtles. 1957. Mar. Observ. 27 (175): 4-5.

School of 45 to 50 turtles sighted 23 February 1956 about 13 miles from Mexican coast—18°N, 103°21' W.

Turtles come to Britain. 1967*b*. Nature (London) 215 (5096): 5-6.

Turtles with a new lease on life. 1970*b*. Southern Liv. 5: 27, 29.

Short article on conservation efforts with *Caretta caretta* stock nesting on Sanibel and Captiva islands on the west coast of Florida. In 1969, 2,952 hatchlings from artificial nests reared to yearling size (8% mortality) and released.

TWEEDIE, M. W. F. 1953. The breeding of the leathery turtle. Proc. Zool. Soc. London 123(2): 273-275.

Brief account of personal observations of *Dermochelys coriacea* breeding on Trengganu coast in July 1952.

UCHIDA, I. 1967. On the growth of the loggerhead turtle, *Caretta caretta*, under rearing conditions. Bull Jap. Soc. Scient. Fish. 33(6): 497-506.

Growth rate (carapace length and body weight) from 1.5 to 4.5 years follows logistic curve of Robertson formula. Formulas for relation of age, weight, and carapace length given. Turtles will attain a maximum of 1,040 mm Cl and 110 kilograms in six to seven years. Relation of certain meristic characters expressed by the formula of allometric equations. Inflection point in carapace length to carapace width relation found at 57.25 mm Cl, suggesting ecological or physiological changes occurring.

URBAN, EMIL K. 1970. Nesting of the green turtle (*Chelonia mydas*) in the Dahlak Archipelago, Ethiopia. Copeia 1970(2): 393-394.

Eighteen nest sites observed on four islands during 18-25 March 1969. Since this Archipelago contains a group of several hundred islands, an important nesting area may be present that was previously unknown.

U.S. COMMISSION OF FISH AND FISHERIES. 1896. Florida Fisheries. Rept. U.S. Comm. Fish Fish. 23: 132.

VAILIANT. 1896. Remarques sur l'appareil digestif et le mode d'alimentation de la Tortue luth. Comptes Rendus Acad. Sci. 123.

VALENTRY, DUANE. 1967. Solving the great turtle mystery. Sea Frontiers 13(3): 137.

Brief account of Carr's methods of studying migration at Ascension Island.

VAN DER JAGT, E. R. 1932. The origin and development of the anterior lymph sac in the sea-turtle (*Thalassochelys caretta*). Quart. J. Microsc. Sci. 75(1): 151-163.

Histological study based on serial sections reconstructed.

VERRILL, A. HYATT. 1940. Wonder creatures of the sea. W. Appleton-Century Co., New York.

Sea turtles not mentioned in this popular account.

VERSLUYS, J. 1913. Phylogeny of the carapace and on the affinities of the leathery turtle *D. coriacea*. Rept. 83rd Meeting Brit. Assn. Adv. Sci. Birmingham, pp. 791-807.

VERSLUYS, J. 1914. Ueber die Phylogenie des Panzers der Schildkröten und über die Verwandtschaft der Lederschildkröten (*Dermochelys coriacea*). Paleont. Zeitschr. Berlin 1: 321-347.

VICENTE, J. JULIO, and ELIAS DOS SANTOS. 1968. Terceira especie do genero "Tonaudia" Travassos, 1918 (Nematoda, Kathlaniidae). Atlas Soc. Biol. Rio de Janeiro 12(2): 55-56.

T. freitasi described from the stomach of *Chelone mydas* captured from the state of Ceara, Brazil.

VILLIERS, A. 1955. Tortues et crocodiles de l'Afrique Noire française. Initiations Africaines. 345 pp.

Extensive work on turtles and crocodiles. Covers structure and function, general biology, physiology, systematics, and their relation to man. Keys given for genera within each family and for species within each genus. Section on sea turtles included.

VILLIERS, A. 1962. West African tortoises, turtles, and terrapins. African Wildlife 16(1): 39-52.

Five species of marine turtles are found on West African coast: *Dermochelys coriacea*, *Eretmochelys imbricata*, *Chelonia mydas*, *Caretta caretta*, and *Lepidochelys olivacea*. Green is most common and ridley is most rare. Coloration, general biology, and behavior briefly discussed. All species eaten by natives.

VIOSCA, PERCY. 1961. Turtles tame and truculent. La. Conserv. 13(7-8): 5-8.

Of 32 species of turtles in Louisiana, 5 are marine. *Lepidochelys olivacea kempii* gray sea turtle or ridley most abundant. *Chelonia mydas mydas*, *Caretta caretta caretta*, and *Dermochelys coriacea* all listed as rare. Ridley purported to nest on the beaches of the Chandeleur Island chain.

VIRCHOW. 1926. Die Halswirbelsäule der Schildkröten (Cervical vertebrae of turtles). Verhandl. Anat. Ges. 1926: 214-221.

A highly technical account of the structures and variations in vertebrae.

VOLKER, H. 1913. Ueber das Stamm-Gliedmassen und Hautskelet von *Dermochelys coriacea*. L. Zool. Jahrb. 33: 431-552, pls. 30-33.

VOLLBRECHT, JOHN L. 1947. Skeeter turtle hunt. Fla. Outdoors, June 1947, pp. 6-7.

Summary of a trip in specially built beach wagon and subsequent discovery of a female sea turtle laying eggs. Several notes on loggerhead turtles included.

VON ZITTEL, K. A. 1902. Textbook of palaeontology, Vol. II.

WALKER, WARREN F. 1959. Closure of the nostrils in the Atlantic loggerhead and other sea turtles. Copeia 1959(3): 257-259.

Closure of nostrils by the meeting of bulges from the laterodorsal and medioventral walls of the nasal passages observed frequently in the loggerhead and twice in the ridley and in the green. Observed only when the turtles were at rest. Suggested that this adaptation prevents water entering or air leaving the respiratory passages when stimuli might cause the glottis to open reflexively or during periods of low muscle tonus.

WALKER, WARREN F. 1971. Swimming in sea turtles of the family Cheloniidae. Copeia 1971(2): 229-233.

Swimming of green, hawksbill, ridley, and loggerhead turtles observed and photographed at Marineland, Florida. Four species show no significant differences in major aspects of limb movement. Swim by moving the blade of their pectoral flipper up and down along a line inclined from 40° to 70° from the horizontal plane. Downstroke is the main propulsive stroke, but some propulsive components generated on the upstroke. Analysis of movement with regard to body structure and vector forces included.

WALLACE. 1881. Island life. London.
For Seychelles Islands lists only *Chelonia imbricata*.
WALLS, G. L. 1934. The reptilian retina. 1. A new concept of visual cell evolution. Amer. J. Opthalmology, Ser. 3. 17(1): 892-915.
That excessive rod and cone development is physiological not morphological is developed. Evidence for the theory as well as a discussion of the optic apparatus of all reptiles, including turtles, is discussed.
WANGERSKY, E. D., and C. E. LANE. 1960. Interaction between the plasma of the loggerhead turtle and toxin of the Portuguese Man-of-War. Nature 185(4706): 330-331.
Results suggest that the loggerhead turtle lacks blood immune bodies for the toxin of the jellyfish. Apparent insensitivity of these turtles to this toxin might be due to localized tissue antibodies.
WATSON, D. M. S. 1914. *Eunotosaurus africanus* Seeley, and the ancestors of Chelonia. Proc. Zool. Soc. London, Pt. 2.
WEGNER, R. N. 1959. Der Schädelbau der Ledershildkröte *Dermochelys coriacea* Linne (1776). Abh. Dtsch. Akad. Wiss. Berl. Klasse Chem. Geol. Biol. 4: 1-80.
Detailed text and plates on the skull structure of *Dermochelys coriacea* with comments on structures in other sea turtles (*Chelonia* and *Caretta*).
WERLER, JOHN E. 1951. Miscellaneous notes on the eggs and young of Texan and Mexican reptiles. Zoologica 36(3): 37-48.
Mentions a nesting of a ridley on Padre Island, Texas in March 1950; 100 eggs (approximately) laid, 18 artificially incubated. Sixty-two days later eggs began to hatch. Size and coloration given for four hatchlings at 120 days of age.
WERMUTH, H. 1956. Versuch der Deutung einiger bisher übersehener Schildkrötennamen. Zool. Beitr. 2(2-3): 399-423.
WERMUTH, H., and R. MERTENS. 1961. Schildkröten, Krokodile, Brückenechsen, VEB Gustav Fischer Verlag, Jena. 422 pp.
List of synonymies and key given for marine turtles.
WESTERMAN. 1948. Unpublished report instigated by Dr. Westerlund and sent by Dr. A. A. Aberson, Chairman, Caribbean Coordination Commission, Netherlands, to E. S. Pembleton, Deputy Chairman of Caribbean Research Council, Kent House, Port-of-Spain, Trinidad.
WETMORE, A. 1925. Sleeping *Chelonia mydas*. Expedition to Hawaii. Nat. Geogr. Mag. 79: 577-602.
Turtles seem to bask upon beaches.
WHEELER, J. F. G., and G. D. OMMANEY. 1953. Report on the Mauritus-Scychelles Fisheries Survey 1948-49. Great Britain Colonial Office, Fishery Publications: No. 3. 145 pp.
Greatest number of green turtles is at southern islands in the Aldabras group. Comments on preparation of turtle oil from fat, eggs, guts, and heart. Green turtles on Assumption, Aldabras, and Cosmoledo overexploited. Breeding grounds of green are at Alda-

bras February to September, and grazing areas relatively unknown. Conservation measures discussed, also turtle products and the need for improving efficiency of manufacture and transportation.

WILCOX, WILLIAM A. 1896. Commercial fisheries of Indian River, Florida. Rept. U.S. Comm. Fish Fish. 22:249-262.

WILL, L. 1892. Zur Kenntnis der Schildkrötengastrula. Biol. Centralbl., pp. 182-192, 4 figs.

WILLGOHS, JOHAN F. 1952. Common loggerhead *Caretta caretta* stranded in Western Norway. Univ. Bergen Abork. Naturv. rekke 1952(17): 1-8.

Found near Tviberg in western Norway in December 1951. First record from Scandinavian waters, specimen intact and had four enlarged inframarginals.

WILLGOHS, JOHAN F. 1956. Nye funn av leerskilpadde i Nordsjoen, og Litt om Artens utbredelse og levevis. Saertrykk av "Naturen" 9: 532-544.

WILLGOHS, JOHAN F. 1958. Har laerskilpadden (*Dermochelys coriacea*) ogsa overvintet i vare farvann? -nytt funn i versteralen. Saertrykk av "Naturen" 8: 508-510.

WILLIAMS, ERNEST E., ALICE G. C. GRANDISON, and ARCHIE CARR. 1967. *Chelonia depressa* Garman re-investigated. Breviora No. 271. 15 pp.

Aggregative nesting may give rise to nascent or genuine species. It is proposed that *C. depressa* of Australia is a separate and distinct species from *C. mydas*. Brief account of earlier work; 15 external characters checked on 40 known specimens (listed in table). Most are not key characters; two characters in combination define *C. depressa*: 1. postocular scale count of 3; 2. areas of wrinkled skin distally on fore and hind limbs. Variation in postocular count of *C. mydas* makes character unsuitable when used alone. Most characters of *depressa* involve what appears to be a general weakening or reduction of scalation. Further studies are needed.

WILLIAMS, M. WOODBRIDGE, and KARL W. KENYON. 1950. The turtle hunters of Scammon's Lagoon. Pacific Discovery 3(4): 4-16.

Scammon's Lagoon is located on Pacific coast of Baja, California. Hunters used two or more 8-foot spears and kept turtles in pens for shipment to cannery. About 70 pesos per turtle.

WILLS, J. H., JR. 1967. Sea food toxins. *In* Toxicants occurring naturally in foods. Nat. Acad. Sci., Nat. Res. Conc. Publ. 1354: 147-163.

Lists *Chelonia japonica, Dermochelys coriacea,* and *Eretmochelys imbricata* as turtles that may cause poisoning. Symptoms are nausea, vomiting, diarrhea, weakness, sore lips and throat, hallucinations, coma, and death. Death may occur between 12 hours and 2 weeks after ingestion.

WITHAM, ROSS. 1971. Breeding of a pair of pen-reared green turtles. Quart. J. Fla. Acad. Sci. 33(4): 288-290.

Turtles observed mating early summer 1968; laying occurred on June 2, July 8, and August 1, 1969. Many of the eggs were malformed, and none hatched.

WITHAM, ROSS, and ARCHIE CARR. 1968. Returns of tagged pen-reared green turtles. Quart. J. Fla. Acad. Sci. 31(1): 49-50.

Two returns from 98 yearlings released in Indian River (Gulf coast of Florida). One had traveled 7 miles north in 64 days, and the other was captured 65 miles (Grand Bahamas) away after 30 months.

WOJTUSIAK, ROMAN J. 1932. Ueber den Farbensinn der Schild-kröten. Zeitschr. Wiss. Biol. Abt. C., Zeitschr. Vergleich. Physiol. 18(3): 393-436.

Animals were trained to five colors. They were not only able to tell colors, but could judge intensity. Grays were poorly per-ceived.

WOJTUSIAK, ROMAN J. 1934. Ueber den Formensinn der Schild-kröten. Bull. Internat. Acad. Polonaise Sci. et Lettr. Cl. Sci. Math. et Nat. Ser. B: Sci. Nat. (11) (Zool.) (8, 10): 349-373, 19 figs.

Turtles were able to distinguish figures of the same form but different size, and figures of the same form and size but different position. A discussion of "secondary associations" is also given.

WOLF, SIEGFRIED. 1933. Zur Kenntnis von Bau und Funktion der Reptilienlunge. Zool. Jahrb. Abt. Anat. u. Ont. 57(1): 139-190.

Lungs and respiratory organs of all reptiles including turtles de-scribed.

WOOD, F. G. 1953. Mating behavior of captive loggerhead turtles. Copeia 1953(3): 184-186.

Observed in tank at Marine Studios, Marineland. Male maintained mount on female by grasping edges of carapace with single claw on each flipper for 4 hours 20 minutes, except for release of female for air, despite nudging of porpoises and mutilation of penis by triggerfish, causing intervals of hemorrhaging. During thrusts by male, tail extended straightforward at a slight down-ward angle. Penetration apparently occurred once (about 2 hours after onset) at which time the male tail was flattened out along female's plastron. Behavior of female ranged from passive accept-ance to active dislodging or evading movements.

WOODWARD, A. A. 1887. Leathery turtles, recent and fossil. Proc. Geol. Assoc. 10: 2-14.

WYATT-SMITH, J. 1960. The conservation of the leathery turtle. Malayan Nature J. 1960: 194-199.

YARROW, H. C. 1882. Check-list of North American Reptilia and Batrachia, with catalogue of specimens in U.S. National Museum. Bull. U.S. Nat. Mus., pp. i-v, 1-249.

Of doubtful value in the present connection.

YERGER, R. W. 1965. The leatherback turtle on the Gulf coast of Florida. Copeia 1963(3): 365-366.

Describes sightings of 10 adults and several hatchlings on the Gulf coast. One nesting recorded on north Florida coast. Measurements and weights for two specimens included.

YERKES, R. M. 1901. The formation of habits in the turtle. Popular Sci. Monthly 58: 519-529.

YERKES, R. M. 1904. Space perception of tortoises. J. Comp. Neurol. Psych. 14: 16-26.

Fear of space by dropping from various heights is relative to the amount of time spent on land. Water turtles take greater drop and with less restraint than land turtles.

YONGE, C. M. 1930. A year on the Great Barrier Reef. G. P. Putnam's Sons, pp. 195-199.

Natives get them by diving and with captive *Echenesis naucrates* (mackerel family). Small cannery on Heron Island for *mydas*. Breeding season in the summer. *Imbricata* not common, 1 to 25 shillings per pound for shell. Queensland exported £1,643 in 1929, as much as £3,000 in the past.

ZANGERL, RAINER. 1958. Die oligozenen Meerschildkröten von Glarus. Schweiz. Palaeontol. Abhandl. 73(3): 1-56.

Specimen ascribed to *Chelonia* in 1865 by Heer redescribed under name of *Glarichelys knorri*. Comparisons with *Chelonia, Caretta, Eretmochelys,* and *Lepidochelys*. *G. knorri* and *Chelonia gwinneri* are thought to be forerunners of the tribe Chelonini.

ZANGERL, RAINER, and ROBERT E. SLOAN. 1960. A new specimen of *Desmatochelys iowi* Williston. A primitive chelonid sea turtle from the Cretaceous of South Dakota. Fieldiana: Geol. 14(2): 1-40.

Found in 1953 in Milbank-Ortonville granite district in eastern South Dakota and western Minnesota, the skeleton exhibits a number of features that are seen in toxocheligid, protostergid, and dermochelyid turtles, but its overall morphology makes it a primitive cheloniid.

ZIM, HERBERT S., and HOBART M. SMITH. 1953. Reptiles and amphibians. A guide to familiar American species. Simon and Schuster, New York. 147 pp.

ZULLO, VICTOR A., and J. SHERMAN BLEAKNEY. 1966. The cirriped *Stomatolepas elegans* (Costa) on leatherback turtles from Nova Scotian waters. Can. Field-Nat. 80(3): 162-165.

Most northern record for any platylepadid; found in two leatherbacks. Authors suggest these barnacles settled on the individuals in warmer waters and that information on migration and dispersal of marine turtles might be obtained through a study of the barnacles which they host.

ZULOAGA, GUILLERMO. 1955. The Isla Aves story. Geogr. Rev. 45: 172-178.

Aves is nesting ground for green turtles during the later months of the year. Survey reveals island has shrunk to about one-half the size given on U.S. Hydrographic Chart 1011 (1840s).

SUBJECT INDEX
OF THE BIBLIOGRAPHY

Anatomy

Abel and Ellis 1966; Adams 1947, 1962; Agassiz 1857; American Association of Anatomists 1932; Babcock 1930a, b, 1931; Baur 1887, 1888; Beaufort and Coker 1910; Bojanus 1819-21; Burne 1905; Contu 1953; Deraniyagala 1939a; Detwiller; Dunlap 1955, 1966; Ellis 1964; Ellis and Abel 1964; Francescon 1930; Goodrich 1916, 1919; Granda and Haden 1970; Hadziselimovic and Andelic 1967; Haines 1935; Hasse 1871; Hay 1901, 1922, 1928; Heldt 1933; Kappers, Huber, and Crosby 1936; Knoepffler 1962; Koenig 1934; Larsell 1932, 1933; Lubosch 1933; Martin and Moale 1895; Nick 1912; Noble and Noble 1940; O'Donoghue 1918; Owen 1849; T. Parsons 1958, 1968; Peters 1838; Poglayen-Neuwall 1953a, b; Pritchard 1966b; Risley 1936; Rucker 1929; K. Schmidt 1946; Schmidtgen 1907; Schmidt-Nielsen, Knut, and Fange 1958; Schumacher 1953-54, 1954-55a, b, 1956; Scott 1957; Shah 1962; Shah and Patel 1964; Sieglbauer 1908, 1909; Smith 1961; Starks and Howard 1928; Stieda 1875; Stromsten 1911; Thompson 1932; Van der Jagt 1932; Villiers 1955; Virchow 1926; Volker 1913; Walker 1959, 1971; Wegner 1959.

Behavior

Bustard 1967; Caldwell and M. Caldwell 1962; Carr 1942, 1952, 1962; Carr and Giovannoli 1957; Carr and Hirth 1961; Carr, Hirth, and Ogren 1966; Carr and Ogren 1959, 1960; Daniel and Smith 1947; Detwiller; Ehrenfeld 1968; Ehrenfeld and Carr 1967; Fischer 1964; Harrisson 1955, 1962a; Herrick 1922; Hooker 1908a, 1909, 1911; Kaufmann 1968; Layne 1952; Loveridge 1945; Mast 1911; Mayer 1909; McFarlane 1963; Mellen 1925; Mjoberg 1930; Moorhouse 1933; Mrosovsky 1967, 1968, 1970; Mrosovsky and Carr 1967; Mrosovsky and Pritchard 1971; Mrosovsky and Shettleworth 1968; Parker 1922; Parrish 1958; Parschin 1929; Parsons 1962; Pritchard 1971; Schmidt 1916; Smith 1961; Smith and Daniel 1946; Tinklepaugh 1932; Walker 1959, 1971; Wetmore 1925; Wojtusiak 1932, 1934; Wood 1953; Yerkes 1901, 1904.

Breeding and Life History

Allen and Neil 1957; Bacon 1970; Barth 1962b; Bass and McAllister 1964; Brice 1896b; Bustard and Greenham 1969; Bustard and Tognette 1969; Caldwell 1959a, b, 1962a, d, 1966, 1968, 1969; Caldwell, Berry, Carr, and Ragotzkie 1959; Caldwell, Carr, and Hellier 1956a, b; Caldwell, Carr, and Ogren 1959; Caldwell and Casebeer 1964; Caldwell and Rathjen 1969; Carr 1952, 1963, 1967a, d; Carr and Carr 1970; Carr and Giovannoli 1957; Carr and Hirth 1961, 1962; Carr, Hirth, and Ogren 1966; Carr and Ingle 1959; Carr and Ogren 1959, 1960; Chavez, Contreras, and Hernandez 1967; Chin 1969; Deraniyagala 1936c, 1939a, 1957; Domm, 1971; Dimond 1965; Gallagher and Hollinger 1972; Greaves 1933; Harrisson 1951, 1952, 1954, 1962c; Hendrickson 1958; Hendrickson and Alfred 1961; Hendrickson and Balasingam 1966; Hesse, Alee, and Schmidt 1937; Hirth and Carr 1970; Holbrook 1840; Hoge 1950; Hooker 1908b; Hughes 1970b, c, 1971; Hughes, Bass, and Mentis 1967; Hughes and Mentis 1967, Kaufmann 1968, 1971; Le Buff and Beatly 1971; Limpus 1971; Marquez and Contreras 1967; Mawson 1921; McAllister, Bass, and van Schoor 1965; Monroe 1897; Montoya 1969; Moorhouse 1933; Musgrave and Whitley 1926; Parsons 1962; Penyapol 1958; Peters 1957; Pritchard 1966a, 1969b, d, 1971; Reinhardt

and Lutken 1862; Routa 1967; Schmidt 1916; Schulz 1971; Tweedie 1953; Urban 1970; Villiers 1955; Vollbrecht 1947; Werler 1951; Witham 1971; Wood 1953; Yerger 1965; Yonge 1930; Zuloaga 1955.

Conservation

Aberson 1947; Balasingam 1969; Bravo 1970; Brown 1946; Bustard 1968, 1969a, b; Caldwell and Carr 1957; Carr 1954b, 1967a, 1969a, b,1970; Carr, Hirth, and Ogren 1966; Carr and Ingle 1959; Chavez 1967; Chavez, Contreras, and Hernandez 1967; Department of Commerce and Agriculture, Puerto Rico 1944; De Silva 1969; Garman 1884; Goodrian 1946; Harrisson 1962b, 1964a, b, 1969a, b; Hendrickson 1958, 1969; Hendrickson and Alfred 1961; Hendrickson and Winterflood 1961; Hillaby 1963, 1968; Hirth 1969; Hughes 1969b; Laycock 1969; McAllister, Bass, and van Schoor 1965; McNeill 1955; Marine turtles 1968; Montoya 1969; Moorhouse 1933; Parsons 1962; Pritchard 1967, 1969a, b, c, d, 1971; C. Schmidt 1962; J. Schmidt 1916; Schmidt and Witham 1961; Schroeder 1966; Schulz 1969; Smith 1950; Thompson 1945, 1947; Turtles with a new lease on life 1970; Westerman 1948; Wyatt-Smith 1960.

Cultivation

Barney 1922; Boeke 1907; Coker 1906, 1920; Garman 1884; Goodrian 1946; Heffington 1970; Hendrickson 1958; Hildebrand 1929; Hildebrand and Hatsel 1927; Mitsukuri 1904; Monroe 1897; Montalbano 1973; Moorhouse 1933; Schroeder 1966; Witham 1971.

Ecology

Agassiz 1888; Bustard 1970; Bustard and Tognette 1969; Caldwell 1959a; Carr and Goodman 1970; Hendrickson 1958; Hendrickson and Balasingam 1966; Moorhouse 1933; Ragotzkie 1959; J. Schmidt 1916; True 1884.

Embryology

L. Agassiz 1857a; Albert 1898; Brachet 1935; Bustard and Greenham 1968; Bustard, Simkiss, and Jenkins 1969; Cunningham and Hurwitz 1936; Davenport 1896; Deraniyagala 1932a, 1936b, 1939a; Dimond 1965; Fujiwara 1966; Goette 1899; Gregory 1900; Harrisson 1952, 1961; Haycroft 1891; Hendrickson 1958; Hendrickson and Winterflood 1961; Hildebrand 1938, Hirth and Carr 1970; Hughes 1969a; Hughes, Bass, and Mentis 1967, Krabbe 1935; Luther 1959; Parker 1880; Penyapol 1958; Procter 1922; Ragotzkie 1959; Rathke 1846, 1848; Simkiss 1962; Tomita 1929.

Enemies

Barth 1962a; Bustard and Limpus 1969; Caldwell 1959a; Caldwell and Caldwell 1969; N. Caldwell 1951; Carr 1952, 1967d; Hendrickson 1958; Hirth and Carr 1970; Limpus 1971; McAllister, Bass, and van Schoor 1965; Moorhouse 1933; Pritchard 1971; Raven 1946.

Feeding Habits

Bleakney 1965, 1967a; Brongersma 1969, 1972; Catesby 1731-43; Carr 1952; Deraniyagala 1939a; Dobie, Ogren, and Fitzpatrick 1961; Ferreira 1968; Harrisson 1955; Hirth and Carr 1970; Pritchard 1969d, 1971; Seale 1917; Steinbeck and Ricketts 1941; True 1887; Villiers 1955; Witham and Carr 1968.

Fisheries

Bahamas Fisheries

Catesby 1731, Nye 1886.

Bermuda Fisheries

Babcock 1938, Garman 1884, Mowbray and Caldwell 1958.

Caribbean Fisheries

Boeke 1907; Brown 1946; Caldwell 1961; Carr 1954b, 1956a, 1969a, 1970; Craig 1966; Duerden 1901; Fiedler et al. 1943a, b, c, d; Goodrian 1946; Long 1774, Mortensen 1907; Pritchard 1969d; Schmidt 1916; Swingle, Dammann, and Yntema 1969; Thompson 1945, 1946, 1947.

Cuban Fisheries

Cuba's fishing industry 1958, 1959; Martinez 1948.

Mexican Fisheries

Caldwell 1963b; Carranza 1967, Linder 1948.

U.S. Fisheries

Alexander 1902a; Anderson and Power 1948, 1951, 1955, 1956a, b, 1957; Annual summaries 1953, 1957, 1962, 1963, 1965, 1967, 1969, 1970, 1971; Annual summary 1950, 1952-1969; Audubon 1834; Brice 1896b; Caldwell 1960; Caldwell and Carr 1957; Carr and Caldwell 1956; Collins and Smith 1891; Earll 1887; Everman and Bean 1896; Evermann 1901; Fiedler 1928a, b, 1938, 1940, 1941; Fiedler, Manning, and Johnson 1932, 1934; Florida State Board of Conservation 1940, 1942, 1944, 1946; Ingle 1972; Lyles 1965, 1966, 1967, 1968, 1969; Monroe 1897; Power 1958, 1959, 1960, 1961, 1962, 1963; Power and Lyles 1964; Schroeder 1924; Sette 1924, 1925; Simoneaux 1934; Stearns 1886, 1887; Stevenson 1889; U.S.

Commission of Fisheries 1896; True 1887.

Other Fisheries

Banks 1937; Bruhl 1930; Cadenat 1954; N. Caldwell 1951; Chari 1964; Copley 1956; Deraniyagala 1939a; Domantay 1952-53; Harrisson 1950, 1951; Hendrickson 1958; Hendrickson and Alfred 1961; Hornell 1927, 1950; Jones and Fernando 1968; McCarthy 1955; Report on Kenya Fisheries 1957-1965; Seale 1917; Stejneger 1907; Wheeler and Ommaney 1953; Williams and Kenyon 1950; Yonge 1930.

Food Poisoning

Bierdrager 1936, Deraniyagala 1939a; Gadow 1909; Halstead 1956; Wills 1967.

General Biology

Abbott 1894; Angel 1946; Babcock 1938; Balasingam 1969; Beebe 1924; Bustard 1966; Caldwell 1959a, 1960; Caldwell and Caldwell 1962; Carr 1952, 1956a, 1967; Deraniyagala 1939a; Ditmars 1910, 1936; Garman 1884; Heldt 1933; Hendrickson 1958; Hirth and Carr 1970; Laycock 1969; Loveridge and Williams 1957; Moorhouse 1933; Parsons 1962; Pope 1939; Pritchard 1971; Schmidt 1916; Villiers 1955.

Growth and Age

Banks 1937; Caldwell 1962b, c; Carr 1952; Carr and Goodman 1970; Deraniyagala 1936c, 1939a; Flower 1925, 1937; Harrisson 1955, 1956a, 1963; Hendrickson 1958; Hildebrand 1932; Kaufmann 1967; Kluger 1931; Loveridge and Williams 1957; Mattox 1936; Parker 1926; Pritchard 1971; Sachsse 1970; Uchida 1967.

Marketing

Carr 1952; Fiedler 1928a, b; Parsons 1962; Thompson 1945,

1947; Tressler 1923; Tressler and Lemon 1951.

Methods and Gear

Alexander 1902a, b; Catesby 1731-43; Craig 1966; Decary 1950; Hornell 1950; Jones and Fernando 1968; Loveridge 1945; McCarthy 1955; Parsons 1962; Steinbeck and Ricketts 1941; Thompson 1947; True 1884; Yonge 1930.

Migration

Brongersma 1972; Caldwell 1968, 1969; Caldwell and M. Caldwell 1962; Caldwell, Carr, and Ogren 1959; Carr 1952, 1954a, b, 1962, 1964a, b, 1965, 1967a, c, e; Carr and Caldwell 1956; Carr and Giovannoli 1957; Carr, Hirth, and Ogren 1966; Carr and Ogren 1960; Chopard 1966; Do turtles sniff their way to Ascension 1969; Duerden 1901; Ehrenfeld and Kock 1967; Fischer 1964; Harrisson 1956b, c, 1959, 1969; Hendrickson 1958; Hirth and Carr 1970; Koch, Carr, and Ehrenfeld 1969; Moorhouse 1933; Oliver 1946; Pearse 1923; Pinner 1967; Pritchard 1971; Schmidt 1916; Sweat 1968; Valentry 1967.

Parasites

Braun 1899; Brongersma 1969; Caballero y Caballero 1959, 1962; Dunlap 1955; Ghai 1931; Gupta 1961; Hamerton 1935; Hendrickson 1958; Hunt 1957; Inglis 1957; Leared 1862; Linton 1910; Looss 1899, 1902; Luhman 1935; Mac Callum and MacCallum 1918; Manter 1932; Martin and Bamberger 1952; McAllister, Bass, and van Schoor 1965; Mehra 1932; Monticelli 1896; Nigrelli 1940, 1941, 1942; Nigrelli and Smith 1943; Nilsson-Cantell 1932; Pearse 1949; Pratt 1914; Price

1939; Richards 1930; Schmid 1933; Simha and Rani 1969; Smith and Coates 1938, 1939; Smith, Coates, and Nigrelli 1941; Vicente and Santos 1968.

Physiology

Abel and Ellis 1966; Banks 1937; Belkin 1963, 1968; Bemmelen 1896; Benedict 1932; Berkson 1966; Cate 1936; Ellis 1964; Faulkner and Binger 1927; Gage 1886; Graper 1932; Hermann and Merklen 1926; Hirth 1962; Holmes 1965; Holmes and Mc Bean 1964; Jacobs 1939; Johlin and Moreland 1933; Lucke and Schlumberger 1942; Ludicke 1936, 1940; Lumsden 1923; 1924; McGinnis 1968; Murphy et al. 1934; Parker 1925, 1928; Pearse, Lepkovsky, and Hintze 1925; Phisalix 1934; Remlinger and Baily 1931; Ridgway, Palin, Anderson, Wever, and McCormick 1969; Rodbard 1948; Saentz 1931; Scheer 1938; Schmidt-Nielsen and Fange 1958; Shaw and Baldwin 1935; Smith 1929; Tercafs, Schoffeniels, and Goussel 1963; Thorson 1963; Villiers 1955; Walls 1934; Wangersky and Lane 1960.

Shell and other Products

Atwater 1888; Carlton and Coates 1958; Chandrasekharan 1969; Deraniyagala 1939a; Giral 1955; Hooper and Ackman 1970; Minato and Otomo 1969; Pathak and Dey 1956; Pax and Arndt 1930; Penyapol 1958; Pufahl 1915; Richard and Thi-Lau 1961; Somadikarta and Anggordi 1962; Stevenson 1898; Thompson 1947; Tominaga 1955; Tressler 1923; Tressler and Lemon 1951; Yonge 1930.

Taxonomy and Distribution

Agassiz 1857b; Agassiz and Cope 1871; Aguayo 1953; Ahrenfeldt 1945; Allen and Neill 1957; Angel 1946; Babcock 1919; Barth 1965; Baur 1890; Bell 1827-28; Bemmelen 1928; Bleakney 1955, 1965; Bocourt 1868; Boulenger 1889; Brattstrom 1955; Brongersma 1961, 1967a, 1968a, b, f, g, 1969, 1972; Burt and Burt 1932; Bustard and Limpus 1969; Cadenat 1954; Caldwell 1960, 1961, 1962d, 1963a; Caldwell and Erdman 1969; Caldwell, Rathjen, and Hsu 1969; Capocaccia 1968; Carr 1952, 1954a, 1957, 1961a, b; Carr and Caldwell 1956, 1958; Carr and Giovannoli 1957; Carr and Goin 1955; Carr and Hirth 1962; Carr, Hirth, and Ogren 1966; Carr and Ogren 1959, 1960; Chavez, Contreras, and Hernandez 1967; Cogger 1960; Cogger and Lindner 1969; Collins and Lynn 1936; Conant 1958; Cooker 1905, 1910; Cope 1875, 1887a, 1896; de Betta 1874; Decary 1950; Deraniyagala 1930a, b, 1932a, 1933, 1934a, b, 1936a, 1938a, b, 1939a, b, c, d, 1943, 1945, 1946, 1952, 1953, 1957, 1961, 1964; de Rooij 1915; De Silva 1969; de Sola 1931; de Sola and Abrams 1933; Despott 1930; Dobie, Ogren, and Fitzpatrick 1961; Dollo 1901; Domm 1971; Donoso-Barros 1964a, b; Duellman 1961; Dunn 1944; Faber 1883; Fahy 1954; Fitzinger 1843; Forbes and McKey-Fender 1968; Forrest 1931; Flores 1966; Freiberg 1967; Fry 1913; Fugler and Webb 1957; Fujinoki and Tonegauna 1957; Gadow 1899, 1905, 1909; Garman 1880, 1884; Gaymer 1968; Goin 1968; Grant 1956; Gray 1855, 1869; Green 1971; Harlan 1827; A. Hardy 1959; J. Hardy 1962; Harrisson 1950, 1959, 1960, 1966, 1969a;

INDEX

laws regulating fishing. *See* fishing
leatherback turtle, *Dermochelys coriacea coriacea:* breeding, 79-83; captivity, 45; description, 19, 28, 29; distribution, 15, 19, 34; economic importance, 30, 100, 124, 126; eggs, 29, 30, 82, 83; embryology, 67; enemies, 56; fishing and industry, 124, 126, 129; food, 55; growth rate, 45; habitat, 47-48; illness, 56; mating, 82; maturity, 45, 83; migration, 87; nesting, 81-83; parasites, 49, 56; physiology, 88-89; protection, 118; size, 30, 35, 45; taxonomy, 19; weight, 30, 45; young, 29, 83
Lepidochelys kempii. See Kemp's ridley turtle
Lepidochelys olivacea. See olive ridley turtle
limbs: of green, 23; of hawksbill, 26; of leatherback, 29; of loggerhead, 26
Little Cumberland Island, rookery for loggerhead, 74
loggerhead turtle, *Caretta caretta caretta:* age, 40; breeding, 74-77; captivity, 44, 53; description, 20, 26-28; distribution, 15, 17, 32-33; economic importance, 28, 120, 124; eggs, 53, 76, 83; enemies, 53; fishing and industry, 112-13, 114, 116, 119, 124, 127, 129, 132, 135, 137; food, 52-53; growth rate, 40-44; habitat, 47; history in Caribbean, 28; mating, 74; maturity, 40, 43, 75; migration, 86-87; mortality, 44; nesting, 74-75; parasites, 49, 53; physiology, 89, 90, 91-92; protection of, 118, 120; size, 26, 27, 28, 35, 40; taxonomy, 17, 27; weight, 27, 40; young, 27, 40-44, 53, 72, 76-77, 92, 93

luth turtle. *See* leatherback turtle

Malaya: economic importance of green, 97; rookery for green, 58; rookery for leatherback, 80, 81
Manila Bay, type locality for olive ridley, 17
marginal, 23; of hawksbill, 26, 99
mating, 50; green, 50, 57-58, 63-64; hawksbill, 72; leatherback, 82; loggerhead, 74
maturity: green, 37, 65-66; hawksbill, 39, 73; leatherback, 45, 83; loggerhead, 40, 43, 75; ridley, 44, 78
metabolism, 91
Mexico: fishing and industry, 137-38; rookery for hawksbill, 73; rookery for Kemp's ridley, 79; rookery for leatherback, 82
migration, 141; extension, 86, 87; green, 60, 84; hawksbill, 84, 86; leatherback, 87; loggerhead, 86-87; mechanism of, 85-86; for nesting, 60, 86
Monserrate, fishing and industry, 125
mortality, 140, 142; diamondback terrapin in captivity, 103; due to barnacles, 49; due to cold, 111; due to papilloma, 49; of eggs, 105-6; of green, 49, 89, 109; of green young, 106; of loggerhead in captivity, 44

nesting, 57, 141; green: 58-66; cycles, of green, 60-63; migration for, of green, 60; season for, green, 58, 127, 129, 134, 136; hawksbill, 72-73, 120, 124, 129, 134, 136; leatherback, 81-83, 124, 127, 129, 134, 136; loggerhead, 74-75, 127, 129, 136; ridley, 77-79; secretion of tears in, 91
Netherland Antilles, fishing and industry, 136-37

neural, 20
Nevis: fishing and industry, 125; rookery for leatherback, 80
Nicaragua: fishing and industry, 113, 134-35; rookery for leatherback, 80
North Carolina: rookery for green, 59; rookery for loggerhead, 74
nuchal: 23; of loggerhead, 26

olive ridley turtle, *Lepidochelys olivacea:* breeding, 77-78; description, 20, 28; distribution, 15, 17, 33; economic importance, 28, 100; eggs, 55, 78, 79, 100; enemies, 55; fishing and industry, 113-14; food, 54; growth rate, 44; habitat, 47; homing, 86; maturity, 44, 78; nesting, 77-78; physiology, 88, 90; protection, 118; size, 28, 35, 44; taxonomy, 17; weight, 44; young, 78
Old Providence Islands, economic importance of hawksbill, 99
optimum environmental temperature, 89
orientation, 92; hatchlings, 92; nesting females, 85
osmoregulation, 91

Pacific ridley. *See* olive ridley turtle
Palermo, type locality for leatherback, 19
Panama: fishing and industry, 131; rookery for hawksbill, 73
parasites, 49; amoebae, 49; barnacles, 49; barnacles on hawksbill, 52; barnacles on leatherback, 56; leeches, 49; nematode worms, 68
Persian Gulf, economic importance of leatherback, 30
physiological activity, 88; when diving, 89, 90-91
plastron, 23; green, 23; hawksbill, 26, 99; loggerhead, 26

poisoning, from eating: hawksbill, 99, leatherback, 100
pressure resistance, 91
Puerto Rico: fishing and protection, 124; rookery for hawksbill, 124; rookery for leatherback, 80, 124
Puntarenas, rookery for green, 59

Quintana Roo, fishing, 28

reaction to light, in hatchlings, 92
respiration: 88, 89-90; importance of blood circulation, 91; nitrogen poisoning, 91; oxygen poisoning, 89

Saint Croix, rookery for leatherback, 80
Saint Kitts: fishing and industry, 125; rookery for leatherback, 80
Saint Thomas, rookery for leatherback, 80
Saint Vincent, fishing and industry, 125-26
San Andrés Island, economic importance of hawksbill, 99
Sarawak: economic importance of green, 97; rookery for green, 58, 60, 61, 64
scales, prefrontals: of green, 23; of hawksbill, 26; of loggerhead, 26; of ridley, 28
secretory glands, 92
sex ratio, in diamondback terrapin, 103-4
sexual dimorphism: green, 24; hawksbill, 26; leatherback, 29; loggerhead, 27
Seychelles Islands: rookery for green, 58, 61; rookery for hawksbill, 73
shell, 23; green, 24; hawksbill, 26, 99-100. *See also* carapace and plastron
size, 35, 141; green, 35, 36, 38; leatherback, 30, 35, 45; loggerhead, 26, 27, 28, 35, 40; rid-

leatherback, 30, 45; loggerhead, 27, 40
West Africa: rookery for leatherback, 82; rookery for ridley,
77

young: destruction, 114;
diamondback terrapin, 102-3;
enemies, 102; enemies of
green, 51-52, 106; enemies of
hawksbill, 52; enemies of loggerhead, 53; food of green, 49;
food of hawksbill, 52; green,
23, 24, 32, 38, 50-52, 69-72,
92, 99; growth of green, 38;
growth of hawksbill, 39-40;
growth of loggerhead, 40-44;
hawksbill, 52; leatherback, 29,
83; loggerhead, 27, 72, 76-77,
92, 93; movements, 93-94;
orientation, 92-93
Yucatán: fishing and industry, 28,
137-38; rookery for green, 59